Passion of the People?

D0294100

CRITICAL STUDIES IN
LATIN AMERICAN AND IBERIAN CULTURE

SERIES EDITORS:

James Dunkerley
John King

This major series – the first of its kind to appear in English – is designed to map the field of contemporary Latin American culture, which has enjoyed increasing popularity in Britain and the United States in recent years.

Six titles will offer a critical introduction to twentieth-century developments in painting, poetry, music, fiction, cinema and 'popular culture'. Further volumes will explore more specialized areas of interest within the field.

The series aims to broaden the scope of criticism of Latin American culture, which tends still to extol the virtues of a few established 'master' works and to examine cultural production within the context of twentieth-century history. These clear, accessible studies are aimed at those who wish to know more about some of the most important and influential cultural works and movements of our time.

Other Titles in the Series

DRAWING THE LINE: ART AND CULTURAL IDENTITY IN CONTEMPORARY LATIN AMERICA by Oriana Baddeley and Valerie Fraser

PLOTTING WOMEN: GENDER AND REPRESENTATION IN MEXICO by Jean Franco

JOURNEYS THROUGH THE LABYRINTH: LATIN AMERICAN FICTION IN THE TWENTIETH CENTURY by Gerald Martin

MAGICAL REELS: A HISTORY OF CINEMA IN LATIN AMERICA by John King

MEMORY AND MODERNITY: POPULAR CULTURE IN LATIN AMERICA by William Rowe and Vivian Schelling

MISPLACED IDEAS: ESSAYS ON BRAZILIAN CULTURE by Roberto Schwarz

THE GATHERING OF VOICES: THE TWENTIETH-CENTURY POETRY OF LATIN AMERICA by Mike Gonzalez and David Treece

DESIRE UNLIMITED: THE CINEMA OF PEDRO ALMÓDOVAR by Paul Julian Smith

JORGE LUIS BORGES: A WRITER ON THE EDGE by Beatriz Sarlo

Passion of the People?

Football in South America

◆

TONY MASON

VERSO
London · New York

First published by Verso 1995
© Verso 1995
All rights reserved

Verso
UK: 6 Meard Street, London W1V 3HR
USA: 180 Varick Street, New York, NY 10014

Verso is the imprint of New Left Books

ISBN 0 86091 403 8
ISBN 0 86091 667 7 (pbk)

British Library Cataloguing in Publication Data
A catalogue record for this book is available from the British Library

Library of Congress Cataloging-in-Publication Data
A catalog record for this book is available from the Library of Congress

Typeset by Type Study, Scarborough
Printed and bound in Great Britain by Biddles Ltd, Guildford and King's Lynn

CONTENTS

INTRODUCTION

There are two types of football, prose and poetry. European
teams are prose, tough, premeditated, systematic, collective.
Latin American ones are poetry, ductile, spontaneous,
individual, erotic.
Pier Paolo Pasolini, nd

Most people would agree that football is an important part of the popular
culture of South America but it is surprising how many histories exclude it
from their accounts. Edwin Williamson's *Penguin History of Latin
America* can find no space for it in 631 pages. The *Cambridge Encyclopedia
of Latin America* (1989 edn) has only the briefest of references, as does E.
Bradford Burns's one-volume history of Brazil. Rory Miller ignores
sporting contacts in his *Britain and Latin America in the Nineteenth and
Twentieth Centuries* (1993). The list could be extended, and even Janet
Lever's pioneering study of football in Brazil, *Soccer Madness* (1983), was
more concerned with the place of the sport in the Brazil of the 1970s than
with its role in the social history of twentieth-century Brazil.[1] Football has
been and remains a popular activity to which historians and sociologists
have been reluctant to pay attention. This attempt to remedy the deficiency
is essentially for an English-speaking audience although not, I hope, too
ethnocentric in its approach. It is an exploration of the place of football in
the history of its three most successful South American exponents,
Argentina, Brazil and Uruguay, with the emphasis inevitably on the
experience of the two larger countries.

Why is football the world's number-one sport? Although there may be
complicated reasons for this, its list of attractions is well known. It can be
played anywhere, from waste ground, in the streets, on the beach in parts
of Brazil, and on a range of properly marked out pitches from the humblest
village to the most sophisticated metropolitan stadium. The players do not

require special equipment or even a commercially produced ball. Football is cheap and economical with time, and anyone can play by finding his or her own level. In that sense it is a world open to talent. But it is not only about playing. Many can watch others play a game which most of the spectators will also have played. This enables them to imagine themselves as the actors on the field and gives an edge to their critical appreciation of the play. Watching (and then discussing and reading about) football has become part of the leisure lives of so many people in many places during the twentieth century. Football clubs rapidly became part of competitive structures, the clubs themselves based on organizations and territory – schools, villages, factories, towns, cities, countries – so becoming part of the identity of players and supporters. Individual footballers, like other sporting heroes, rise and decline, but many football teams go on for ever and the loyalties of supporters can last a lifetime. Football is a team game in which individual glory is not denied, a stage for individual virtuosity which fits neatly with South American ideas of manliness. Each year brings a new season of matches, always a fresh start, a new chance to win. A final ingredient is fate, with luck, both good and bad, being ever present in the world of football.

Football provides a collection of comforting rituals. In many respects it is a stable social world in which the pitch, the rules, the spectators' place on the ground, the pattern of the play itself do not change much. Yet it provides the opportunity for excitement and the chance to indulge in forms of behaviour which would be frowned upon in other social contexts. On the football ground ordinary life is forgotten and time is suspended. It can touch off emotional highs and lows rarely attained elsewhere. Its phrases enter every language and the play itself provides unending material for comment, conversation, memory and sociability. Its jokes are international. In Minas Gerais, Córdoba, Montevideo and Scunthorpe the wife accuses the husband, 'You only think about football. I bet you don't even remember the day we got married.' The husband replies, 'Of course I do. It was the day before the game between Santos and Corinthians, Talleres and Boca, Nacional and Peñarol, Scunthorpe and Grimsby...' For the significant minority of the world's population which likes it, football is not only twenty-two men kicking a ball about. In many countries it has been a part of the culture for over one hundred years. It has a history all of its own and has become a 'tradition' or a characteristic of the lifestyle of many peoples. Its professional sector offers opportunities for material and social advancement to many, though few are able to take full advantage. South

America is probably the site of football's most remarkable triumph, with Brazil the most spectacular example.

All football followers and many people who take little interest in the sport have an image of South American football and especially Brazilian football. It is of players who are maestros with the ball, who have at their instant disposal a selection of tricks, back-heels, overhead kicks, chips and swerving shots which set them apart from most players in other cultures, however talented. It is a football based on the dribble and the rapid exchange of short passes. Above all it is a football based on attack, a joyful game of individual self-expression which owes little to coaching or schools of excellence. One thing we shall try to do in the pages which follow is to see how far this image is supported by the study of football in South America, both past and present.

Chapter 1 will focus on the early history of organized football in Argentina, Brazil and Uruguay, noting the role played by foreigners in general and the British in particular. The part played by the British also features strongly in Chapter 2, where an assessment is made of the contribution of British touring teams to the development of football in South America. Chapter 3 examines the first impact of the South American game on Europe and describes the spectacular success of Uruguay in the Olympic Games of 1924 and 1928 and the first World Cup in 1930. Professionalism was openly accepted in Argentina, Brazil and Uruguay in the 1930s, and that process is examined in Chapter 4. Chapter 5 would probably not exist in a book on British football but in South America football and politics have had a longstanding if complex relationship. 'The Reign of Pelé' is a title that more or less speaks for itself, while in Chapter 7, 'Passion of the People?', an attempt is made to probe the intensity with which the game is followed in the south. The book ends with a discussion of some possible interpretations of football, more especially in Argentina and Brazil, and wonders if South American football is all it used to be. Finally, there is some description and analysis of the South American performance in USA '94.

This book would not have been written without the help and encouragement of many people, but especially deserving are the editors of the series, James Dunkerley and John King, and colleagues Jim Obelkevich and Nick Tiratsoo. The Research and Innovations fund at the University of Warwick provided crucial financial support for a visit to the FIFA archive, where Andreas Herren was friendly and helpful. The Institute of Latin American Studies in London also made a small grant in support of the work and asked only for a paper in return. Eduardo Archetti, Richard Holt, Pierre Lanfranchi and Bill Murray provided me with a lot of stimulating reading and some anxiety-inducing comments, and David Ward introduced me to American press coverage of their World Cup. Bob Turner shared with me some of his memories of being a referee in Argentina. David Toole provided me with old copies of *World Soccer* from his collection and Julian Germain and Dean Walton contributed ideas about illustrations. I would also like to thank Robert Castle, David Martin, Julio Marne Rodríguez, Claudio Rojo and Eric Weil. Deirdre Hewitt typed the manuscript splendidly. Finally, thanks to all those people who translated material, but especially Raquel Dias, Julian Sago and last but not least Clare Wightman.

CHAPTER ONE

ORIGINS

*It almost seems that the English have the preference in
everything pertaining to the business and business interests of
the country . . . They are 'in' everything, except politics, as
intimately as though it were a British colony.*
United States Consul in Buenos Aires, quoted by J. Smith in
*Illusions of Conflict: Anglo-American Diplomacy Toward
Latin America, 1865–1896*, Pittsburgh, 1979, p. 191

The first groups of young men to play something like the modern game of
football in nineteenth-century Latin America were probably British
sailors. Coming ashore at the ports of Rio de Janeiro, Santos, Montevideo
and Buenos Aires, football provided exercise and an enjoyable activity for
the spare time while the ships were unloaded and loaded. Football became
so popular a pastime among the crews of ships docking in Buenos Aires
that by the 1920s there was a thriving Merchant Service Football League
there with sixty-nine teams.[1] Some of the early games were not much more
than kick-abouts but they provided locals with their first sight of football.

In Argentina and Uruguay at least, their second sight was almost
certainly provided by members of the British community in those places.
This was partly a reflection of the fact that the British community in
Buenos Aires was one of the largest and wealthiest outside the countries of
the Empire. By the 1890s it was about 40,000 strong with its own schools,
clubs, churches, hospitals and two daily newspapers. Most of the settlers
had come as technicians and employees of British business, which had
substantial investments in railways and other public utilities, meat-packing
plants, banks, land and government loans. Britain was Argentina's leading
trading partner. The British brought with them their sports: cricket, golf,
polo, rowing, rugby, tennis and football. The British were responsible for
the birth of organized football in the River Plate. A cricket club had already

been set up in Buenos Aires when Thomas Hogg, his brother James and William Heald formed the Buenos Aires Football Club. It was the first in South America, but it was something of a false start. After a few games in 1867 and 1868 the club turned to the rugby game. It was to be the schools and colleges set up by the British for their children and later for those of the Argentinian elite in which sport in general and football in particular was to flourish. The Flores Collegiate High School, for example, included in its curriculum a programme of physical activities when it was founded in 1870 by R. P. Spilsbury. But if there was one moment more important than any other it was the arrival of Alexander Watson Hutton in February 1882. A graduate of the University of Edinburgh, he had come to teach at St Andrew's Scottish School but did not stay there long. He appears to have fallen out with the school managers due to their refusal to spend more money on the gymnasium and the playing fields. In 1884 he started his own English High School and brought over a teacher from England to teach games and physical education; football was one of the games. During the next few years, other schools took it up and it appears that it was a teacher at St Andrew's who suggested the formation of a championship in 1891. It did not last, and two years later Watson Hutton made a second attempt with his Argentine Association Football League (AAFL). It began with five clubs and in one guise or another it has been going ever since.[2]

By 1893, some Argentine colleges had also taken up the game. More clubs were formed, prompting the setting up of a Second Division in 1899 quickly followed by a Third for players attending the full day session of the schools and under the age of seventeen.[3] Lomas Athletic Club won the first championship of 1893. They were a British foundation set up by old boys of Bedford School living and working in Buenos Aires. The club also had sections for golf, rugby and tennis and a membership of 259 by 1900.[4] Had they won the league in that year it would have been their third successive victory and they would have kept the trophy. But the club staunchly agreed at its annual general meeting that a new winner had provided 'a great stimulus' for football.

Other British sportsmen had founded the Belgrano Athletic Club in 1896 and native-born Argentinians, having set up the Gimnasia y Esgrima (gymnastics and fencing) at La Plata in 1887 added the now fashionable football to its attractions in 1901. By that time the AAFL had a Fourth Division and clubs were beginning to appear which would become household names, not only in Argentina but first throughout South

America and later in the widening sphere of world football: River Plate (1901), Racing Club (1903), Independiente and Boca Juniors (1905).

There were also clear signs that football was spreading outside Buenos Aires. In 1892 Lobos Athletic Club had become the first *equipo de campo* (team from the countryside). The Central Argentine Railway Company had two teams in Rosario, one for the managers, Rosario Athletic, the other for the workers, Rosario Central. In 1905 the bosses beat the workers 2–0 in the Copa Competencia and actually won the final against that other team of railwaymen from Montevideo, Peñarol. Also in that year the Liga Rosarina, the Rosario League, began. Two years before, Newells Old Boys had been founded. Football clubs were starting up, disbanding and often reforming all over the Buenos Aires metropolitan area by the first years of the twentieth century. In 1905, seventy-seven clubs made up the various divisions of the league and 500 matches were played. June 1 of that year was an historic day in the annals of Argentine football. Fifty-two teams played, involving 600 players and referees with an average crowd of 200 spectators per match. Soon, four-figure crowds became common, supporting what was the biggest league outside Great Britain. Its games were reported widely in both the Spanish and English newspapers. *La Argentina*, for example, published the names of teams looking for grounds. Even the main establishment newspaper, *La Nación*, reported on football regularly from 1903 and by 1912 the press would be complaining that they merited specialist accommodation. Tickets for the grandstand were no longer enough.[5]

The club which most clearly symbolized the British origins and control of football in Argentina at this time was Alumni. In October 1898 the English High School Athletic Club had been set up with the active participation of students and ex-students. It joined the Second Division of the league in 1899. In 1900 the club went into the First Division, recruiting some old boys of the school who had been playing with other clubs, and won the championship.[6] The club also won a trophy donated by the English-language newspaper the *Buenos Aires Herald* for the team voted the most popular by its readers. For the next eleven years, Alumni remained the pre-eminent club in Buenos Aires football. They had changed their name from English High School in order to distinguish themselves from the school teams of the Third Division. Their success attracted a growing number of spectators to their matches, especially after they had become the first team to defeat visiting foreign tourists, a team from South Africa, in 1906.[7] By 1910 Alumni, Belgrano and Quilmes were the three

First Division teams containing 'the largest proportion of Britishers' and the team which beat River Plate in May of that year was certainly full of British names: Goodman, J. G. Brown and J. D. Brown, P. B. Browne, E. H. Brown and Jacobs, Weiss, A. C. Brown, Watson Hutton (son of the founder of the AAFL), E. Brown and J. H. Lawrie. In fact, most of them were probably Anglo-Argentinians rather than British-born immigrants, the sons, or even grandsons, of British settlers in Argentina. What seems clear is that they tried to uphold what they considered to be British ideas of fair play, 'to play well without passion' and certainly to avoid unseemly conflicts on the field.[8] The red and whites of Alumni won a lot of matches but disliked those who put success before sportsmanship. Once, playing Estudiantes and 2–1 down, the referee gave Alumni a penalty. The Estudiantes supporters protested and Watson Hutton changed the referee's decision, saying that there had not been a foul. Virtue was rewarded when Alumni later equalized. Alumni were the social equivalent of the English Corinthians and it is a pity and a surprise that that team of gentlemen never reached as far south as Buenos Aires. A match between Alumni and Corinthians would have been a real gentleman's cup final.

By 1912 Alumni had disbanded and their red and white stripes were seen no more. The team was ageing – though several of the players clearly had a good deal of life left in them because they joined Quilmes, who went from last place in 1911 to top of the league in 1912 – and the pool of good players from the English High School was no longer enough to succeed in the growing competitive atmosphere of Argentine football. Although Alumni's most important games had attracted big crowds, the club had made no effort to develop its ground. In fact, they had often leased the better-appointed grounds of other clubs. Profits from their matches tended to be given to charities like the British hospital, or to the governing body of the game. Other local clubs had been investing for the future and the future of Argentine football could hardly lie with the British. The British community in Argentina was not big enough to sustain winning football teams once the game had spread to the Argentines. Another sign of this was the failure of the annual match between Argentinos and Británicos, which had been played since 1894. After the 1910 game, which the Británicos lost 5–1, the British could not produce a team that could make a match of it and the fixture lapsed.[9] Alumni were overtaken by the criollization of the game.

The shift to Argentine control came quite quickly. As recently as 1903 the AAFL had changed its name to the Argentine Football Association (AFA) and affiliated to the Football Association in London. But in the same year the rules had been drafted in Spanish and the meetings were no longer conducted in English. In February 1905 the *Buenos Aires Herald* quoted from a letter written by the secretary of the San Isidro Athletic Club to his counterpart in the AFA suggesting that the name be changed again to La Asociación Argentina de Football. The writer stressed that the AFA was an Argentine institution, the majority of members were Argentines and that to keep an English name was therefore anomalous and unintelligible to a large proportion of club members and supporters.[10] It was no surprise on the eve of the 1905 season that the AFA should print a pamphlet on the laws of the game in English and Spanish.[11] The AFA finally changed its name to Asociación Argentina de Football in 1912, by which time there was a rival organization in the field.

Why were two bodies struggling for control of football in Argentina in 1912? It was partly about money. Football in Argentina was facing the problems of success. Tours of foreign clubs had proved very lucrative, but not all the local clubs shared in the profits. Not every club was good enough to merit a fixture against the British visitors, yet they were forbidden to play on those days when the tourists had fixtures. This meant no receipts on eight Sundays and feast days.[12] Club expenses were increasing and members' subscriptions were not enough, particularly to meet the cost of ground improvements. It was not only a matter of providing better accommodation, but also of draining and levelling playing areas. Moreover the context was one of a city and its suburbs which were expanding rapidly. The builders would drive clubs further and further out if they could not afford to buy and develop existing grounds and buying was expensive. Belgrano, for example, moved several times and then decided to raise the capital to buy a ground. Belgrano, Quilmes and Estudiantes had plans to build stands in 1906 and San Isidro had already begun work on theirs.

When the first tours took place most of the games were played on the ground of the Sociedad Sportiva at Palermo. It was by far the best-appointed ground in Buenos Aires and the Sociedad did well out of their agreement with the AFA which allowed them 40 per cent of all net proceeds. But they were tempted by the remainder. If they were the ruling body in Argentine football all the profits would be theirs. Exploiting discord among some of the clubs the Sociedad Sportiva set up a rival body to the AFA, the Asociación Argentina de Football in 1908.[13] But it did not last long.

In 1912 the Sportiva ground could not be used for the visit of Swindon

Town due to disputes over ownership. By that time the best alternative was the ground of Gimnasia y Esgrima. This club had been gradually improving their ground, opening a grandstand in 1909 until, by 1912, it had a capacity of about 25,000 and 'was probably the biggest and best-equipped athletic club in South America'.[14] That placed them in a strong position when the AFA approached them about staging the games with Swindon. When the Council of the AFA offered Gimnasia 20 per cent of the profits from a game with the Uruguayan League, the club said it was not enough. The AFA replied that they made the rules so Gimnasia withdrew from the AFA and began taking steps to set up a rival organization, the Federación Argentina de Football.[15]

Like the Sociedad Sportiva before them, Gimnasia were able to exploit the feelings of other disgruntled clubs. In the early years of a national football organization much of the detail of the every day is worked out only after trial and error. Important matters such as player eligibility and registration and agreeing a system of promotion and relegation often provoke controversy. It is not surprising when some individuals and some clubs feel badly treated. Alumni's failure to resign from the league but instead to concede walkovers to their opponents until they forfeited their place upset Independiente who had finished second in Division Two in 1911 and would have been promoted if Alumni had not entered a team for Division One. Estudiantes de la Plata had their ground closed for the remainder of the season in May 1912 after an assault on a referee following a game with Estudiantes of Buenos Aires. Two of their players had been suspended for a similar period, having been found guilty of inciting the spectators to attack the referee and one of them also insulted the official. Estudiantes de la Plata withdrew from the AFA and Porteño followed suit.[16] Some football people argued that what was needed was a special meeting of the AFA to elect a new Council, and not a new organization.

But the struggle was about power as well as money. Argentine football had made rapid strides among the elite of the country, British-born, Anglo-Argentine and Argentine. The Secretary and Treasurer of the AFA were both British, although with twenty years' residence in Argentina. Hugo Wilson, President of the AFA, was also President of the Jockey Club, one of the most elitist in Buenos Aires. The opposition was also led by well-connected professional people such as the President of Gimnasia, Dr R. C. Aldao. Football had status among the local elites. Southampton's first match in 1904 was watched by the President of Argentina and the Minister of War. When Everton played Tottenham on the Sportiva ground in 1909, the President of the Republic attended the match and the teams were presented to him.[17] He later gave a trophy to be competed for by the clubs of the new Federación.[18] Football was already something worth having control over. By the end of July 1912 there were two separate leagues running side by side. The AFA meanwhile was bent on reforming itself, or at least the manner in which its Council was elected. In future, this was to be done by the clubs and not at a general meeting, in the pious hope that this would avoid 'cliques and combines'.[19]

As for the rival Federación, they were soon petitioning the Argentine Congress for a subsidy of three thousand dollars a month in order to meet their running costs, as their member clubs were keeping all the match receipts. They were also finding, like the AFA before them, that the course of sporting administration did not run smooth. In the last match of the 1912 season, Independiente won their championship by beating Argentinos de Quilmes 5–0. This meant that they had finished level on points with Porteño but had a superior goal average. But the result caused some resentment among the supporters of Porteño who accused Argentinos of sending a weakened team for the match with Independiente. The Federación decided that justice would be done, and more money earned, if Porteño and Independiente played off for the title. The game was indecisively drawn, on. goal each, Independiente equalizing only three minutes from the end with a disputed goal. But it ended in disorder. The referee had awarded a corner, but the players of Independiente claimed the ball had already crossed the line and should have been a goal. In the ensuing discussion, he sent off three of the players of Independiente and the rest refused to continue. The referee was assaulted, the crowd invaded the field, the match was abandoned. Later, a Federación disciplinary tribunal suspended two Independiente players and reprimanded another and awarded the championship to Porteño.[20]

In spite of the split, football in Argentina by 1912 was a thriving and prosperous amateur sport. In June the AFA was affiliated to FIFA and it had already begun to forge footballing links with other countries in South America, most notably its closest neighbour, Uruguay. Only 109 miles and nine hours away by boat, the journey to Montevideo was already a familiar one to players and supporters from both sides of the River Plate.

As in Argentina, in Uruguay football was a game for the elite at first and an important part of the cultural baggage of the British. Young British professional workers founded cricket and rowing clubs in Montevideo but it was the schools which were the crucial institutions in teaching the game and organizing teams and fixtures. An English High School was founded in 1874 and a British School in 1885. A teacher at the former, William Leslie Poole, was a games enthusiast and one of those who founded the Albion Cricket Club in May 1891. A football section was also established and the club as a whole claimed fifty members in 1893.[21] Albion was soon playing against British clubs in Buenos Aires. In the winter of 1898, for example, they met Belgrano, Lomas and Lobos. Poole was still a playing member and A. C. Lichtenberger the captain. The latter's father was Brazilian, his mother English, but his ancestors came from Alsace. He later worked for the Sun Insurance Company and was one of the prime movers in the setting up of the Uruguayan Association Football League in March 1900. Poole was its first President. It was a split among the Albion members which led to the formation of the Montevideo Wanderers in 1902, by which time several clubs were making football a new winter attraction in Montevideo. An interesting sign of this growing popularity was the initiative taken by a local tramway company, who opened Grand Central Park in Montevideo in May 1900 and recouped some of their investment by encouraging football to be played there. Teams and spectators used the company's cars to get to the new ground.[22]

One of the most popular clubs was the Central Uruguay Railway Cricket Club. Formed by young British engineers with 118 founder members in September 1891, it also had tennis and football sections. It clearly had the support of the railway company because its chief administrator, Frank Hudson, was its first President, but this support did not last. By 1906, by which time the football team was well known on both sides of the estuary, a new chief administrator with stricter ideas about making the company pay was beginning to question the support given by company to club. The footballers played in a suburb of Montevideo in which the railway yards were located. This eventually gave them a new name, Peñarol, and they were soon attracting a crowd, doubtless helped by their winning three out of the first five championships of the Uruguayan League. But relations with the company deteriorated. It is alleged by some writers that the last straw followed a match against Montevideo which was abandoned after a collision between one of the opposition and the Peñarol goalkeeper. He was taken to hospital and rumours of his death provoked some Peñarol supporters to set on fire the carriages in which the Montevideo team were travelling back to the city... Whatever the truth of the matter the club became independent of the company, probably part of the process of the criollization of Uruguayan football. In 1905, the name of

the Uruguayan Association Football League was changed to the Liga
Uruguaya del Football. Another important moment in the same process
had been the establishment in 1899 of Club Nacional de Football. Formed
by Uruguayans, it was the fruit of a union between Montevideo and
Uruguay Athletic. But its significance was that it was the first clearly
national club, though its players were mainly college students until about
1911. Nacional and Peñarol became the great club rivals of Uruguayan
football. The standard of play of those two clubs made very rapid strides in
a very short time. So much so, that in 1911 the visiting Swindon Town
Secretary-Manager, spending a Sunday in Montevideo en route for Buenos
Aires, was very impressed with a match that he saw between the clubs:

> I have been Secretary of Swindon Town for seventeen years, and the play I saw
> yesterday was as good as any I have seen between any two amateur teams. It
> could not be beaten as an amateur match in any part of England, and two or three
> of the players would have been carefully watched by every club representative.[23]

The British role in the origins and early history of football in both
Argentina and Uruguay cannot be gainsaid. Britons were present at the
birth of the game in Brazil, too, but the birth there was more complicated.
For one thing other European migrants were important in football's early
stages there. But it is well known that association football first came to
Brazil in 1894 and that it was Charles Miller who introduced it. There had
been earlier sightings – the usual sailors' games in the 1860s and 1870s,
rumours of a priest introducing it in a São Paulo school also in the 1870s,
and games played among British and Brazilians working for the São Paulo
Railway in 1882. São Paulo therefore deserves the title of pioneer, but only
by a narrow margin from the then Federal capital and deadly rival Rio de
Janeiro.

It was to São Paulo that Miller returned from England in 1894. Twenty
years before, he had been born in the coffee capital to English parents who
packed him off to school in the old country at the age of ten. He spent some
time at the Bannister Court School in Southampton but does not appear to
have played for Southampton St Marys in the early nineties as is often
claimed. At the age of nineteen he certainly played for Hampshire against
the touring Corinthians in a match which the home side lost 4–0 in 1893.[24]
A year later he was back home in Brazil, having brought with him a couple
of footballs. He later claimed to have played for the first time in São Paulo
in 1895 on ground in the Varzea do Carmo near the junction between the

Avenue Gasometro and Santa Rosa Street.[25] He collected together a group of young Englishmen from the local Gas Company, the London and Brazilian Bank and the São Paulo Railway, picked two sides and played the first game of football in Brazil in the modern era. The ball used was alleged to have been the one used in the Hampshire–Corinthians match of 1894, given to Miller by William Pickford, a future President of the Football Association. Another game soon followed the first. The next crucial step was when the São Paulo Athletic Club added football to its list of physical activities. The club had been formed for cricket in 1888 by British professionals working in Brazil. Miller joined with his footballs. In April 1895 picked teams from the Gas Company and the São Paulo Railway played a recognizable match which the trainmen won 4–2. Most of the players were São Paulo Athletic Club members and, as the participants enjoyed it, further games were arranged. Miller himself seems to have worked for the Railway Company then moved to the London and Brazilian Bank and, in 1899, to Phoenix Insurance where he eventually became manager. He played football for São Paulo until 1910 and refereed until he was forty.[26]

It was not only the British in São Paulo who were interested in football. The first club for Brazilians was also located there, in Mackenzie College. Mackenzie had been founded by American Methodist missionaries and remains a respected centre of higher education. The students may have seen the early British kick-abouts and it seems that they started their own some time in 1895–6. One story, probably apocryphal, tells of a teacher returning from the United States with a basketball, which the students proceeded to use for football. They had certainly founded an Associação Atlética and a football club by 1898. A pitch was marked out on the college recreation ground. It was probably students from Mackenzie, who lived in the port of Santos, who first played football there. By the early twentieth century football was common in the private schools as several of the distinguished Brazilian sociologist Gilberto Freyre's interviewees later affirmed.[27]

It was not only the young British immigrants who were keen on football. Hans Nobiling arrived in São Paulo from Hamburg in 1897. He also brought with him, as well as a ball, the rules of the German club of which he had been a member. A German gymnastic club already existed in São Paulo. Not surprisingly, Nobiling found his way there and persuaded some of its members to try football. It seems entirely in keeping with the exotic image of Brazil in the European imagination that these young men are reported to have practised, after work, on moonlit nights between 8 and 10 p.m.

By the close of the 1890s, Athletic Club (AC) São Paulo, Mackenzie and the Germans were all playing football and early in 1899 a Nobiling team played a college team. Although there were no goals, the players liked it sufficiently to arrange another match and then a third. Then the British from AC São Paulo played Mackenzie. The Germans then played the British and, it is alleged, an audience of sixty saw AC win 1–0. Interest in football was growing, enough for a local shop, Casa Fuchs, to begin importing playing equipment from Europe in 1900. In August 1899 Sport Club Internacional was founded by twenty-five young men of various nationalities including Brazilians, Germans, French, Portuguese and English. They were soon building a city-centre clubhouse with all the trappings of the aspiring commercial and professional men's club: reading room, games room, fencing room, gymnastic area and bars. But the ethnic pull remained strong and Nobiling and the Germans left early to form Sport Club Germania. Following a match with Mackenzie the Germania players celebrated with traditional German beer.[28]

If São Paulo was the place where the first organized football clubs emerged in Brazil then Rio de Janeiro was not far behind. Football in Rio had many pioneers. The British were in the van, of course, setting up the Paissandu Cricket Club in the 1870s, but football did not become established until the foundation of the Rio Cricket Sud in what is now Niteroi. British, Brazilians and Anglo-Brazilians seem to have been playing the game in the later 1890s. But there were probably only three teams in the Rio area in 1900. Oscar Cox was an important figure. From an Anglo-Brazilian family, he had been educated in Europe and while in Switzerland met several other young men from his country at a college in Lausanne. One of these was António Casemiro Da Costa. This connection was important. Da Costa was a Paulista who played with SC Internacional and late in 1901 he had written a letter to a local newspaper suggesting that football clubs in São Paulo should form a league. He also thought that the public might be interested enough to pay to watch the games. Any money thus taken could be divided equally between the clubs and the league. Eventually Internacional, AC São Paulo, FC Germania, Mackenzie College and CA Paulistano formed the Liga Paulista de Football in December of 1901. Da Costa promised a cup for the winners and in 1902 it was presented to the first champions, AC São Paulo. It was also in 1901 that a team of Brazilians beat a team of British players for the first time.[29]

But the most significant event for the development of Brazilian football in 1901 was the fact that the football circles of São Paulo and Rio made contact for the first time. It was Oscar Cox of Rio and Rene Vanorden of São Paulo who organized the first representative match between the two cities. It was a social as well as a sporting occasion. These were young men from Brazil's social elite who could afford the cost of travel, food and accommodation that such a venture involved. The Rio players went to São Paulo on the overnight train on 18 October 1901. Two matches were played, on the 19th and 20th, and both were drawn. After the games the two teams dined together in the Rotisserie Sport restaurant. Various toasts were drunk, including one to the honesty of the referee and one to Charles Miller, 'the best all-round sportsman'. The meal was ended by Da Costa drinking a toast not only to the President of Brazil, Campos Salles, but also to King Edward VII. This underlines the continued influence of the British. A look at the names of the two teams also suggests the international flavour of the occasion. The Rio team was Schuback, M. Friar, Nóbrega, Oscar Cox, Wright, MacCullock (*sic*) Walter, Costa Santos, J. Morais, E. Morais and F. Frias. The reserves were Moutinho and Rocha. São Paulo was represented by Holland, Duarte, Nobiling, Vanorden, Jeffery, Meiss, Salles, Boyes, Da Costa, Miller and de Carvalho.

The next few years would see football establish itself as an organized recreation in both of Brazil's great urban centres. It would also see the foundation of those clubs which would become household names in Brazil and eventually achieve fame wherever football was played. Oscar Cox and his young friends formed the elegant and aristocratic Fluminense club in 1902, Cox becoming its first President at the age of twenty-two. Its ground was located in a highly desirable part of Rio, Retiro da Guanabara. It was a club for well-off young men, often from the best families. It was alleged that they travelled to away matches in dinner jackets. As one Brazilian scholar has written, in order to join the Flu,

> the player had to live the same life as an Oscar Cox, Felix Frias or Horácio da Costa Santos, a Waterman, a Francis Walter, or an Etchergary, all chiefs of companies, sons of rich fathers, educated in Europe, used to spending money. It was a hard life. Those who did not have a good salary and money in their pocket couldn't take it.[30]

In 1904 three new football clubs were formed in Rio: América, Botafogo and Bangu. The first league championship took place in 1906. The América club was named after the continent which had become so hospitable to migrants from Europe. Botafogo was founded by students at the Alfredo Gomez College. The Glorioso, or the black and whites, as happens with many football clubs everywhere, had moved grounds three times by 1908. It was the foundation of Bangu that pointed to a less socially elitist future for football in Brazil. Bangu was a suburb in the North Zone of Rio, well away from the fashionable city centre. It was the first club from outside the Federal District. It was set up by the British managers of the textile firm Companhia Progresso Industrial do Brasil, who provided the ground. It may have been aimed at the young British managers and supervisors at first but it soon began to provide playing opportunities for ordinary workers. The club would soon be more important than the factory. In 1912 another elite side appeared, Flamengo, grafted on to the rowing club of that name, a club which already had 6,000 members.[31]

As we have already seen, similar developments were taking place in São Paulo with new clubs joining São Paulo Athletic such as Paulistano, AA Ponte Preta and Sport Club Corinthians Paulistano, the latter founded in 1910 by five Brazilians, a house painter and four railway workers, after the tour to Brazil in that year by the famous English amateur club Corinthians. The São Paulo team made such progress that it joined the Liga Paulista in 1913 and won the title in 1914 after the aristocratic clubs had left the league as a protest against lower-class opponents. Two leagues existed in São Paulo until 1917.[32] Santos had been founded in 1912 and Exeter City practised on their rough little ground during their short stopover in Brazil en route for Argentina in 1914.

As in Argentina and Uruguay, football in Brazil began as a game for young men from the well-off, educated elite. Mazzoni in his history looked at the careers of nine of São Paulo's leading players from the pre-1914 era together with about thirty of the less well-known footballers. They were engineers, building contractors and merchants, in the main, with a scattering of accountants, doctors, bankers, army officers, professors, architects and one 'poet–schoolteacher'. They were mostly professional men either involved in the coffee or sugar trades, or working in the new urban growth industries of tramways, electricity generation and gas production, together with the older one of railways. Football in Brazil was an elite game, a fact underlined by the *Gazetta* after a match in Rio in 1908 in which América had beaten Botafogo 2–0: '... after the arguments and the matches, footballers are always friends. They are polite young men from our society and respect each other. They do not fight seriously.'[33] Football matches between the leading clubs were social occasions where young men from good families could display their masculine qualities and young women could look on and admire. Could anything be more civilized, more European, than Ana Amélia's poem 'The Leap' which she sent to the Fluminense goalkeeper.

> When I saw you today, executing your relaxed, daring and vigorous leap like a figure from the *Iliad* I trembled in the most intimate part of my being, swept by a frenetic impulse as if I was before a Greek, the hero of an Olympiad. Shaken like Dryad before Apollo, I measure his magnificent figure. Against the incomparable background of a pale twilight you threw yourself into space, tensed all your muscles, enrapt by the roar of the crowd's enthusiastic applause. Like an agile God that graciously came down from Olympus, you touched the ground, glorious, fervent and fearless, perfect in the beauty of the classic Greek sculpture.[34]

Ana's Olympic God was Marcos de Mendonça, who became her husband, kept goal for the Brazilian team in the 1919 South American championships, became a banker and industrialist, President of Fluminense and author of several books on Brazilian history.

But it was unlikely that football would remain entirely at the feet of a social elite. In fact in all three countries it was spreading downwards with remarkable speed. Six years after *Gazetta's* complacent pronouncement, the chairman of Exeter City, on tour with his team of British professionals, rushed off the boat when it stopped at Rio when they saw, not far from the dockside, a game of football in progress. The group who went to investigate were astonished 'to discover that the match was between junior teams of about 18 to 20 years of age. They were all niggers, as black as your hat, and most of them playing in bare feet.' It was the future, but it did not seem so in 1914.[35]

CHAPTER TWO

ENGLISH LESSONS

*Belgrano Athletic Club v English High School Athletic Club.
Should the weather be fine today and tomorrow this match will
take place at Coghlan on Sunday, commencing on the arrival of
the 1-20 pm train from Retiro. 31 March 1900.*

*Belgrano AC. There will be a pick-up game today (Thursday)
and on Sunday at 3 o'clock on the old ground Calle Patepa. All
comers will be welcome and are requested to take the 2-25 train
from Retiro. 12 April 1900.*[1]

As we have already seen, the British played a particularly important part in
the growth of football in Argentina. Buenos Aires contained a sizeable
British community and the British had controlling interests in most sectors
of the economy. Not surprisingly it was a confident community,
convinced of its own moral superiority, quite prepared to criticize the
customs of the country as the *Herald* did in May 1900 when it suggested it
was about time that employers and the government should bring in a
half-day holiday on Saturdays. Argentine young men were compelled to
drill in the National Guard on Sundays and even the frequent feast days
were insufficient compensation. Moreover all those holidays were bad for
business. The editorial confidently predicted that Saturday early closing, *el
sábado inglés*, the English Saturday, had to come in time.[2]

But what did please the editorial writers of the *Herald* was the fact that
'English sports and pastimes have taken root on Argentine soil, and
become the favourite outdoor amusements of Argentines of all ranks and
ages'. Cricket had not yet captured the hearts of many Argentines but
football had, probably because it appealed 'more to the Argentine's natural
love of excitement than the comparatively placid summer pastimes beloved
of the contemplative and more phlegmatic Briton . . .'[3] Indeed the game had

reached a level where it was time to test the best of the local teams against the acknowledged masters from Britain.

In 1904 the Argentine Hippic Club invited Southampton to play a series of matches on the shores of the River Plate. The Hippic was a sports club for the elite whose President was Baron Antonio de Marchi, a 'typical sportsman' who had 'interested himself personally in the arrangements of the tour'.[4] That it was an important social as well as sporting event is illustrated by the large crowds at the games. The *crème de la crème* of Buenos Aires society turned up for the first match against Alumni, including the President of the Republic, General Julio Roca, accompanied by his Minister of War and an escort of lancers. This was particularly appropriate as football had just been introduced into the Argentine Army. A local newspaper described the scene on the grounds of the Hippic club at Hipódromo.

> The football field proper was fenced in with a strong and neat wire fence at the back of which was a space of about five yards in width, followed by a continuous row of stands on all sides of the field with the lowest row of benches well raised, so that their occupants could easily see over the heads of those using the standing room in front. Opposite the centre of the field on each side were the reserved seats, and on the south west side was a break in the stands, occupied by the box for the use of the President and the official guests. The seats to the north of the President's box being reserved for members of the Hippic club and their families. Long before 2 o'clock the seats were well filled, and at five minutes past two, the band of the 3rd Battalion of the line struck up 'Hail to the Chief' and the carriage of General Roca was seen to be approaching ... Great applause greeted his appearance, which he gracefully acknowledged.[5]

It is not clear why Southampton was chosen. It was, at the time, one of the leading professional teams in the Southern League and had twice been losing finalists in the FA Cup, in 1900 and 1902. The team swept through their five matches in Buenos Aires and one in Montevideo like an irresistible force. The day after they got off the boat they beat Alumni 3–0. A team of Britishers was savaged 10–0, Belgrano destroyed 6–1: much was made of the first goal to be scored against 'foreigners' by Arthur Forester in that game. An Argentine eleven was then beaten 8–0 and a team representative of the league in Buenos Aires lost 5–3 to the triumphant visitors. On the way home a Uruguayan combination was similarly despatched 8–1 in Montevideo.[6]

Southampton were still talked about twenty years later, especially their 'magnificent work with head and feet, their skilful blending of brains and boots'. They aroused the 'admiration of local followers of the great winter game as no other team since has succeeded in doing'.[7] They doubtless confirmed the belief in the British section of the local football community of the superiority of the players from the Mother Country. At any rate the visit of Southampton only served to whet the appetite. In 1905 Nottingham Forest were persuaded to follow in the footsteps of the 'Saints'.

Forest stopped off in Uruguay first and on 12 June 1905 they defeated Peñarol, representing the Liga Uruguaya, by 6–1 at the Parque Central in Montevideo. A muddy pitch probably kept the score down and the rain restricted the attendance to about 4,000.[8] Next stop was Rosario where a team drawn from the Athletic and Central clubs could not score against the Forest and conceded five. All the principal Rosario families went to the match as did a number of people from the outlying rural areas. The ground at Plaza Jewell was *en fête* for the occasion, the police band played and the gate receipts were devoted to relieving the victims of recent flooding in the area.[9] This was an important social as well as sporting event in the Rosario calendar.

Forest played their first match in Buenos Aires against Belgrano, a team of British and Anglo-Argentines, but who went the way of the rest; 7–0 was the score but more interesting was the record crowd, estimated to have been between seven and nine thousand. For some reason Forest kept them waiting and were gently chided in the English-language press and reminded that punctuality was one of the characteristics of *los ingleses* in Argentina. Again it is clear that this was a social event of some importance with many of the best-known families and ladies being present.[10]

The third game of the tour was 'an international that was not an international', when the British players of Argentina took on the Britishers as represented by Nottingham Forest. Of course Forest were bound to win but not by the ten goals that Southampton had managed the previous year. The correspondent of the *Herald* was right about that, as the visiting team won 13–1. It was 'want of condition' in the second half that told against the home players.[11] Forest then went back to Rosario and recorded another easy victory, 6–1, but it had only been 1–0 at half time and the feeling was that the Rosarinos had proved the toughest opponents yet.[12]

The highlight of the Forest tour was the match against Alumni on 25 June. About 10,000 were thought to have turned up at the Palermo ground of the Sociedad Sportiva and some of them got in without paying. Many of them did not like Forest's six goal to nil victory but the British referee who had accompanied the tourists was not to be put off by the whistling and shouting of the biggest crowd to watch a football match in Latin America up to that time. The tour was completed by relatively easy wins against an Argentine representative eleven, 5–0, and the local league by 10–1. At the farewell dinner at Monschi's Restaurant the Forest club was presented with a gold medal and the members of the team received silver ones. The form of the visitors so impressed the newly formed Independiente club that it decided to adopt the Forest red shirt as its own colours.[13]

The third successive winter footballing visitors to the River Plate were a team of South Africans who came in 1906. Southampton and Forest were English professional teams. The South Africans, eight of them British and seven South African-born, were gentlemen amateurs or sportsmen and gentlemen, as some critics emphasized. This did not inhibit their Zulu dance before each game. The Corinthians had already made extensive tours to the Cape in 1897 and 1903 and it was clear that football among the European migrants there was booming. The South Africans arrived late, owing to rough weather, but quickly got into their footballing stride. Victories were recorded against San Martín, 6–0, and a selection of university students who were physically overpowered 14–0. But there then occurred an historic moment in the history of Argentine football. Before another record crowd, probably exceeding that which had watched Alumni lose to Forest, Alumni beat the tourists 1–0, thus providing the Argentinians with their first win against overseas opposition. According to the *Herald* Alumni were lucky but the winning goal was marked by people cheering 'until they were hoarse; hats and sticks and papers were flung into the air; highly respectable, portly and usually sedate members of the community actually danced with joy and even a "vigilante" was seen frantically waving his helmet'. At the end of the game spectators ran on to the field and carried the Alumni players off shoulder high. Both captains were congratulated by the President of the Argentine Republic at the end.[14]

That level of excitement could hardly be maintained and the remainder of the tour was downhill all the way for the home teams. Belgrano were overcome 6–0, a Rosario combination lost 9–0, Británicos 4–1, Argentinos 1–0, Estudiantes a surprisingly narrow 3–2, the Argentine League 4–1, Alumni 2–0 the second time around and Quilmes 5–1. But this was not the end for the South Africans. After defeating Quilmes, they travelled to Brazil and became the first foreign football team to play in that country. On 31 July they met a combined team from the Liga Paulistano and before the usual upper-crust crowd at the Velodrome scored six unanswered goals.[15]

There were no British visiting teams in 1907 or 1908 but in 1909 Everton and Tottenham Hotspur both visited Argentina and both also played a match in Uruguay. On paper these were stronger than any of the previous tourists. Forest were in the English First Division in 1905 but they had only just escaped relegation to the Second whereas Everton were runners-up in the First Division in 1909, and Tottenham had won promotion from the Second Division. The two English clubs played each other twice, drawing 2–2 a day after leaving the ship and Everton winning 4–0 later. A record crowd in Montevideo saw Everton beat the Uruguayan League 2–1 and they also defeated Alumni 4–0 and the Argentine League 4–1. Tottenham also beat the Argentine League 4–1, a combined Rosario team 9–0, Alumni 5–0 and Argentinos 1–0. On their only trip across the River Plate they dismantled the Uruguayan League 8–0. Yet Argentine football opinion concluded that the tour of the two clubs at the same time was not a success. It is not entirely clear why this was, but the crowds at the two games featuring the English clubs only were disappointingly small. The local paper said it might have helped if the visitors had worn numbers on the backs of their shirts. At least then spectators could have identified the twenty-two total strangers who made up both teams. Shirt numbering did not become compulsory in the English League until thirty years later.[16] What really attracted the people was seeing their own champions take on the foreigners.

In 1910 Fluminense of Rio invited the Corinthians to visit Brazil and in the late August and early September of that year the famous English amateurs played three games in Rio and three in São Paulo, winning all of them comfortably. Fluminense scored in the first minute of their match but still lost 10–1. A combined team from several Rio clubs was then beaten 8–1 and a picked Brazilian XI 5–2. A cricket match was played against the English Cricket Club. Fluminense provided the usual farewell dinner and then it was off to São Paulo. The Velodrome ground there was thought to be narrow but it did not inhibit the muscular English. Palmeiras were beaten 2–0, Paulistano 5–0 and Os Estrangeiros 8–2. Not only top people attended these matches, as in one of the games a controversial decision by the referee brought on to the field 'a small black boy' who kicked the bottom of a Corinthian and then ran off to 'intense amusement'.[17]

Three years later the Corinthians were back. Maybe they were not quite as strong but almost certainly the Brazilians had improved. The matches in 1913 were much tougher and although the tourists had an enjoyable time, they found it harder to win. Indeed they actually lost the first game of the tour 2–1 to a Rio combination containing Englishmen Harry Robinson in goal and Harry Welfare at centre-forward, the latter scoring the decisive goal. Estrangeiros were then beaten 4–0 and a Brazilian XI 2–1. In São Paulo the Liga Paulista lost 2–1 in a game refereed by Charles Miller, Mackenzie College 8–2, but Palmeiras forced a 1–1 draw. The matches were well supported, with crowds of between six and ten thousand. That football in Brazil retained an essentially elitist character may be inferred from the fact that for the game against the Brasileiros in Rio, the American and British Ambassadors and several members of the Brazilian Cabinet were among the spectators. One of the Corinthians offered a sober judgement on the state of football in Brazil when he said they would probably find it hard to beat an English university side, especially in England. But he won top marks for prophecy by his declaration that there was 'no doubt that a brilliant future is in store for Brazilian football...'[18]

The most successful tour of Argentina, in all senses, was that of Swindon Town in 1912. Like Southampton before them, Swindon were a successful Southern League side who had reached, and only narrowly lost in, the FA Cup semi-finals of 1910 and 1912. In 1912 Swindon played six times in Buenos Aires, and once each in Rosario and Montevideo. The first match against the Northern Suburbs was a 2–2 draw, as was the game against the Liga Argentina. This latter was played only a day after the Rosario match and followed a bumpy and presumably sleepless, all-night train journey back to the capital. All the other matches were won but the home teams were often very competitive, a fact which undoubtedly encouraged the record crowds which turned up at several of the matches, including 14,000 to see the British team take on Northern Suburbs, 15,000 for the game with the Southern Suburbs, 20,000 to see the match against the Argentine League and in excess of 20,000 for the final match against a representative Argentinian eleven, a game played on a public holiday. Swindon enjoyed it all hugely and their Secretary-Manager, Sam Allen, was very enthusiastic. It all showed what a future football must have in South America.

> I have never seen such enthusiasm for the game as shown by the two Republics and everywhere one sees the hold it has taken on the people. Boys in the street, on the seashore, down alleys, soldiers on the barrack ground – all have the fever and when I say that one firm alone in Buenos Aires has just given an order in England for 5,000 of one particular make of football the immense attraction the game has out there will be realised. The picked teams we met were really good, clever, fast and gave us each match as much as we wanted.[19]

He told the *Herald* just before the Swindon party left for home,

> The standard of play was much higher than we had been led to expect when we were in England ... Many of the men who have played in the more important teams out here could very easily earn a living in England as professionals...[20]

The final visit of an English team to South America before the First World War was that of Exeter City in 1914. Again it is not clear why they were invited. They were a modest Southern League side, having finished twelfth in that competition in the 1913–14 season just ended in England. Yet of eight matches which they played in Argentina only the first, against the Northern Suburbs, was lost, six were won and a goalless draw was played out with a representative team of Argentinos. Only three goals were let in by the 'Grecians', as they were nicknamed at home, and in spite of wet weather good crowds saw their matches. Yet there appears to have been a good deal of dissatisfaction on the side both of the AFA and of Exeter City. There was an early problem about where the matches should be played. This was the result of a controversy surrounding the ownership of the Sociedad Sportiva ground. In the event they were all played on the ground of Racing at nearby Avellaneda. Racing was the champion club of the Argentinian League in that year, yet Exeter beat them 2–0. Nevertheless, critics claimed their football lacked style and sparkle. They were physically strong players, good at tackling and heading, but this was felt to be not enough. Yet they were obviously difficult to beat. Torino of Italy, the first visitors from continental Europe, also played three matches in Argentina in 1914 and lost two of them, including one to Racing. Perhaps the novelty of the British footballer was wearing off.[21] As the game developed in Europe there would be other exemplars to which Argentinian players could turn.

While calling at Rio on their way out to Buenos Aires Exeter had arranged to play three matches there on the way back. The third of these carved out for them a place in the football history of Brazil. Against a Brazilian national selection, the red and whites from Devon lost 2–0 and the Brazilian football authorities were so pleased with the performance that the same team was selected to play Argentina in Buenos Aires for the General Roca Cup two months later.[22]

Why did British football clubs undertake what were arduous trips at the end of long, hard domestic seasons? After all, travelling to South America was not like going to Europe where the Channel could be crossed in two hours and the rest relatively easily achieved on Europe's sophisticated railway network. Going to South America meant six weeks on a boat, three out and three back. It was not easy to maintain physical or psychological fitness on such monotonous journeys, broken only by short shore stops at Vigo, Lisbon, Madeira, Bahia, Rio, Santos and Montevideo. Of course on board was the usual round of concerts and competitions, but it was mostly eating – a lot of that – sleeping and sitting, although there were occasional excitements such as those experienced by the Corinthians on their way to Brazil in 1913 when they were diverted by a wedding, a birth, a suicide and the antics of a ship's cook driven mad by it all. The South Africans took twenty-seven days to reach Buenos Aires from the Cape in 1906 due to bad weather. The Corinthians probably thought of their trips as part holiday and part football missionary work. They were forced to look abroad for fixtures after 1907 because they had joined the renegade Amateur Football Association, which had broken away from the FA and were therefore unable to arrange fixtures with its member clubs.[23] For the professionals, a long season followed by a long voyage and the expectation that they would stride straight down the gangplank and perform must have seemed more like work than a holiday. These were young, British working-class males in foreign countries, whose languages they did not speak and whose food they sniffed suspiciously. The Exeter players would not eat what was offered to them at Rosario because of the way it was cooked.[24]

Above all they needed entertaining as there was a lot of time to be filled in between training and matches. The AFA were aware of this and set up an entertainments committee, and the British community did their bit. An Everton director said of his trip in 1909 that it was one continuous round of pleasure, but he did not have to play in any of the matches, nor was he a young man away from his summer haunts and mates. Everyone went to the *frigorífico*, the meat freezing and packing works, and to an *estancia*, a country house and estate, for demonstrations of lassoing and horsebreaking. The South Africans in 1906 combined the *frigorífico* with the dubious pleasures of the Central Produce Market in Buenos Aires. A couple of days later came a ride in a special tram over the whole of the lines of the Anglo-Argentine Company in order to see the expanding city. Three days later the Zoological Gardens were seen and in the evening a Choral Union concert attended. Next day came a visit to Tigre on the river followed later by an English Literary Society concert and next day the races at Palermo. The following evening a trip to the San Martín theatre was arranged. Four days later came the journey to the *estancia* and after that visits to a butter factory and a bag factory. After that came excursions to La Plata and Hurlingham, where a cricket match was played. Motor cars were regularly put at the disposal of the team although the reported eccentricities of local drivers made such trips more of a trial than a pleasure. Concerts and dinners were commonplace until the farewell banquet and some of the meals were grand affairs. The Exeter players may have had problems with their first taste of Rosarinian cuisine but after the match the dinner at the Station Hotel was sumptuous, the excellent food being supported by the finest wines and the best cigars. Speeches and a sing song rounded off a memorable evening. Swindon found that the meals at their hotel were too French and not substantial enough to train on, so a special English diet was provided.[25] The Swindon players were delighted by Buenos Aires and could not tear themselves away from the city-centre shops. To them the city fully merited its title of the 'Paris of South America'. Exeter City in 1914, on the other hand, felt that the entertainment had not been well organized. A month in Argentina left the players resentful and homesick. They had not had the good time which they had been led to expect. What they had expected, apparently, was a holiday with amusements every night. The best part of the trip had been the hotel and the nightly card schools.[26] The players felt that they had been left too much to their own devices in a foreign land.

But of course an important factor for British professional clubs was money. Tours helped to pay summer wages and could make a profit besides. In 1904 Southampton asked for a guarantee of £100 from the AFA but later realized this was not enough. They then requested and received another £100.[27] Season tickets were sold for Nottingham Forest's games in Buenos Aires in 1905. A director of Everton claimed that their 1909 tour had made a profit of £300. But it was the visit of Swindon Town which showed how popular football had become in Argentina and the money that could be made. Receipts for the six matches in Buenos Aires grossed 64,154 dollars. This left an overall profit of 20,479, and this after the Swindon party's travel expenses (19,821) had been met, and their hotel charges (861), and Gimnasia y Esgrima paid for the use of the ground. In a later account of the tour Sam Allen said that the match receipts for the eight games totalled £8,000 and that future visitors ought to ask for 10 per cent of the gross takings or 40 per cent after expenses.[28]

Whether the visits helped to improve the play of the local teams is difficult to say. The *Buenos Aires Herald* took a purist line in 1906.

What could be the lasting benefit of suspending all local matches for a month while foreign teams come and perform? The standard of play is, or should be, a matter of minor consideration. As long as the game is played in a gentlemanly manner and is kept free from the taint of money-making and professionalism, all other considerations are of comparatively trifling importance.[29]

Apart from the contradiction at the core the British could express exactly the opposite opinion, as in 1910 during an international tournament in Buenos Aires when the *Herald* claimed that both Uruguay and Argentina benefited from the visits of British professionals. They had shown the virtues of training and practice, were physically stronger and better at heading. The short-passing game of Southampton, for example, had made a big impression on local players as had the longer-ball game of Nottingham Forest.[30]

What seems unarguable is that the visits of the British teams helped boost interest in the game. These 'international' matches, covered extensively by the Spanish as well as the English newspapers, made football better known and more popular and began to erode its elitist character. The growing numbers prepared to pay to watch is another indication of football's developing grip on the popular imagination. The local game was also helped by British coaches: men like Walter Bull of Tottenham, who stayed behind for a couple of years after the Spurs visit of 1909 coaching the players of Gimnasia y Esgrima; by John Harley, the Scot who first played for and then managed Peñarol before settling in Montevideo and dying there in 1959; and John Hamilton, thought to be the first professional trainer appointed by a Brazilian club when he was invited by CA Paulistano in 1907.[31]

Some writers see the spread of modern sports from the developed imperial centres such as America and Britain as a form of cultural imperialism, buttressing the economic and political control designed to maintain the dependence of the colonial state. The British clearly had major economic influence, especially in Argentina, Uruguay and Chile, but their cultural influence is more difficult to measure. They took their football with them and, of course, were pleased when other nations did take it up because many of them were convinced of its social value. As the *Buenos Aires Herald* wrote in 1905, 'this peaceful conquest of British customs is one that naturally pleases us'.[32] But even in the relatively early days of the growth of Argentine football, for example, it developed a style of its own which led to a clash of ideas about what the game was. When Tottenham beat the Argentinos in 1909 neither the home team nor the home crowd liked the English shoulder-charging. Argentine referees regularly penalized it as too violent. When a team of Argentinians visited Brazil in 1912 *O Estado de São Paulo* much preferred their style of play to that of the Corinthians:

> In striking contrast to our players the Argentines were always simply marvellous. What magnificent combination, what marksmanship; how resourceful, how tenacious, how splendid the defence, how brilliant the attack. Yet all without charging – always gentle and polite! The play of the Argentines was better than the best we have ever witnessed. Even the Corinthians were inferior. They may have been more vigorous but they were less brilliant.

And presumably less influential. Could the gaucho sports have survived in the growing metropolis of Buenos Aires?

Of course the English connection was strong in the early stages of football's growth in South America. English terms were taken over to describe the match so that, for example, the *Jornal do Comercio*, reporting a match in São Paulo in 1904, talked about kick-off, goal, corner kick, half time and out sid (*sic*) left, about captain, team and dribblings (*sic*) and shotta (*sic*). Fútbol did not replace football in the title of Argentina's ruling association until 1934 and had not universally become futebol in Brazil until the 1950s. But such matters were phases. The nationalization or criollization of football would be in place long before the railways were removed from foreign control. Soon only a handful of club names, most famously in Buenos Aires, River Plate, in Rosario, Newells Old Boys, in La Paz, The Strongest, Always Ready, in Chile Everton, Montevideo Wanderers and of course, Corinthians of São Paulo, remained to remind later comers how it had all begun.

In August 1914 the Corinthians were actually sailing west on their third visit to Brazil in five years when news was received that war had broken out in Europe. Four of the party, who were reservist officers, left the ship at Pernambuco and the rest barely had time to take in the physical wonders of Rio before returning to Britain. Exeter City, meanwhile, also on their way home, had reached Madeira when they heard that war had broken out and spent an exciting few days dodging probably imaginary German submarines. By 1914 football in South America had been well and truly launched. The influence of the British would decline from that moment. Even so it had been worth it. As an Everton director wrote on returning to Liverpool from Argentina and Uruguay in 1909, the tour 'had not only contributed something to the sport of nations' but helped to break down 'many of the old standing prejudices peculiar to foreigners ... and at no cost'. What could be better than that?[33]

CHAPTER THREE

INTERNATIONAL TRIUMPHS

*... the Committee believes that competitive sports by teams, as
illustrated by soccer football which is played all over the world
under uniform rules, are of increasing importance in bringing
nations together, when true ideals of sportsmanship are adhered
to ... we recommend the teaching of soccer ... with emphasis
on the proper standards of conduct, as part of the international
education programme ...*
Part of a resolution adopted by the World Federation of
Education Associations at its meeting in Toronto, Canada,
August 1927

At the 1919 South American football championships held in Rio de Janeiro
the few Chilean fans who attended travelled by boat, train and mule. It
took them two months. In a continent of huge distances punctuated by
jungles and mountains, transport was always difficult and often unpredictable. It is not surprising therefore that international football contests began
around the River Plate. As early as 1888 young Britons resident in Buenos
Aires and Montevideo organized a football match to celebrate the birthday
of Queen Victoria. It was played on 15 August and was repeated each year
until 1894.[1] Once organized football developed in Argentina and Uruguay
it was almost inevitable that regular internationals would be played and
they were, forty-one times between 1901 and 1914. This pairing would
soon overtake, and leave well behind, England against Scotland as the most
frequently played international football match. Both countries liked to feel
that some trophy was at stake and their rivalry was stimulated by the
presentation of a silver challenge cup for annual competition by the British
entrepreneur and sportsman Sir Thomas Lipton in 1905. It was to be
played for in Buenos Aires and Montevideo in alternate years, always on a
feast day, with the proceeds going to charity.[2] Argentina–Uruguay football

relations would not always be good, but this often served only to add extra spice to the fixtures.

A major step forward was the AFA's organization of a tournament to coincide in 1910 with the centenary celebrations of the establishment of the first autonomous government in Argentina. It was more football festival than international tournament. Chile joined Uruguay in sending a team although Brazil, who had been invited, did not come. The matches began on 27 May on the Belgrano ground – Mrs G. D. Ferguson served the teas – where a combined Argentine team beat the Chileans 3–1. An interesting incident was the missing of a penalty by the home team, though the kicker did shoot at goal, to the cries of 'kick it out' from the stands.[3] It shows the persistence of the view of some Englishmen that gentlemen did not deliberately commit fouls and that the award of a penalty was therefore unnecessary and offensive. Chile then met Uruguay and suffered the expected defeat. The Uruguayans got the Argentinian equivalent of the bird for protesting about two disallowed goals, the crowd cheered on the Chileans and 'play became somewhat rough and several free kicks were awarded principally against the Orientales, who are old offenders in doubtful tricks . . .' The crowd chaired off the Chilean goalkeeper at the end.[4] Most of the Chileans were not native born and the Uruguayans also included Buck and Harley, born in the United Kingdom. This raised the question of whether Argentina should adopt the same approach. It is not clear how this was resolved.[5]

What was clear was that the winners of the festival would be either Uruguay or Argentina. The *Buenos Aires Herald* began its preview, 'Today's international may be described as the most important association football match played in this country since upon the result depends the championship of South America.' There was talk of a big crowd and rumours that if the home team were losing a certain element would invade the field and prevent the game from finishing in revenge for an earlier transgression across the water. In the event Argentina won 4–1 with about 10,000 watching, not including about a thousand who had a free view from the new embankment of the Central Argentine Railway Company.[6]

Argentine players had visited Brazil for the first time in 1907, winning six of seven games. The AFA received a further invitation to play against the Rio and São Paulo leagues in 1912. This time the Argentines lost the first match but won the rest. In São Paulo the visitors were entertained grandly by the Paulistano club and the elite of the city attended the reception and garden party in their honour. The first two proper internationals were not long delayed. In 1914 the Argentine General Julio A. Roca presented a cup for competition between the footballers of the two countries. His aim was 'to encourage the young people who play such noble sport and to cultivate good relations between our countries'.[7] The Brazilians sent the team that had just beaten Exeter City and after a couple of friendlies which provided one win each the big match took place on 27 September. The Argentine Ministers of Foreign Affairs and Justice represented the government and the Foreign Minister presented the cup after the only goal had been scored by the Brazilian Friedenreich. The Argentinian team was actually chosen not by the AFA but by the breakaway Federación Argentina de Football. One moment in the game was a witness to the amateur purity of the players. Argentina appeared to equalize. But the ball had been handled into the goal and both the Argentine linesman and some of their players told the referee that it was not a goal.[8]

These continental footballing contacts and the first matches between teams representing their countries prompted the circulation of ideas about whether or not the time was ripe for a real South American football confederation which, among other things, would be able to organize a proper championship. In 1912 a meeting between the AFA and the Rosario and Uruguayan Leagues discussed the possibility of a confederation of the River Plate. FIFA, Fédération Internationale de Football Associations, already existed as a kind of model, having been formed by seven European countries in 1904. The man most closely associated with the idea of a confederation was a Uruguayan, Hector R. Gómez. He saw it as a powerful governing centre which would reduce the danger of the kind of breakaway currently seen in Argentina. It might even have the effect of attracting those clubs who had formed rebel groups. Nothing happened in 1912 but Gómez, a teacher, member of the Uruguayan Parliament, President of Montevideo Wanderers and sometime chairman of the Uruguayan League and the Uruguayan League of Physical Sports, persisted. In August 1915 he published an article in *El Hogar* insisting that a South American Football Confederation was 'an institution we need'.[9] Gómez used the occasion of a tournament promoted by the AFA to mark the centenary of Argentina's declaration of independence from Spain in 1916 to bring his idea to fruition. 'The purpose of the South American Football Confederation is to join under one common authority all the institutions from every member country that rule the amateur football associations.' Gómez directed its operations from an office in Montevideo.

An early task was to schedule the first four South American championships to be held respectively in Montevideo 1917, Rio 1919, Viña del Mar 1920 and Buenos Aires 1921. The CSF was the first of its kind in the football world.

As for that 1916 tournament, for which a cup had been donated by the Argentine Ministry of Foreign Affairs, it was characterized by two of the issues which were to bedevil football in Latin America. A Chilean journalist accused Uruguay of including two African professionals. The two players were Gradín and Delgado. In fact they were 'Uruguayans born of slaves' and entertainers in the Montevidean Carnival celebrations. The Chilean delegates apologized but only after the issue had been taken up at diplomatic level. In Brazil in particular, racism in football would not go away.[10] Professionalism, too, would have to be faced, as we shall see in the next chapter.

Second, although no reader would know it from the official centenary history, the Argentina–Uruguay game scheduled for 16 July never started. More tickets were sold than there were places and the ground of Gimnasia y Esgrima was overwhelmed by far more potential spectators than it could ever hope to accommodate.[11] When it was clear that the match could not be played, a section of the crowd took naphtha from the lights of cars waiting behind the stands to set fire to them. The fire lasted for four hours. Only the central official pavilion remained unscathed. The match was replayed the following Thursday afternoon and 10,000 turned up to watch on a working day. It was a goalless draw, which meant that Uruguay won the tournament. Uruguay also won the first official South American championship in Montevideo the following year. The Parque Pereira ground was especially built for the tournament and the home team did not concede a goal in matches against Chile and Brazil, both won 4–0, and Argentina 1–0. Uruguay was also the first country to win away from home in Viña del Mar in 1920. It was Uruguay which was to place South America firmly on the map of world football when, in 1924, like a wolf on the fold, its team swept down on the Paris Olympics and devoured all opponents, astonishing the Europeans.

One of the ways by which the International Olympic Committee marked the eighth Olympiad in 1924 was by producing a silk scarf covered with the flags of the competing nations. All, that is, save one: Uruguay's was the missing flag.[12] The Olympic football tournament was effectively a world championship but not all the leading contenders were there. There were no other teams from South America, none from Germany and none from the British Isles, yet football was becoming one of the most popular sports of the Olympics. A total of 280,000 spectators saw the twenty-two matches in the fifteen days of play and the final in the Colombes stadium was watched by a crowd of 60,000 with ten thousand more locked out.

Uruguay began by demolishing Yugoslavia 7–0 in the preliminary round. The United States were then beaten 3–1, which brought Uruguay up against the host nation. Uruguay won 5–1 and inside-right Scarone scored four.[13] It was a staggering victory. The press agreed that although the French had done well in the first half and had been only 2–1 down at half time, in the second period they had been outclassed. The Uruguayans had superior technique and better tactics and the French, obliged to compensate for their inferior skill by employing unlimited energy, simply ran out of steam. Uruguay scored three more goals in the last fifteen minutes. As for the Uruguayans, the commentators noted, they were good but they liked the ball too much. They only let go of it to shoot with regret.

In the semi-finals Switzerland beat Sweden and Uruguay found Holland tough opponents. Not only did the Dutch lead 1–0 at half time, Uruguay had missed a penalty. But two goals in the second half produced another South American victory. The final was much easier, with Switzerland beaten 3–0. Petrone and Cea with shots got the first two and Romano headed the third. It was clear by then that a powerful new footballing nation had arrived, and it had come from 10,000 miles away. Gabriel Hanot, a leading French writer on the game, was almost ecstatic.

It is the best of the twenty-two teams which has won the championship ... The principal quality of the victors was a marvellous virtuosity in receiving the ball, controlling it and using it. They have such a complete technique that they also have the necessary leisure to note the position of partners and team mates. They do not stand still waiting for a pass. They are on the move, away from markers, to make it easy for team mates ... To an impeccable technique is added a stout foot and a good eye ... The English professionals are excellent at geometry and remarkable surveyors ... They play a tight game with vigour and some inflexibility. The Uruguayans are supple disciples of the spirit of fitness rather than geometry. They have pushed towards perfection the art of the feint and swerve and the dodge, but they know also how to play directly and quickly. They are not only ball jugglers ... They created a beautiful football, elegant but at the same time varied, rapid, powerful and effective ... Before these fine athletes, who are to the English professionals like Arab thoroughbreds next to farm horses, the Swiss were disconcerted.[14]

Uruguay led the way, at least in football, and not surprisingly the players returned home to Montevideo to be welcomed as heroes. Crowds thronged the streets to witness their passing. The government declared a national holiday, gave presents to these amateur players and issued stamps in three different prices each embossed with the words 'Uruguay Campeón de Football'. This was a big moment for a small, democratic republic. Not only had European–South American football relations been turned upside down: the new world had shown the old world that it could excel in a modern, civilized activity. In the six years since the end of the war European clubs had travelled to South America and had not found victories easy. But they had not been the best in the best of condition. Uruguay had won, in Europe, against probably the best amateur teams there. Overnight, it was the players and clubs of South America who were in demand in Europe.

In 1925 three leading South American club sides found themselves in Europe at the same time and all made powerful impressions. Nacional of Montevideo embarked on the football equivalent of a royal progress. Promoters in France, keen to exploit Uruguayan brilliance and success, secured Nacional, presumably with tempting financial guarantees, because they had provided seven or eight of the winning Olympic team. The tour was an astonishing campaign worthy of a chapter in its own right. The team left Montevideo in February 1925 and did not return until August. In that time it played thirty-eight matches, won twenty-six, drew seven and lost only five, scoring 130 goals and conceding only 30. About 700,000 people or an average crowd of 20,000 watched matches played in nine countries and twenty-three different cities in 160 days. This was about one game every four days and suggests a nightmare of slow trains, station to stadium, play, back to the night train and on to the next station/stadium with a few hotels to break the monotony. The team once played in two places on the same day. While one eleven were beating a local combination in Brussels 2–1, the remainder of the party were in Paris putting paid to a combined French/Swiss team 3–0. There was obviously money to be made, sometimes after a little flutter. At Roubaix the local directors bet the Nacional management that they would not score five; they shot seven. Not surprisingly the Uruguayan championship was not played in 1925.[15] Two years later Nacional was cashing in on its fame in the United States, Mexico and Cuba. This tour was not quite so strenuous, although it lasted five months and twenty-two matches of which three were lost and two drawn. Two of the defeats were in Boston and Chicago, the other in Havana.

Boca Juniors spent most of their 1925 tour in Spain, where they played thirteen matches, mainly against scratch or combined teams. Only three were lost. Of five games in Germany and one in France, none was lost. Boca had been runaway champions of the Asociación Argentina in 1924, winning eighteen of nineteen matches, drawing the other and conceding only eight goals. The other twenty-one teams were probably glad to see them permitted to miss the 1925 championship, save for the dent in their match receipts, but the success of the tour meant that Boca were proclaimed 'honourable champions' on their return anyway.[16]

Finally AC Paulistano were the first Brazilian football club to cross the Atlantic. The trip was partly a conscious attempt by their much-travelled President, António Prado Júnior, to reward the dedication of leading club members like himself. But it was also its purpose to promote, using football, the image of Brazil abroad. The party included two journalists from O Estado de São Paulo and São Paulo Esportivo. The games were played mainly in France and Switzerland, ten of them, and only one, against Cette, was lost. In some respects the best came first when the tourists beat a French national selection in Paris by 7–2 on a cold, wet day before 25,000. This performance stimulated Le Journal to christen the visitors Les Rois du Football, obviously having forgotten that the Uruguayans already held the title. Le Miroir des Sports thought that they were more balanced than Uruguay but not so good in defence. Le Soir also bombarded Paulistano with compliments. Their football was 'nervous, magic and brilliant ... an outstanding way of playing'. Here was another team from the new world who could run, pass precisely, change the direction of play unpredictably and score goals. Needless to say Artur Friedenreich, 'El Tigre', impressed everyone, not just by his eleven goals but by the way he led the forwards and brought colleagues into the game, as well as his renowned dribbling and shooting. AC Paulistano's players were probably really amateurs. Eleven of the party had degrees.[17] A great reception awaited them on their return to Brazil. The accompanying journalists had played their part almost as well as the players. Crowds turned out to greet them when the boat had short stops in Bahia and Rio. The Confederação Brasileira de Desportos (CBD) put on a banquet and further good dinners were digested in Santos and São Paulo. Local journalists organized a victory parade. A celebratory match against the crack Fluminense was played and won in Rio, and much was made of this voluntary effort which had done so much to place the name of Brazil before influential Europeans. As Senhor Prado remarked, it had all been achieved by the club. There had been no state aid. In fact the club was so pleased about the tour that it built a monument to commemorate it. This was the first occasion that the image of Brazil had been promoted abroad through sport.

Uruguay's win in the 1924 Olympics probably caused as much astonishment in South America as it did in European footballing circles. But it was a surprise tinged with resentment, especially in Argentina. The feeling among football people there was that Argentina could beat Uruguay. After all, they had done so often enough. If Argentina had been in Paris they would have now been Olympic champions! When the Uruguayans had returned and recovered from the euphoric reception, they found themselves challenged by their neighbours to two money-spinning games. The first was in Montevideo where Uruguay, including nine of the Olympic victors, hung on for a 1–1 draw in face of considerable Argentine pressure. An additional satisfaction for the Argentines was that this showed they were better than all the European amateurs. The return match was to be played the following week in Buenos Aires on the ground of Sportivo Barracas.[18] It turned out to be another of those mismanaged affairs. The teams left the field after only five minutes' play because of crowd encroachment. Police and conscripts managed to force the crowd behind the touchlines and the hope was that play would continue. The Uruguayans, however, were not too keen in the circumstances and the match was abandoned. Fortunately the efforts of a 'rowdy element' to destroy the stadium failed, though several ticket kiosks were upset. It was agreed to try again the following Thursday on the same ground. It was also decided that in order to prevent the crowd invading the pitch a twelve-metre-high wire netting fence should be built around it. This was an important moment in Latin American football. It was the first fence to go up aimed at keeping the spectators from the players and officials. It would become part of the game on most grounds in South America, later supplemented by moats in the grander stadiums. It became a symbol, suggesting that the South American football crowd was more volatile than its Western European or North American counterpart.

The replay provided an example of why fences were needed. The crowd was large, 35,000, with an estimated further 5,000 locked out. The game ended four minutes early when the Uruguayan players walked off. They were losing 2–1 at the time. The crowd was hostile towards the visitors anyway, a hostility perhaps exacerbated by the feeling that Uruguay should have continued the first match. But the game itself was one of the hardest fought ever seen in Buenos Aires, though tarnished, according to the English-language *Herald*, by the rough play and bad behaviour of some of the Uruguayan players. It was one all at half time, the Argentine goal coming direct from a corner, a score only allowed by a recent amendment to the laws of the game. The Argentina right back, Celli, broke his leg and was replaced by Bidoglio. Argentina had the best of the second half, their passing was impressive and they launched many attacks. They also kept possession skilfully, especially after Tarascone had given them the lead. It was then that the rough play of the Uruguayans led to some of the crowd throwing pebbles at them. The referee stopped play for a few minutes while the Argentine captain told them to stop. The referee, from Uruguay, then failed to award Argentina a penalty, Andrade charged Onzari violently from behind and 'a shower of pebbles fell on the offending darkie'.[19] Play was stopped and some of the Uruguayan players threw the pebbles back. The referee asked them not to and they walked off. The Argentine players remained on the field until the referee blew for the end of the match. While the police were trying to restrain the Uruguayan players from throwing pebbles, Scarone kicked a policeman and was arrested. When the Uruguayans went home the next day, a crowd, not entirely composed of well-wishers, gathered to see them off. There was an exchange of coal between ship and shore. But the Argentine newspaper *La Prensa* could be lofty. 'The loss of a football match does not inflict any injury on the sovereignty of the country of the losing team or imperil the safety of the nation ...'[20] This paper would not always be so sensible. There was a longstanding rivalry between the two neighbouring republics and on the football field there were plenty of opportunities to indulge it. The South American championships began only nine days after the match just described. They were held in Montevideo and the first match was Argentina against Paraguay. The crowd was not large but it was lively, cheering on the Paraguayans, whistling the Argentinians and carrying members of the Paraguay team off shoulder high at the end of their goalless draw ...[21]

Argentina were determined to enter the Olympics of 1928. The split in its football, which had produced two leagues since 1919, had healed. The Amsterdam football tournament included eighteen teams with Chile and Uruguay joining Argentina as representatives of South America. From being exotic and mysterious in 1924, the South Americans found themselves among the favourites in 1928, although the overall competition was tougher. Holland were playing at home, Germany were included and

Italy much improved. The draw gave Uruguay by far the hardest passage. They played the Dutch first and there was tremendous interest in this game, special trains bringing supporters from all parts of Holland. Tickets were fetching twelve times their face value on the black market. The Amsterdam City Council voted to attend the match and were among a full house of 40,000 which saw Uruguay win 2–1. If that had been close the second game, against Germany, was very bad-tempered. The Egyptian referee had his hands full from the start and there was some suggestion that he turned a blind eye to Uruguayan misdemeanours. On the other hand, the French papers blamed the Germans, who had two players sent off. The Uruguayans lost their captain but still won 4–1. The champions were then faced with another hard match against Italy. This was as brilliant a game as the one against Germany had been soiled and tasteless. The better team won but the Olympic champions prevailed only by 3–2. Andrade had one of his last great games and at the end all the players of both sides shook hands and cheered each other.[22]

Argentina, meanwhile, had had a relatively easy passage. They were far too sophisticated for the United States, winning 11–2, their speed and passing overwhelming the Americans. Belgium caused a few anxieties. After sixteen minutes Argentina led 3–0, Belgium then drew level but Argentina pulled away to win comfortably enough in the end by 6–3. In the semi-final they met surprise packets Egypt, but again it was another six-goal victory. So now it was Argentina versus Uruguay for the 102nd time since that first meeting only twenty-seven years before, and this time the prize was the Olympic Football Championship.

The interest in the two South American republics was enormous. It provides one of the key moments in the process by which football became the people's passion. Most of the papers in Buenos Aires and Montevideo devoted several pages to the final match. Many men in Buenos Aires and Montevideo found their lives structured around the cables from Europe which provided minute-by-minute accounts of the progress of the matches. During the game between Argentina and the USA the correspondent from *La Prensa* sent, by small telegrams of fifteen words each, 10,000 francs' worth of messages. Before the end of the game he was being criticized by his editor for having delayed giving the name of the scorer of the first of the eleven Argentine goals. The news could not be detailed or quick enough. *La Nación* claimed one flash from Amsterdam reached their office in only fifty-two seconds.[23]

Every square in the centre of Buenos Aires had loudspeakers fitted so that the public could hear the progress of the game, and crowds also gathered outside radio shops. The most spectacular gathering was in front of *La Prensa*'s offices. The crowd completely blocked the street from the Plaza de Mayo for two squares via the Avenida de Mayo and the Calle Peru connecting with the Calle Victoria. All the balconies within hearing distance of the three loudspeakers were also filled to capacity. The crowd behaved as if they were at the game. Cheers, shrill whistling, groans and sighs were the responses to the loudspeakers' descriptions of the progress of the game. There was, of course, no running commentary. Episodes were described after they had taken place, based on the cable information.

> In between the intermittent episodes broadcast, excited comment would burst forth from the crowd but as soon as the voice of the loudspeakers was heard again sss-s-s-s went the crowd, and it would have been something akin to suicide to have spoken another word until the voice had stopped ... The silence of the grave, broken only by the monotonous drone of the loudspeaker and an occasional distant snort of a motor horn seemed to hang over just those few squares.[24]

Football fever had broken out in Europe too. The tournament was watched by enormous crowds – 249,560 paid £44,905 for seventeen matches – and for the final 250,000 requests for tickets were received from all over the continent for places in a stadium which held only 40,000. Otto Busche left Switzerland for Amsterdam on foot on 5 May and arrived on 6 June just in time to buy a ticket for the final. He would be joined in the stadium by Prince Henry of the Netherlands and most of the local diplomatic corps, who did not have to undergo the indignity of paying.[25]

It took two games to decide the final. The first was a 1–1 draw in which both teams played cautiously. The replay was much better and characterized by the 'savage ardour' of both sets of players. No one, it seemed, wanted to rely on the drawing of lots which another equal outcome would produce. It was end-to-end excitement. Uruguay had brought in three fresh forwards, Arremón, Borjas and Figueroa replacing Petrone, Urdinaran and Castro who, some commentators thought, were not the players they had been in 1924. Uruguay won 2–1, the winning goal coming from Scarone in the second half. But it was the wonderful play of their defence, especially the backs Arispe and the captain Nasazzi, and the brilliance of goalkeeper Mazali, which ensured the victory. The last two were better than they had been in 1924. The crowd had supported the Argentinians as underdogs and the general verdict was that they had been unlucky to lose.

Back in Buenos Aires, the crowd outside *La Prensa* could hardly contain itself when the second Uruguayan goal was scored. Faces fell as the loudspeaker announced only two or three minutes to go with Argentina engaged in a *'violenta ofensiva'*. Some began to leave, muttering, *'Ya está terminado todo'* and disappearing into the mist which had descended. The loudspeaker then announced *'Uruguayos dos Argentina uno'*. At the same moment the crowds in the Plaza Independencia and other parts of Montevideo were beginning the celebrations.

Was South America the new centre of world football? Jules Rimet, the French President of FIFA, thought that Argentina and Uruguay could hold their own against the best of British professionals. The Chilean delegate Juan Livingstone agreed: 'It was the best match I have ever seen. I think the South Americans have given a lesson in technique to European football.'[26] But *Le Miroir des Sports* was doubtful. The Uruguayans and the Argentinians were not yet in the physical condition of the British, who never tired. But the paper agreed that the Latin Americans were the artists, the British the robust artisans. Who was better? How could the professionals be brought up against the amateurs – if they were amateurs? A tournament was needed in which all could legitimately take part, a genuine world championship. That was one straw in the wind. Another was the talk of the individual players whose finesse, elegance and skill had seduced the crowds in Amsterdam. Orsi, for example, the Argentine left-winger. He would soon be playing his football closer to Amsterdam than Buenos Aires after receiving an offer from Juventus which he could not refuse.

The idea of a world championship had been discussed at several FIFA meetings. In 1926 the Secretary, Henri Delauney, had said, 'Today international football can no longer be held within the confines of the Olympics, and many countries where professionalism is now recognised and organised cannot any longer be represented there by their best players.' By 1928 it was agreed to put on such a tournament. The only questions were when and where? Uruguay would hardly have come into the reckoning before 1924. One writer claims that a Uruguayan diplomat, Dr Enrique Buero, discussed the possibilities with Jules Rimet in Geneva in 1925.[27] Several European countries were interested in staging the event. Uruguay appears to have been chosen partly because of the country's triumphs on the field in 1924 and 1928, but mainly because their authorities offered to pay the travel and hotel expenses of all the participating teams and to build a large, modern stadium. Uruguay was enjoying a good standard of living in the 1920s, based on a combination of meat and wool exports and stable government, which had built something akin to a welfare state including the first legal eight-hour day in the Western hemisphere. If the tournament were to be held in July 1930, then it could form part of the centenary celebrations of the adoption of Uruguay's first constitution.

The Centenario Stadium was built in the middle of a park in central Montevideo named after the man who had twice been President of the Republic, José Batlle y Ordóñez. Building did not begin until February 1930 and it was therefore not ready for the first matches. It was officially opened by the President of the Republic for Uruguay's match against Peru on 18 July. The Centenario was not modern in design, but was reminiscent of the Roman Coliseum except that it was built with reinforced concrete. As Jules Rimet later wrote, it was built only for one sport and was a 'temple of football'. It contained accommodation for about 80,000 spectators and the three tribunes were called Colombes, Amsterdam and Montevideo, the first two in recognition of the Olympic triumphs, the third in expectation of the completion of a hat-trick of victories. It was easily the biggest stadium in South America and had very little competition from Europe either in size or elegance.

Unfortunately few Europeans crossed the Atlantic either to play or sit in it. Only France, Belgium, Rumania and Yugoslavia sent teams. That Italy and Spain failed to do so was very disappointing to the hosts, as was the refusal of the British. The English Football Association replied to their invitation in the most cursory manner. Dated 30 November 1929, their note said:

Dear Sir,
The letter of the 10th ultimo from the Asociacion Uruguaya de Football inviting a Representative Team of the Football Association to visit Uruguay in July and August next to play in the Worlds Championship [sic] in Montevideo has been considered by our International Committee.
    I am instructed to express regret at our inability to accept the invitation.
                                                                      F.J. Wall, sec.

The Uruguayan Chargé d'Affaires in London was told by a representative of the Foreign Office that there was nothing to be done.[28]

The four European teams were joined by Mexico, the USA and seven representatives from South America: Argentina, Bolivia, Brazil, Chile, Paraguay, Peru and the hosts. A cumbersome thirteen meant three groups of three and one of four, the winners to meet in semi-finals. Uruguay and

Argentina looked unstoppable but Argentina had a narrow squeak against France. Leading 1–0 but under pressure and hanging on, a potential French equalizer was prevented by the referee ending the game six minutes early. He was persuaded to restart it but the danger had passed. The Uruguayan crowd supported the French and catcalled the Argentinians, who were so upset they threatened to withdraw from the tournament. The President of Uruguay gave a personal guarantee as to their safety, so they played on. They beat Mexico 6–3 in a match of five penalties, but against Chile became involved in a little local difficulty. Again the Uruguayan crowd had been supporting their opponents and probably whistling the men from across the water. Just before half time Monti fouled the Chilean Torres. In their next encounter Torres punched him on the nose. A fight ensued, rapidly involving most of the other players. Some spectators joined in but policemen and championship officials eventually sorted it out, enabling Argentina to complete their 3–1 victory.[29] The semi-final provided an easy victory over a United States team which contained five Scots and one Englishman. Once Monti had scored the first goal it was a matter of how many Argentina would win by. It was 6–1 in the end. Several thousand fans went over the River Plate to watch the game while an estimated 20,000 listened to it over newspaper loudspeakers in the centre of Buenos Aires.[30]

Uruguay entered the final having conceded only one goal in four matches. That was in the semi-final, against the Yugoslavian team, who fought well in the first half but were eventually overwhelmed 6–1. Several of the Yugoslavs played professionally in France, and they had eliminated Brazil in the first phase of the competition. So the stage was set for a repeat of the 1928 Olympic Final.

For those few July days Buenos Aires and Montevideo were ravished by the passion for football. For many Argentine supporters the first task was to obtain a passage either on one of the river steamers which regularly criss-crossed the Plate or on one of the Atlantic liners which would call at Montevideo on the way out. It was easy for some, such as the six National Deputies who made the crossing in a government barge towed by a tugboat. The Postmaster General chartered a cargo steamer for favoured subordinates and the rich took their private yachts or went by plane. As for the rest, there was heavy advance booking of the steamers from Saturday afternoon once it was known Argentina were in the final. On Monday, ten thousand fans besieged the shipping offices for most of the day, even though it had been announced at noon that all places on boats sailing on Tuesday night – the final was on Wednesday – had been sold.[31]

Wednesday's newspapers were full of descriptions and pictures of the 'exodus'. No one really knew how many had travelled although it was claimed that fifteen thousand had gone and twice as many had wanted to. Thousands turned up at the South Basin to watch the boats depart, some hoping to take the place of those ticket holders who did not turn up, others in order to leap from dockside to boatdeck as the vessels pulled away. The slightly less adventurous climbed dockside cranes and conducted community singing, which was punctuated by cries of '*Argentina Si, Uruguaya No*'. After the departing ships had been cheered on their journey groups of young men paraded through the city with optimistically worded banners.[32]

Business was most certainly not as usual on that Platense Wednesday. Many firms and offices closed for the day, including the General Motors plant in Buenos Aires. The Chamber of Deputies abandoned its afternoon session because most of the members had gone to the match or arranged to listen to it on the radio. Many offices brought in radios around which the staff huddled; indeed many had done so from the start of the tournament. One estimate claimed that fifty thousand fans gathered in front of newspaper offices in the city to listen to broadcast descriptions of the game. Although they did not know it they were better placed than some of those who had actually obtained places on the steamers. Several became fogbound in the river overnight and their passengers never reached the Centenario Stadium.

But the largest crowd ever to witness a football match in South America up to that time – about 80,000 – were there. They saw an exciting match in which Uruguay went ahead, but by half time Argentina led 2–1. Uruguay equalized early in the second half, after which the Argentine forward Varallo was injured and limped badly for the rest of the game. Uruguay were now on top with the Argentine half-backs unable to win possession. Constant pressure on the Argentine defence eventually produced goals for Iriarte after seventy-five minutes and Castro three minutes from the end. By that time the Argentine goalkeeper had hurt an arm.

Jules Rimet thought he had rarely seen such a storm of enthusiasm and released emotions in a stadium at the end of a match. He assumed it was due to the fact that a little country had beaten the world. Both teams received an ovation as they left the field. The disappointment of the Argentinians was obvious. But in Montevideo an all-night celebration preceded a national holiday declared by the President.

Many of the smaller bars in working-class districts kept open house all night serving free wine or beer or anything else, only ejecting customers when they became too obnoxiously drunk … Throughout the night processions of fans marched through the city singing, shouting, proclaiming their victory through great megaphones …[33]

It was lively in Buenos Aires too, rather like London on the day war broke out in 1914 or on the day it ended, as one, presumably British, commentator opined. A woman on a balcony in the Avenida de Mayo waved the Uruguayan flag and cheered, only to be met with stones. Both the Uruguayan Consulate and the Oriental Club were stoned and their windows broken. In the Avenida groups of youths went along dismally chanting, '*Ar-gen-ti-nos Ar-gen-ti-nos*'. Many were armed with stones and bits of wood. It took several charges by mounted police to clear the area. In the evening, groups of youths played *Sacarse el sombrero*. This was a traditional Buenos Aires activity involving a marching column led with the national flag. Passers-by were ordered to salute the colours. If they did not, they could be chastised. Two people were allegedly shot. It was after midnight before the last of such gangs had been broken up.[34] The disappointment was palpable. One evening paper had invited every football enthusiast in Buenos Aires to gather in front of its offices after the match for a huge procession which would parade all round the city, and thousands had done so, many bringing their own flags. Their homeward plod with furled flags was a sorry sight.

As for the papers themselves, there was sense and sensibility on the one hand and disappointed thrashing about on the other. *La Prensa* claimed the Uruguayans had won by excessively rough play and criticized the Argentinians for failing to adopt similar tactics.

Argentine teams sent abroad to represent the prestige of the country in any form of sport should not be composed of men who have anything the matter with them … We don't need men who fall at the first blow, who are in danger of fainting at the first onslaught even if they are clever in their footwork … These 'lady-players' should be eliminated … we must also get rid of those leaders who manage, speculate, and deal in football as if it were a purely commercial affair …

La Nación, on the other hand, condemned the wilder reactions to defeat as 'marks of ill-breeding'. It criticized groups who misused the Argentine National Anthem on such occasions.

We quite understand the vehement desire on the part of the people to see the Argentine side win the match and the championship; we can make allowances for the passionate enthusiasm of the crowd. But this is not the sort of conflict which calls either for acts of ruffianism, and then, on top of that, a sudden call to pseudo-patriotism, in the shape of the National Anthem, to prevent the police from taking repressive measures. Above football ... comes the grade of culture which we hope we have achieved, and it is the business of the authorities to take whatever steps they deem necessary to maintain that culture. This is something we ought to take care never to lose.[35]

The Asociación Amateurs Argentina de Football lost that culture, for a time at least. A combination of disappointment and the extravagances of players and press persuaded it to break off footballing relations with Uruguay. No matches were played in 1931 but the only two internationals played by Argentina the following year were against the Orientals.[36] The Uruguayans did not visit Europe to defend the world title in 1934 nor did they go to France in 1938. The complications brought about by the introduction of professionalism in South American football were probably the reason, although there was some suggestion that it was in retaliation for the poor European turnout in Montevideo. As for Argentina, the team did compete in Italy in 1934 but was eliminated in the first match by Sweden, 3–2 the score, the winning goal coming ten minutes from the end. None of the 1930 finalists played. But Monti and Orsi had become professionals in Italy and played for the Italians on the basis of parental nationality. The Asociación del Fútbol Argentino, as by 1936 it had become, was keen to stage the 1938 championships, but FIFA chose France instead and Argentina refused to send a team. Brazil's undistinguished performance of 1930 was repeated in Genoa four years later when its team lost 3–1 to Spain after missing a penalty. Again the complications accompanying the introduction of professionalism and Rio–São Paulo rivalries did not allow the strongest side to be selected. There were no Paulistas in the team.

But in the 1938 championships Brazil made its mark. Led by the brilliant black centre-forward, Leonidas da Silva, Brazil first defeated Poland 6–5 after extra time on a waterlogged pitch in Strasbourg. At one point Leonidas took off his boots and threw them towards the training bench with the obvious intention of playing on without them. But the Swedish referee made him put them back on. He scored four goals with them.[37] Brazil next met Czechoslovakia in Bordeaux and in one of those unpredictable but anarchic matches characteristic of Latin American football had two players sent off. The Czechs lost one and suffered several injuries in a drawn match. The replay involved fifteen new players, nine Brazilians and six Czechs, and this time there were no problems and Brazil won 2–1. Were Brazil really as confident as the history books now suggest?

It is alleged, for example, that the main party left Bordeaux for Marseilles, where the semi-final was to be played, before the end of the match with Czechoslovakia; that on arrival there, they booked all the places on the plane to Paris, so sure were they that they would beat Italy in the semi-final; and that they rested Leonidas and Tim, in order that they would be fresh for the final. Each Brazilian player was promised a house and a share of the final receipts if the team won. But Brazil lost more convincingly than the 2–1 score suggests. Nevertheless, two more goals from Leonidas helped them to beat Sweden and take third place. They were still complaining to FIFA about the organization of the tournament in 1943.[38] Uruguay, Argentina and now Brazil had shown themselves to be world powers in football. The FIFA Congress of 1938 awarded the 1942 championship to Brazil. In 1946, Spanish became one of the three official languages of FIFA. The balance of football power was beginning to shift.

CHAPTER FOUR

PROFESSIONALS

*Professionals are in this respect quite outside the frames of the
Football organisations. They are artists, good or bad, such as
men generally are. The more you pay them the more interest
they will show, but this has nothing to do with the sport spirit
... and aim of sport, and it is not for the benefit of artists that
countries and towns subsidise sport and numerous people in all
countries spend time and work for the interest of Football.
Sportsmen as Professionals are a mistake. Professionals as
Artists are the proof of the fact that both leaders and footballers
forget the ideals of sport. Sport [is] for every young man in the
country, for the health of the nations and not for the purse of
some players.*
Louis Oestrup, former Vice-President of FIFA, December
1928, *Fédération Internationale* 33, 1928

In many respects the coming of professional football has the same causes
everywhere. As football becomes a more popular activity and ceases to be
the monopoly of an elite, so more people begin to watch as well as play.
Ambitious clubs start to invest in better facilities, to charge spectators an
entrance fee, to seek the best players. Inducements are offered to the
players, jobs perhaps, or cash in the boots. The pretence that all is above
board may persist, even though everyone knows what is happening. Some
members or owners will try to stamp out what they consider an offence
against the purity of sport. Sometimes there are struggles between those
clubs, usually the smaller or medium-sized ones, who see professionalism
as annihilating healthy competition and producing a football world based
on money, and the bigger clubs for whom it is the obvious next stage in
an historical process. Moreover, it facilitates control of the players. In
South America this process was complicated by splits among the elites
who ran the game. But the key moment came when leading players in

Argentina, Brazil and Uruguay were systematically recruited by European clubs.

As early as 1906 complaints appeared in the Argentine newspapers that some clubs were trying to poach players belonging to their competitors. Not long after there were allegations that Uruguayans were coming over the Plate to play for Buenos Aires clubs. Was it for love of the game alone? Boca Juniors, Racing as well as Estudiantes de la Plata had had Uruguayan players since 1911 and by 1913 *La Nación* could talk of a disguised professionalism preparing the way for future evolution.[1] Some clubs were becoming powerful, most notably Gimnasia y Esgrima. By 1912 it was the biggest and best-equipped athletic club, if not in the whole of Latin America, certainly in Buenos Aires. Not only did it boast a splendid gymnasium and a fencing school, as befitted its name, but as we have seen it had a football ground with accommodation for 25,000 people, a spacious swimming bath and tennis courts. The President, Ricardo Aldao, was an important member of the Buenos Aires elite, a lawyer and businessman, member of the IOC and the Asociación Gentlemen del Deporte with a long record of public office. It was not surprising that he was involved in the first breakaway from the Asociación Argentina de Football and presided over the rebel Federación Argentina de Football during its three years of life between 1912 and 1914.[2] But the AFA retained the strongest league including Boca, Huracán, Racing and River Plate.

By 1915 unity had been rebuilt, but it was to prove fragile. Four years later a more serious division occurred. It was triggered by conflicts between the clubs and dissatisfaction with the way in which these conflicts were dealt with by the AFA. At the end of the 1918 season it was clear that Argentinos de Quilmes were going to be relegated from the First Division. Either Ferrocarril Oeste or Columbia seemed most likely to accompany Quilmes and they still had to play each other. When Columbia won it looked as though they must stay up, but Ferrocarril protested that Columbia had fielded an ineligible player. Two other clubs down near the bottom supported them in their protest. The Disciplinary Council of the AFA agreed with the protesters and docked Columbia eleven points, but on appeal changed its mind. Columbia stayed up, Ferrocarril went down. Meanwhile another problem surfaced in the Intermediate League where Vélez Sarsfield were hoping to win promotion to the First Division. But the club had eight points removed by the AFA for fielding a suspended player. In fact it was his brother who had played and the AFA found in favour of Vélez on appeal. Some clubs protested and the whole issue spiralled out of control. A special assembly of the AFA to decide the issue was thwarted by an organized filibuster. It was clear that some of the bigger clubs were spoiling for a fight. There were complaints of AFA arbitrariness when six clubs were suspended, others threatened with expulsion and the 1919 championship collapsed after a few weeks. The upshot was that thirteen of the leading clubs formed their own league, under the title of Asociación Amateurs de Football. When their invitation to Vélez Sarsfield to join was accepted it meant that the rebels could run a fourteen-club championship which included Racing, River, San Lorenzo and Independiente, while the AFA was left with a rump of six including Boca, Estudiantes de la Plata and Huracán in their First Division. The rift lasted until 1926 and required the intervention of the President of the Republic before it was resolved. In 1927 the Asociación Amateurs Argentina de Football presided over a revamped First Division of thirty-four clubs.[3]

It is not clear how much any of this was linked to the issue of professionalism. But what is clear is that by the middle of the 1920s many players in the Argentine leagues were being paid to play. *El Gráfico*, the main football paper, set out the issues clearly enough in 1926 without actually naming any names. When the British or students had made up most of the players, they had paid for themselves. But the increase in the number of clubs, the growth of competition and the expansion in the numbers of spectators meant the game had spread beyond the social elite. Good players drawn from the poorer sections of society were given football gear, free membership and even suits to wear. Club directors sought players who would boost the prestige of their institutions. Tempting offers of employment were soon followed by payment for playing. As all this was under the counter, it gave the initiative to the players. They changed clubs when they felt like it and the directors had little control. The implication was that above-board professionalism was necessary.[4] The English-speaking press put it rather more graphically. The idea that the Argentine footballer was amateur was a 'criollo joke':

> The men who compose our leading local teams are every bit as professional as the hardest-headed big leagues in England ... Argentine football players play the game winter and summer and train every day ... Nominally they are engaged to work for gentlemen financially interested in the big teams ...[5]

While in Argentina the existence of professionalism continued to be denied, in several European countries it had been openly adopted. Once the club tours and the Olympic performances showed what a reservoir of talent existed in South America, it was inevitable that European clubs would be attracted. It is not clear when the first Argentinian footballer made his way to Italy, but it was probably Julio Libonatti of Newells Old Boys who in 1925 signed for Torino. After the Amsterdam Olympics of 1928 Raimondo Orsi was tempted by Juventus with a monthly salary of 8,000 lire, a fee of 100,000 and a Fiat 509. Soon others followed, especially when it became clear that those *oriundi*, the sons of Italian immigrants to South America, were qualified to play for Italy. Both Orsi and the notorious centre-half Luis Monti, who had also been signed by Juventus, played for Italy in the Mitropa Cup in 1931 and, along with Guaita, in the World Cup of 1934, and there were other less famous migrants. Perhaps open professionalism at home, it was felt, would staunch the flow.

There was also some feeling that the revamped First Division of 1927 itself was in need of rationalization. In 1930 it contained thirty-six clubs who played each other only once. This meant the attractive matches between the five top clubs were not duplicated home and away as they would have been in a smaller league. The players too felt the fixture arrangements left something to be desired. The season seemed to be extending into the summer and the dangers of this were dramatically underlined in March 1931 when a player of Sportivo Barracas died of sunstroke following a match against Gimnasia y Esgrima.[6] Before the start of the 1931 season some players actually went on strike. What they appeared to be demanding was freedom of contract, which suggested that they were already professionals as no club could compel an amateur player to remain on the retained list. A deputation marched through Buenos Aires and had a brief interview with the President of the Republic. He turned the problem over to the Mayor of Buenos Aires, who allegedly told the clubs that the strike of players and professionalism were really the same issue. The clubs agreed, even if the players were more doubtful. On 9 May 1931 twelve clubs declared themselves to be professional: Atlanta, Boca Juniors, Chacarita Juniors, Estudiantes de la Plata, Ferrocarril Oeste, Gimnasia y Esgrima de la Plata, Lanus, Platense, Racing, San Lorenzo, Talleres and Tigre. Independiente and River Plate could hardly stay out and eighteen clubs kicked off the Liga Argentina de Football on 31 May 1931. The clubs said it would be better for the players and, as the Vice-President of Boca explained, it would end all this nonsense about 'brooms and sawdust', tinkering with the accounts to conceal the illegal payments. The players did not get freedom of contract.[7]

Some tidying up remained. The Asociación Argentina de Football retained the country's affiliation to FIFA even though the biggest clubs and the best players were now with the professional league. With a World Cup scheduled for 1934, efforts were made to bring the two organizations together. They eventually succeeded but not early enough to send the strongest possible Argentinian team to Italy. Of the amateurs, only Sportivo Barracas held out. That year saw the formation of the Asociación del Fútbol Argentino, with the President of the professional league, Tiburcio Padilla, also becoming President of the new body. He was a professor and surgeon in the Faculty of Medicine at the University of Buenos Aires, a political activist in the Unión Cívica Radical and an important holder of office in the Department of National Hygiene and a National Deputy for the Federal Capital. He was also President of Chacarita Juniors. Professionalism had not fractured the connection between football and the Argentinian elite.[8]

In Uruguay there had also been divisions within the football establishment. Not surprisingly this had been related to the troubles across the water in Buenos Aires. Clubs in Montevideo had been tempted into playing teams from the rebel Asociación Amateurs de Football. This had been forbidden by the UFA, who maintained relations with the AAF. The result was the suspension in 1922 of two clubs, Central and Peñarol, the latter one of the two giants of the Uruguayan game. The rift lasted for three years and after the mediation of the National Committee of Physical Education had failed a settlement was reached only following the intervention of the President of the Republic in 1925. It will be recalled that 1925 was also the year of Nacional's epic European tour and it is hard to believe that the leading Uruguayan players were amateurs, whatever definition is used. And with Argentina having a publicly professional sector by 1931, could Uruguay afford to be far behind?

In Brazil things were different. For one thing elite control over football was probably stronger there than in either Argentina or Uruguay. Leading gentlemen sportsmen were firmly attached to amateurism. But the whole issue of professionalism in Brazil was complicated by the presence of race as well as class.

In Rio the championship had been dominated by elite teams. Between 1906 and 1922, no team with a black or mulatto player won a championship match. The President of Brazil forbade the selection of black players for the South American championships in Buenos Aires in 1921. But in 1923 Vasco da Gama were promoted to the First Division. Playing four blacks or mulattos (their occupations were taxi driver, wall painter, stevedore and truck driver) and four illiterate whites, Vasco won the league in their first season. They beat the young students, professionals and businessmen who made up the elevens of Flamengo and Fluminense, América and Botafogo. They were a sensation and big crowds flocked to their matches. They seemed fitter than their rivals and usually came on strongly in the second half. Not only did they play poor whites and blacks; they also paid them. The money was called *bicho* (animal) because it was sometimes a dog, 5,000 reis, at other times a rabbit, 10,000 reis, or a turkey, 20,000 reis. A chicken was 50,000 reis, and a cow 100,000.[9] The reaction to this success and the manner of its achievement was startling. The big five Rio teams, América, Bangu, Botafogo, Flamengo and Fluminense, left the Liga Metropolitana de Desportos Terrestres (LMDT) and created the Associação Metropolitana de Esportes Atléticos (AMEA) but did not invite Vasco to join them.

In 1924 two leagues ran side by side in Rio. But more spectators went to see Vasco repeat their championship win of the previous year in the LMDT than to watch the big five. So in 1925 Vasco were asked to join the new league, along with São Cristóvão and Andarai. But in an astonishing attempt to check shamateurism and to keep top football for the better-off player they introduced the AMEA card. Before each game every player had to complete one in the presence of officials and include the name, nationality, date of birth, place of study and workplace of the player. In a country where neither education nor literacy was widespread this was a test intended to exclude the poor white as well as the black player. The process was supervised by a three-man commission of the league. Players had to prove to the Commission that they really worked for a living. Visits to employers were made and players were banned. Some newspapers opposed such authoritarian policies. Vasco's response was to send some of its players to night school, but learning by rote did not always satisfy the investigators. The system remained in place until 1929 which, coincidentally, was the next year Vasco won the championship. Abolishing the card was an important moment on the road to professionalism.

As in Argentina, the loss of players abroad also persuaded some powerful men in Brazilian football that professionalism had to come. The Fantoni brothers were among the first Brazilians who went to Italy from Atlético Mineiro in 1930. Seven left São Paulo for Italy soon after and three top Fluminense players left, saying they were fed up with being exploited by the football bosses. Several went to Argentina and five were on the books of San Lorenzo in the early 1930s when it won the LAF in 1933. In

1931 Vasco, on its tour to Spain, lost two of its stars, Fausto and Jaguaré, who defected to Barcelona happy with a 30,000 peseta signing-on fee, a proper contract and a salary plus bonuses. The coming of professionalism in Argentina and Uruguay served only to underline the urgency. As one of the players bound for Italy, Amilcar, warned:

> I'm off to Italy. I am tired of being an amateur in football when such a condition has stopped existing a long time ago, masked by a hypocritical system of tips which clubs give to their players while keeping most of their income for themselves. For 20 years I have offered my modest services to Brazilian football. What has happened? The clubs got rich and I have nothing. I am going to the country that knows how to pay for the players' skill.[10]

The loss of the best players, a suggestion of a decline in the size of the paying crowd and the fact that many clubs used money made from football to support their other social and sporting activities also helped to concentrate the minds of some scions of Rio football. Fluminense in particular lost important players and by the early thirties could show only two championships in twelve years. Their President, Oscar da Costa, was in favour of recognizing professionalism, although it was the President of América, Antonio Gomez de Avelar, who in 1932 was the first to announce that his club paid its players. Bangu and Vasco soon came out in support with Flamengo, Botafogo and São Cristóvão against. The Fla–Flu rivalry was as intense off the field as on, with both sides competing vigorously in the search for top players and both Presidents looking to control whatever new organization the reform of football might bring. Rivadávia Meyer, President of both Flamengo and AMEA, showed that there was a battle to be fought when he castigated the player who wanted to become a professional as like:

> a gigolo who exploits a prostitute. The club gives him all the material necessary to play football and to enjoy himself with the game and he wants to earn money as well? I will not allow this in Flamengo. Professionalism degrades the man.[11]

Argentina and Uruguay each had but one major football centre. But in Brazil there was São Paulo as well as Rio and what happened there was clearly going to be a vital factor in determining how the conflict within the football elites was resolved. We have noted earlier the formation of the Liga Paulista de Football. But in 1913 several leading clubs led by CA Paulistano set up a rival organization, the Associação Paulista de Esportes Atléticos (APEA). It seems clear that they did this in order to keep out teams, like

Corinthians, made up of working-class players. Indeed they expelled one of their founder members, the Scottish Wanderers, for paying their players in 1916. But by 1917 the Corinthians and Palestra Italia were together again with the Paulista aristocrats recruiting players from and being supported by a very different class to the gentleman who ran CA Paulistano. For some years a blind eye was turned to the professionalism that undoubtedly existed. As Rivadávia Meyer said after Brazil failed to win a match in the 1923 South American championship with a team made up only of players from Rio, it was better to do that than to have 'taken the Paulista mercenaries who only run after the ball for money'.[12]

In 1924 CA Paulistano ran out of patience and, with seven other clubs, formed the Liga de Amadores de Futebol – the Amateur Football League (LAF). It was an organization supported by the coffee aristocracy. Indeed the President of Paulistano and their leader on that famous 1925 tour to Europe, Antonio Prado Junior, was a producer and exporter of coffee. Apart from the fact that such people were about to be seriously hit by the Great Depression, when the Corinthians returned to APEA after only one season the writing was on the wall for the league for amateur purity, and its final championship was held in 1929. In that year CA Paulistano stopped playing football although some of their directors joined with those of AA Palmeiras to form the São Paulo Football Club. They were soon offering salaries to players.

Blacks were excluded from São Paulo's white sports world, but they had been forming their own athletic clubs even before 1914. Some of them soon had good football teams and in 1927, apparently on the initiative of black leaders, a black versus white football match became part of the celebration of Abolition Day, 13 May, the date on which slavery in Brazil had been abolished in 1888. Blacks won the first two matches, much to the surprise of some local journalists, and these successes probably hastened the recruitment of the best black players by the leading white clubs.[13] It is worth noting that sport in the United States was firmly segregated in this period.

By 1930 Italian recruiting agents were making regular trips to Brazil, visiting Rio but especially São Paulo with its large Italian immigrant community. Of course with no formal professionalism and therefore no formal contracts players could leave as and when they liked. No transfer fee was involved and Corinthians soon lost four and Palestra three of their best men. It was alleged that Como, Fiorentina, Lazio and Roma took thirty-nine Brazilian players in 1931. Then there were the losses to

Argentina and Uruguay, including Leonidas da Silva and Domingos da Guia to Montevideo, where they stayed for only one year. This was the context which propelled those in Rio and São Paulo who thought professionalism the only answer to start talks about creating a professional league. There was a good deal of confusion, the newspapers were divided and the opposition to professionalism still vigorous.

But on 12 January 1933 the deed was done. Or rather, a set of rules governing professionalism was drawn up and in Rio, a new league, the Liga Carioca de Futebol, the Carioca Football League, was formed. There followed a piece of delicious irony. Vasco had new directors and they joined the opposition to professionalism and the new league! But the Council of the club was in favour and a special meeting forced the directors to resign. Under fresh bosses, the club returned to its support for professionalism. Botafogo, Flamengo and São Cristóvão were against it but Flamengo reconsidered after six months. How could it afford to lose its matches with América, Bangu, Vasco and, above all, Fluminense? Still two leagues existed side by side for four seasons between 1933 and 1936. The LCF and the APEA at last got together to dot the i's and cross the t's. Club members were rewarded with free admission to all home games or to the grounds where their team was playing. The revenue from all matches was to be split between the teams. In the first professional game in São Paulo in March 1933, São Paulo beat Santos 5–1 and the legendary Friedenreich scored the first goal at the improbable age of thirty-eight. The first game in Rio was a few weeks later when Vasco met América. There was one last twist in this complicated and confused tale. The CBD was against professionalism and in August 1933 the two professional leagues of São Paulo and Rio met to create the Federação Brasileira de Futebol, the Federation of Brazilian Football (FBF). It was chaired by Arnoldo Guinle, Vice-President of Fluminense and a member of one of Rio's oldest and richest families. The aim was to take the place of the CBD as the representative of Brazilian football on FIFA. In the event the CBD kept its power by recognizing professionalism in 1937. But in his 1935 letter to Jules Rimet asking for FIFA recognition for the FBF Guinle made a claim to which we will have to return, that football was already a cultural product inherent to the style of life of the sporting Brazilian.[14]

It would be hard to deny that professionalism was a success. Football's popularity had grown in the 1920s in a context of expanding urbanization produced by the investment of European capital in Brazil after the end of the First World War. Professionalism came as the depression was easing, unemployment falling and a level of economic stability had been achieved. It was certainly good for the clubs. Although admission charges went up, crowds increased, so much so that when the big five clubs in Rio played each other the grounds were not large enough to take all those who wanted to be there. The late 1920s and 1930s saw a round of stadium building. Vasco had opened its São Januário stadium in 1927 in the presence of the President of Brazil and five Ministers of State. The first match encapsulated the rivalry between São Paulo and Rio when Santos, the visitors from the south, won 5–3. Did their centre-forward really say, 'They build a ballroom; we give a show'!?[15] In São Paulo Palestra pulled down the old Parque Antartica and built a new stadium capable of holding over 30,000. It was the biggest there until the municipality built the Pacaembu with a capacity of 70,000 in 1940. The top league games were increasingly played there.

The pro-professional group had always believed in the drawing power and self-sufficiency of football. The aristocratic Fluminense wanted football to be separate from the rest of the club's economic and social life and in order to help ensure this, between 1933 and 1941 established its administrators in a separate office, although on the same street. The facilities at Fluminense had impressed the directors of Plymouth Argyle on their visit in 1924. Not only did they have a stadium with room for 25,000; they also boasted billiard saloons, ballrooms, cafés, sixteen acres of grounds in which were located tennis courts, swimming baths, basketball and netball courts. A gymnasium was being built and there were bedrooms for athletes wishing to sleep there.[16] The club had 4,000 members paying the Brazilian equivalent of £1 per month.

The leading clubs followed the Fluminense pattern. There were two categories of members, an inner circle of voting shareholders, still an elitist preserve in the 1940s and 1950s, and a much larger group of members paying annual subscriptions. Club directorates made policy, as we have seen, and Presidents were powerful figures. But they were elected by shareholders and if they pursued unpopular courses could be turned out, as Vasco's were in 1933. By 1935 Fluminense had 6,500 members, Flamengo 5,500, América 1,700 and Bon Successo 1,200. São Paulo clubs had about 75,000 in total.[17] Later the middle class would join in such numbers that Flamengo boasted 65,000 members by the 1960s and Corinthians 150,000. These were the dominant football clubs in Brazil, so much so that in São Paulo, for example, there was no promotion and relegation between the First and Second Divisions until 1949.

Professionalism stimulated football in the other states too. Of course many of them already had their own championships, Bahia since 1905, Rio Grande do Sul since 1911, Minas Gerais since 1914, Paraná and Pernambuco since 1915. By the end of 1933 Minas Gerais, Paraná and Rio State had adopted professionalism and Espírito Santo followed in 1934. The other side to this was that Rio and São Paulo increasingly sought players from the other states. It would be some years yet before their leading clubs would have any hope of successfully challenging the teams from the political capital and the economic capital. In fact it was 1971 before Atlético Mineiro from Belo Horizonte in Minas Gerais won the inter-club championship of Brazil, first played for in 1933 but a tournament restricted to the clubs of the two biggest cities until 1967.

What did professionalism do for the players? They were paid regularly instead of the 'tips' of the amateur years but often not very well paid. Eventually the stars would do well but others much less so. Moreover contracts were binding. Players did lose a kind of freedom to move as they liked. There would be no more examples from the 1920s like that of Neco who one week played for Palestra against Corinthians, and the next for Corinthians against Palestra.[18] Both the professionals and their coaches were excluded from the social side of the clubs. There were no pensions nor any insurance against disability. By 1940 three-quarters of all professionals were from the lower class. The bigger clubs tried to keep an eye on them by housing them in what were little better than barracks. But most professionals were not with the big clubs. More representative were those like Pelé's father, Dondinho, itinerant semi-pros who often signed for a few matches at a time. There was no players' union until 1946.

As for the blacks, some did all right for a while. Domingos da Guia actually became the first black player to pull on the shirt of Fluminense. The Zona Norte team of Bon Successo, where Leonidas played at first, fielded eleven black players during the thirties and Bangu often as many as eight. Leonidas, the 'Black Diamond', famed for his bicycle kick, became a popular figure among people predominantly of European origin. His photograph filled the pages of magazines, his face was used to advertise toothpaste, he was invited to open new shops and white women were known to ask for his autograph. When his mother went to watch him play she was given banknotes by the wealthier supporters when he scored a goal. He returned from the 1938 World Cup to a hero's welcome. Leonidas ended up as a store manager and later, a television commentator. Another member of that side, Hércules de Miranda, combined paid football with

Table One: Club Membership in Argentina 1926, 1931

	1926	1931
River Plate	3,661	15,686
Boca	3,022	7,728
Racing	2,624	7,071
Independiente	2,601	5,381
San Lorenzo	2,347	15,616
Huracán	1,641	2,986
Estudiantes		7,680

Source: Based on Iwanczuk (1990), p. 243.

further education and professional qualifications to such effect that he was able to buy his mother a house in 1937 and by the 1960s owned land and property in São Paulo and Santos. But there were always suspicions that once their usefulness as players had gone they were quickly discarded. Fausto, one of the great black attacking centre-halves who 'went for the ball like a plate of food', compared himself to an orange which would one day be left as pulp by the white bosses. Was it coincidence that while playing da Guia escaped punishment in 1937 for a motor accident in which he killed a pedestrian, while in 1944, when no longer a celebrity, he was sent to prison for carrying false identity papers?[19] The 1950 defeat by Uruguay which cost Brazil the World Cup was blamed on three black players, Bigode, Juvenal and Barbosa, the last named the goalkeeper who allowed Ghiggia's shot to beat him on the near post. Despite these conditions, the appeal of football to the disadvantaged continued unabated, the number of black players grew, and by the 1960s there were about six thousand professionals in Brazil. Wages were going up for black and white alike.

As we have seen, professionalism came to Buenos Aires in 1931. It seems to have been anticipated with some relish if club membership figures are any indication. In 1926 six of the leading clubs had slightly fewer than 16,000 members between them; in April 1931, on the eve of the professional league, the same six clubs plus Estudiantes de la Plata had over 60,000 *socios*. Attendances cannot be calculated with any precision but numbers of tickets sold per game suggest that after an uncertain start in the first eight years the 1940s and 1950s saw record ticket sales for First Division games. Unfortunately what these averages conceal is the huge crowds which followed the big five and the very small ones which gathered to watch the matches between two of the smaller fry.

Table Two: Tickets Sold per Argentine First Division
Game

1931–35	7,696
1936–40	6,940
1941–45	11,736
1946–50	12,755
1951–55	12,865
1956–60	10,783
1961–65	9,924
1966–70	7,830
1971–75	8,300
1976–80	6,488
1981–85	6,200

Source: Adapted from Scher and Palomino (1988), p. 46.

As in Brazil the early years of professionalism were years of stadium development to cope with the growing popularity of Sunday-afternoon football. A Special Commission of the AFA was set up in 1935 to consider the problem and the next year the Argentine Government showed its support for the professional game by authorizing special loans for stadium construction. The conditions actually benefited the big clubs who owned their grounds. The government justified the arrangements by insisting that institutions so helped should offer their facilities to elementary- and secondary-school children and by emphasizing the importance football had come to have in Argentine life.[20] The great stadiums of River and Boca were built under this scheme.

In many respects the fifteen or so years after the coming of open professionalism were among the most exciting and successful for football in Argentina. Crowds reached record levels and even the third and fourth teams of River Plate might attract 15,000 on occasion.[21] The circulation of the weekly *El Gráfico* almost doubled to 200,000 in the 1940s and the leading players were elevated to heroic status. The rivalry between Boca Juniors and River Plate dominated the championship. Boca won the title in 1934, 1935, 1940, 1943 and 1944; River won in 1932, 1936, 1937, 1941, 1942, 1945 and 1947. In 1943 Boca beat River for the championship by a single point. In the 1947 season River averaged three goals per game.

After a poor season in 1931 River embarked on a spending spree which led to their nickname of 'Millonarios', signing forwards Peucelle and Ferreyra, the latter a formidable goal scorer who drew the crowds, especially when scoring in twelve successive games and netting a record forty-four goals in 1932 and thirty in 1934. Their new stadium was opened in 1938 and provided an elegant but modern setting for two professional and four amateur teams together with 44,000 *socios*, these members having access to a wide range of sporting and social facilities including a two-thousand-seater restaurant. River had the team to match the setting, for this was the era of the forward line known as '*La Máquina*', the machine, because of the precision and harmony of their passing. The play of Muñoz, Moreno, Pedernera, Labruna and Lousteau (or Deambrosi) led many commentators to label them the world's best team.

There was competition from Avellaneda where the '*Diablos Rojos*', the 'Red Devils' of Independiente, won two championships in 1938 and 1939. They were led by the forward trio of de la Mata, Erico and Sastre, Erico a Paraguayan who scored an Argentine record forty-seven goals in 1937 and forty-three and forty in the championship years.[22] Between September 1936 and April 1938 there were no goalless draws in the Argentine First Division. If there had been a World Cup in 1942 Argentina would have been strong contenders.

The players did not always appreciate the restrictions of the professional system. Uruguayan professionals went on strike for four weeks in 1939 and the hero of Paris and Amsterdam, José Nasazzi, was President of an early players' union.[23] In Argentina some players thought that they were not receiving a fair share of this prosperity. A few went to Mexico in 1944 in search of more money. Relations between management and players were not good. An indication of the developing resentment on the players' side can be seen in a story told by the young Argentinian star Alfredo di Stéfano. At the end of 1947 Argentina spectacularly won the South American championships in Ecuador. The players were keen to get back to their families in Argentina for the New Year holiday but found that the AFA bosses accompanying the team had booked themselves on an early flight and the players on one due to leave the following day. Only when the players complained did the directors agree that the party should travel together.[24]

Since the end of 1944 the Argentinian players had had a union, the Fútbolistas Argentinos Agremiados, the FAA. By early 1948 the union was demanding recognition from the AFA, a minimum wage and freedom of contract. As no reply was forthcoming, a strike was declared for April. Union recognition nipped that in the bud but no agreement could be reached on the other demands and the strike began in July. The Argentine

Government then intervened, urging that the players' demands be met. A tribunal was set up to investigate the players' grievances, play restarted, but by November the strike was back on again. This time, the clubs annulled the contracts of the players and said they would finish the championship with amateurs. Attendances declined and in spite of government-inspired press statements that a return to amateurism might be a good thing, a settlement was eventually reached at the beginning of the 1949 season. It is not clear how far the conditions of the players were improved. Some authorities have suggested that the autonomy of club bosses was curtailed by the settlement.[25] It can hardly be without significance that the dispute triggered a new migration of players from Argentina. As many as 105 leading professionals left to follow their trade elsewhere. A similar result followed the five-months-long strike of players in Uruguay.

Many of them went to Colombia. One hundred and nine foreign professionals were playing in Colombia in 1949, fifty-seven of them from Argentina. They were able to do this and avoid the wrath of FIFA due to an internal quarrel between the Colombian Football Association, which was affiliated to FIFA, and the División Mayor del Fútbol Professionel de Bogotá, which was not. The new league introduced professionalism to Colombia in 1948. By 1949 some of the best South Americans, with a sprinkling of Europeans, were turning out for Cali, Medellín and the two leading Bogotá clubs, Independiente Sante Fe and Millonarios. Millonarios in particular with their eight Argentinians, one Brazilian, one Colombian and one Peruvian, made a spectacular if short-lived contribution to the fantasy and reputation of South American football. They won the local championship four years out of five between 1949 and 1953, in 1951 without losing a game. Known as the 'ballet in blue', their supporters claimed that they had elevated football to an art. The forwards were led by Alfredo di Stéfano, who later claimed that their sole method was to attack and to beat the opposition without humiliating them. Once they had scored enough goals to win, the ballet would commence. The ball would pass from one player to another with such precision and speed that sometimes the other side stood and watched in sheer admiration . . .[26] Once FIFA had worked out an agreement which allowed Colombia back into football's league of nations, the Millonarios were able to tour abroad and in 1952 had a triumphant progress through Chile, Argentina, Uruguay, Bolivia, Peru and finally Spain where they won famous victories in Las Palmas, Seville, Valencia and Madrid.

As well as playing like millionaires they allegedly lived like them, with salaries of eight thousand dollars down and five hundred a month for a shorter season compared with the social slavery of Buenos Aires: a maximum wage of five thousand pesos a month, then worth about £85, with win and draw bonuses on top. In fact, once the Second World War was over, the movement of footballers between South American nations and from South America to Europe gathered fresh impetus. Without the introduction of professionalism, of course, the haemorrhage might have been worse. Even so one estimate suggests that at least one hundred players, mostly from Argentina, moved to Italy alone between 1945 and 1961.[27] Fame in South America could be translated into fortune only in Europe.

CHAPTER FIVE

FÚTBOL AND POLITICS

*Gaúcho [meaning from the state of Rio Grande do Sul] from
Bento Gonçalves [his hometown] 64 years old, fan of International in Pôrto Alegre and Botafogo in Rio, brother of two
generals, married, with one daughter, Ernesto Geisel will be
the 23rd president of the Republic.*
Front page, *Jornal do Brasil*, 19 June 1973, quoted by
Janet Lever, *Soccer Madness*, 1983, p. 64

When reigning monarchs and republican presidents patronize football
they are both acknowledging its cultural importance in their society and
adding to it. They are both offering support to football and displaying their
own authority as they present the cup to the winning team. Moreover they
are associating themselves with a popular activity and showing that they
too share the passions of their people. But in South America the
relationship between politicians and football has often been much stronger
than that. Military governments in particular have employed a well-tried
mixture of repression, bread and circuses in order to control their peoples,
and football has played a leading role in the circus. Several writers have
agreed with Uruguayan novelist Mario Benedetti, who pointed to the use
of football as political soporific.[1] In such regimes there is growing evidence
that leading members of the world of football have been important political
figures.[2] What follows will be an attempt to explore the developing
relationship between football and governments in twentieth-century
South America.

We have already noted that in the elite phase of the game powerful
figures would be seen on important footballing occasions. In 1905, the
President of Brazil, Rodrigues Alves, a man of São Paulo, watched
Fluminense play CA Paulistano in Rio, although with some suggestion of a
loss of prestige.[3] In June 1906 President Figuerón Alcarta of Argentina was

the most distinguished member of the record crowd which saw Alumni beat the touring South Africans. Three years later the visiting Everton and Tottenham players were presented to the President at half time during their match in Buenos Aires.[4]

The state began to encourage football in other ways. In 1906 the President of Brazil offered a cup for competition between state teams, an early attempt to establish a national championship. The Argentine Congress had promised, and apparently voted money to provide, a trophy to be competed for annually by Argentine clubs, but somewhat mysteriously it failed to materialize.[5] The Ministry of Education did put up a cup to be played for by Argentina and Uruguay in 1908 and a number of matches were played between that time and 1919. In 1911 the Uruguayan Minister of Education reciprocated, the last game in that series taking place in 1923.[6]

We have already noticed how, as football grew in importance, it began to play a part in national patriotic celebrations. In 1910 and 1916, for example, football tournaments were part of the centenary festivities in Argentina. The South American championships played a similar role in Brazil in 1922 and the first World Cup in Uruguay was arranged in 1930 to coincide with the centenary of that country's independence from Spain. The President of Uruguay attended all of his country's matches in that first world championship. It was clearly no coincidence that both River Plate in 1938, and Boca Juniors in 1940, opened their new stadiums on Independence Day, 25 May.

Leading politicians wanted to be associated with what was fast becoming a major cultural phenomenon. So in 1919 President Pessoa, in the midst of the serious economic and political crisis of that dramatic year, went out of his way to congratulate the Brazilian team which in May won the South American championship for the first time. 'I salute in the name of the nation the victory of the young Brazilian sportsmen.'[7] President Washington Luis was among the crowd at the opening of Vasco da Gama's new stadium in April 1927. He was there again seven months later for the final of the Brazilian championship between teams representing the old rivals of Rio and São Paulo. Before the game the President and his Ministers received an ovation lasting three minutes from the 50,000-strong crowd. The President later said he had never been applauded by so many people in his life. But his day began to go downhill from that moment. The match was a tight one and was still level at 1–1 with twelve minutes left. The home team was then awarded a penalty. The Paulistas, nonplussed, refused to continue. Up in the stands, the President of the Republic, himself a native of São Paulo, sent down one of his minions to tell the São Paulo players that they should get on with it. The captain of the Paulistas allegedly said that *he* gave the orders on the pitch and the team walked off. The referee insisted the penalty be taken even though there was no goalkeeper to oppose it and Rio were declared the winners.[8] The press had a field day and it is hard to escape the view that the image of the President was damaged. Just because you are the President it does not give you the right to intervene in football matches. Three years later he was to be ousted by a military coup, but before he went he showed that he was still interested in the part football could play in promoting Brazilian identity at home and abroad when his government provided the CBD with a special budget to organize the participation of Brazil in the first World Cup.[9]

The Brazilian Government was to take more interest in football during the Presidency and then the dictatorship of Getúlio Vargas, who domi-nated the politics of the country for the best part of the quarter of a century after 1930. His coming to power marked the end of the supremacy of the coffee interests of São Paulo, and his regime eventually was able to redirect the economy away from the unpredictable fluctuations of a coffee-exporting base through a state-guided programme of industrial develop-ment. These economic changes were accompanied by political ones aimed at reducing the power of ᵗʰe separate states and making Brazil more centralized. By the late 1930s Vargas was a dictator, with civil rights curtailed, the press censored, political parties banned and restraints on the activities of the police lifted. Attempts were made to promote feelings of national pride in Brazil. Every radio station had a compulsory Brazilian hour. The regime was also keen to encourage sport and especially football. In April 1941 a National Council of Sports was set up within the Ministry of Education and Culture, its five members, one from the army, one from the air force plus three civilians, all chosen directly by President Vargas.[10] The Vargas era was a turning point in the relationship between football and politics. From this time not only the Federal Government but individual politicians would try to associate themselves with what was becoming an increasingly powerful manifestation of Brazilian popular culture. Not only did the leading football clubs offer social facilities in a country where such things were scarce: the success of Brazilian football abroad, both at club and international level, illuminated the name of Brazil for the rest of the world to see.

There are many examples of politics offering a helping hand to football. In the late 1940s President Dutra gave to Flamengo a prime piece of property close to the centre of Rio. Vargas himself, in his last period as President, also arranged for Flamengo to receive a low-interest government loan so that the club could build a twenty-four-storey office block with spectacular views of the bay. A Governor of Minas Gerais hoped to win votes by building the Magalhaes Pinto stadium in Belo Horizonte in 1965, and there was an orgy of government-inspired stadium building in the 1970s in all parts of this vast country, including Belem, Curitiba, Fortaleza, Maceio, Porto Alegre, Recife and Salvador. Between 1969 and 1975 thirteen new stadiums were built, nine of them in the less developed north and east. By 1978, seven of the world's ten largest stadiums were in Brazil.[11] After the military coup of 1964 football was one of the ways the new dictatorship could associate itself with popular interests. President Medici (1969–74) claimed to be a fan of Flamengo, regularly turned up at their matches, and even tried to influence the selection of the team. He may have been a genuine enthusiast. President Geisel certainly was not, but his publicity machine labelled him a fan of Internacional from Pôrto Alegre in his home state as well as Rio's Botafogo. The famous third World Cup victory in Mexico in 1970 was expertly exploited by the government. Immediately after the final, President Medici made a speech to the nation:

> I feel profound happiness at seeing the joy of our people in this highest form of patriotism. I identify this victory won in the brotherhood of good sportsmanship with the rise of faith in our fight for national development. I identify the success of our [national team] with ... intelligence and bravery, perseverance and serenity in our technical ability, in physical preparation and moral being. Above all, our players won because they know how to ... play for the collective good.[12]

The marching tune written to inspire the World Cup team, 'Forward Brazil', became the theme song of the regime. The nationalistic slogan 'no one will hold Brazil back now' was combined on posters with a picture of Pelé leaping with excitement after one of the goals. The team's first stop after the Mexico victory was Brasilia to meet the President, who had declared the day of the team's return a national holiday. Photographs of Medici with the team were in all the newspapers. He then took the unprecedented step of opening the doors of the presidential palace to the public.

Only one year before, the government had created a lottery based on the national game. It became a very successful promotion of the Department of Finance. Not only did it provide revenue, which was divided between the Departments of Social Security and Education and Culture, but it also penetrated to most corners of this vast country and provided a football-based geography lesson for punters. The lottery almost certainly contributed to the pressure placed on the Brazilian football authorities to organize a genuine national championship. As we have seen, the national championship had been a competition between teams representing individual states. A Rio–São Paulo club tournament had been in existence since 1950 and was expanded in 1967 to include clubs from the other three southern states. Air travel made a national championship for clubs possible especially if the government was prepared to contribute to the cost of the fares. By 1979 ninety-two teams from twenty-two states were involved in a championship which was added on to the state league's season, making football an all-the-year-round business. Both the travel and the playing exhausts the teams and a plethora of games, many of them between teams of grossly unequal strengths, deters the supporters.

Critics have claimed that the development of Brazilian football has been distorted by politics. So far as the military regime was concerned a national championship, like a national lottery, contributed to the overall strategy of national integration. Having at first banned political parties, they then reinvented them, creating a majority government party and a minority opposition one. As winning elections became more difficult, football in general and a place in the national championships in particular, was used in an attempt to sway the electorate. This was made easier by the fact that the Presidency of the government ARENA party in Rio and the Presidency of the CBD were both in the hands of Admiral Hélio Nunes from 1974. Opponents claimed that in areas where ARENA was doing badly the local teams would be given a place in the national championship even if they had not earned one by success on the field. Politics and football remain closely related in Brazil, perhaps one reason why this ludicrously overgrown national championship continued even after democracy was restored in 1985. It is hardly in the interests of the players, and although there are many reasons why they so often follow the siren call of Europe, notably money, the physical and social pressures of too many matches must also play a part in the decision to go. Leading football personalities know that being a football person helps if you want to go into politics in Brazil and if you are a politician an interest in football is a real advantage.[13]

It has been suggested already that there was clear contact between the worlds of football and politics in Argentina. The nation's President was involved in the unification of the two organizations running the game in 1926. It was to the President that a deputation of striking players went in

1931. The nation's leader was also present when Boca Juniors opened their new.ground on 6 July 1924, accompanying his Minister of War, Agustín P. Justo, who was a big fan of the club. General Justo would be President of the Republic himself between 1932 and 1938. The President of Boca 1939–46, Eduard Sáncez Terrero, married Justo's daughter.[14] It is not surprising that Boca and River had financial help from the state to develop their stadiums. A study of AFA Presidents has clearly shown how the spheres of football and politics overlapped. Aldo Cantoni, for example, was President of the Asociación Argentina de Football in 1922–23 and 1926. He was President of Huracán between 1920 and 1923 and again in 1933–4 and also Governor and national senator for the province of San Juan. Ramón Castillo was President of the AFA between 1941 and 1943. He had had no role in football until then but he was the son of the country's President ...[15] This relationship between football and politics would be made more systematic under President Perón.

Perón was a colonel in the army who quickly became an important figure in the military government which seized power in 1943. He was both Minister of War and head of the Department of Labour and Social Welfare. Far from declaring war on labour he promoted the expansion of trade unions in Argentina to such effect that within two years their proportion of the occupied workforce rose from 10 per cent to 66 per cent. In 1945 Perón married the actress María Eva Duarte and in 1946 stood for the Presidency and won. With the support of the unions and the urban middle class Perón created a powerful political organization. He introduced measures to redistribute income in favour of workers and nationalized foreign-owned public utilities like the railways. It was a nationalist impulse that was behind his drive for state-led industrialization in order to reduce Argentine dependence on imports and on the export of food and raw materials. Perón promoted activities designed to further the cultural progress of Argentina and stimulate national unity. Sport in general and football in particular were already popular and it was obvious and easy to use the resources of the state to encourage sport further. Like all governments, he thought such a policy might be a vote winner and take some people's minds off the less satisfactory aspects of his regime.

In 1947 the government created a new sports overseer by fusing together the Argentine Olympic Committee and the Confederation of Argentine Sports. The new authority was chaired by the President of the Supreme Court. 'Perón sponsors sports' and 'Perón, the first sportsman' – echoing the claims made for Mussolini – were slogans designed to draw attention to the way in which sport and sportsmen were to play an important role in constructing the new Argentina 'which we all desire'.[16] Government funds helped with the preparation of the largest team to have been sent to an Olympic Games up to that point, 1948, and it was delighted to associate itself with their considerable if slightly surprising success. Peronist medals were presented to the athletes in a public ceremony in the stadium of River Plate in 1949. In 1951 Argentina organized and won the first Pan-American games, providing opportunities for the Peronist Government to emphasize the civilized state of Argentine culture and its leadership of 'America'. Sporting heroes who won famous victories regularly dedicated them to Juan and Eva. Pascual Pérez, the first Argentine boxer to win a world professional title when he defeated Yoshio Shirai in Tokyo in 1954, grabbed the ring microphone at the end of the contest and cried, 'Mission accomplished my general! I won for Perón and for my country.' Such triumphs were given the maximum publicity in the largely government-controlled newspapers and radio.

Eva Perón also promoted sports through the Social Aid Foundation, which she headed. The first of the Evita Championships took place in 1950. It was a football tournament for children aged between thirteen and fifteen. Anyone could form a team, choose a name, choose its colours – the Foundation supplied all the kit – and enter. The finals were played in Buenos Aires by twenty-four teams. Evita kicked off and in addition to the national anthem, a march was played with the chorus, 'To Evita we owe our club, and for that we are grateful to her.' A total of 150,000 children took part in that first tournament, 200,000 in the second in 1951. The aim was not only to promote participation but also to improve the health of the young. Entry was accompanied by a compulsory medical and an X-ray. The championships were later extended to athletics, basketball and swimming and were yet another public sign of the new Argentina. It appears fashionable to criticize the scheme for its failure to produce many players who would play in the professional league, but it does seem to have been widely enjoyed for the few years it lasted with many small football enthusiasts putting on their first pairs of boots and socks.[17]

Football had many supporters among the Peronist Government, some in influential positions which enabled them to be real benefactors to their favoured clubs. The most famous example was Ramón Cereijo. He was Finance Minister and a passionate supporter of Racing. Though not officially engaged in the management of the club, he was alleged to have taken part in negotiations with other clubs over player transfers. When the best Argentine players were leaving the country for Colombia and Europe during and immediately after the dispute of 1948–9, no one left Racing. The club were champions for three successive seasons, 1949, 1950 and 1951. After the latter triumph most of the team received new Chevrolets. Racing were nicknamed Sportivo (Sporting) Cereijo. As Finance Minister he was central to the cheap loan of three – soon to be eleven – million pesos, which the government advanced to the club so they could build their new ground. It did not need to be repaid for sixty-five years which, given the frequent bouts of inflation, made it a really good deal. No wonder the stadium was named after President Perón, he was given the Presidency of the club, and Eva Perón, Cereijo, Bramuglia (Minister of Foreign Affairs) and Miranda (President of the Central Bank of Argentina) were made honorary members. Both the President and the first lady turned up for the inauguration on 3 September 1950.[18] Few clubs were without a state godfather, although it would be tedious to list them.

Given the attention which the Peronist Government of Argentina focused on football, it is a surprise to find that Argentina failed to send a team to the South American championships of 1949 in Brazil or to the World Cup of 1950, also held in Brazil, and that of 1954 in Switzerland. One possible explanation is that anxiety about defeat led the government to take the decision not to play. This would make sense given that many leading Argentine players had left the country during the strike of 1948–9. Critics have suggested that by not risking defeat the supporters of Argentinian football could still think their team was the best. The President of the AFA at the time was leading Peronist Valentín Suárez. Asked many years later about why Argentina had withdrawn from the 1950 world championships, Suárez reminded his questioner of the strike and the fact that there was some tension between the AFA and the CBD (Brazil). But he also hinted that there was a political factor and that powerful figures in the government thought Argentina was not fit to compete. Such views may not have been decisive but they had to be respected...[19]

Ironically when they did venture outside the River Plate Argentina had victories over Eire (1951), Spain and Portugal (1952). In fact the only defeat inflicted on Argentina between 20 December 1945 and 5 December 1954 – excepting an unofficial match against Uruguay during the dispute of 1948 – was by England at Wembley in a friendly arranged as part of the Festival of Britain celebrations in May 1951. This was the first ever meeting between the two countries and one can imagine that it meant a lot to the visitors. The British had introduced football to Argentina and done much to develop it. In spite of setbacks, the myth of their superiority, as is the way with myths, was reluctant to fade away. England boasted an unbeaten home record against foreigners, with the exception of Eire. The immediate political background was not without tension either as Argentina and Britain had just spent the best part of a year renegotiating their 1949 trade agreement. In general the new terms were more favourable to Argentina but an important result was a small increase in the British meat ration.[20] The match provoked a good deal of interest and a record crowd for an international match played on a midweek afternoon. Argentina scored after eighteen minutes and although mostly on the defensive for the rest of the match were not beaten until England scored two goals in the final eleven minutes. Rugilo, the Vélez Sarsfield goalkeeper, made his name in that match as the 'Lion of Wembley' and in spite of the tears from some of the players at the end it had been an honourable defeat. The party actually received a heroes' welcome on their return to Buenos Aires.

In 1953 England returned the visit. Argentina had again missed the South American championships played in Peru just a few weeks before. Perhaps they were preparing for something they thought more important. After all, Argentina had won many such titles and would have plenty of opportunities to do so again. But the English were not to be taken lightly. For them the visit was part of a tour which also took in matches against Uruguay, Chile and the United States and was the first ever visit to South America of the national team. There were to be two games in Buenos Aires. The first, according to the English, was designed to give the reserve players in the party a game. It was not a full international, but was described in English sources as an FA XI against an Argentinian XI. Not surprisingly Argentina picked its best team. England included only four of their first choices and were soundly beaten 3–1. Argentine joy was more or less unconfined. President Perón declared the day of the match, 14 May, to be 'Footballers' Day' to be celebrated every year.[21] A few days later the full international was played but had to be abandoned after twenty minutes because the pitch was flooded.

There are three further examples of the close links between football and the government of Perón. On the death of Eva Perón in 1952 the AFA and most of its affiliated clubs and leagues sent the most fulsome messages of sympathy to the President. Two years later, in 1954, Alberto Armando of Boca dedicated the championship which they had just won 'to the man who has known how to give Argentinian sport the content and vitality with which it finds itself at the moment, with international repercussions which have gained him acknowledgement as first sportsman of the world'. Finally the AFA gave funds to the Eva Perón Foundation to benefit the victims of the failed coup of 16 June 1955.[22] Of course the government did not run football. They did not decide every issue. But the AFA was run by the President's men: and, as noted earlier, Valentín Suárez emphasized that the views of the government had to be 'respected'. The close relationship between football and politics would not end with the overthrow of Perón. Nor would Peronism end with the overthrow of Perón.

In 1966 FIFA provisionally named Argentina for the venue of the World Cup of 1978. The selection could hardly have been better timed. In 1966 the eighth world championships were held in England. In the quarter finals Argentina met the hosts. When footballing cultures clash they can do so in fascinatingly fruitful ways or deafeningly negative ones. This game was one of the latter. This is not the moment to do more than mention how the English and the Argentinians saw it. The men from Buenos Aires went in for systematic fouling: no one was allowed to pass them. This was buttressed by continual complaints to, and criticism of, the German referee orchestrated by the captain, Boca midfield player Antonio Ubaldo Rattín. The climax came shortly before half time when the referee lost patience and sent Rattín off. For a while it looked as though the Argentinians would not continue. The stoppage lasted eight minutes. Both at this time and at the end of the match there was more trouble between the Argentine players and the officials. Two Argentine players were later suspended for their part in it, Ferreiro for attacking the referee and Onega for spitting at a FIFA official. In spite of being reduced to ten men, the rest of the team played well enough in a close game which either side could have won. England were very relieved by Hurst's sixty-sixth-minute winning goal.

In Argentina the predominant response appears to have been outrage. This was fuelled by the England manager's comment in a post-match interview. 'We have still to produce our best football. It will come against the right type of opposition, a team who come to play football and not act as animals.'[23] Argentina had been insulted as well as cheated. Argentina was the 'moral champion'. President General Juan Carlos Onganía greeted the team on their return to Buenos Aires. A popular daily newspaper *Crónica* published the headline: 'First they [the English] stole the Malvinas from us, and now the World Cup'. The same newspaper later financed an expedition which landed a small plane on the Falkland Islands.[24]

Football remained closely related to the state. Valentín Suárez made it clear enough in January 1967: 'The government never closed its doors and never will close its doors on football clubs.'[25] With many of the leading clubs in financial difficulties it was just as well. The state loaned millions of pesos to football clubs. In return the championship was restructured from 1967 with the Buenos Aires League becoming the Metropolitan championship and a new National championship extending the season to nine months of the year. As with Brazil, political factors were important. The smaller clubs and the provinces of the interior wanted their share of the national obsession. Some Argentines have suggested that football had become a kind of public service. It was inevitable that the 1978 World Cup would be conscripted.

FIFA had confirmed in 1975 that Argentina would be the venue for the next world championships. Little appears to have been done by a Peronist Government overwhelmed by inflation and apparently on the brink of civil war. The government was overthrown by the military in March 1976 with a three-man junta led by General Jorge Videla as President. Some members of the new government suggested the country could not afford to stage the World Cup, but the junta disagreed. In July 1976 the World Cup was declared a national interest and an organizing committee set up. EAM78 – Ente Autárquico Mundial '78 – got off to a bad start when its first President, General Actis, was assassinated. But a lot of hard work and the spending of some 10 per cent of the national budget of Argentina for 1978, 700 million US dollars, produced remodelled stadiums at River Plate, Vélez Sarsfield and Rosario and new ones in the provincial cities of Córdoba, Mar del Plata and Mendoza. A new press centre for the two and a half thousand journalists expected was also constructed, together with new television studios and the introduction of colour TV, a FIFA requirement for the billion people who would watch the games from their own homes.[26] Airports were improved and Buenos Aires smartened up. The organizers claimed that some of this outlay would be recouped by 50,000 tourists, but no more than 10,000 eventually arrived.

From February 1978 EAM and its Coca-Cola allies moved into a propaganda offensive aimed at their opponents both at home and abroad. European civil rights groups were among the most important of the latter. At home radio, television, advertisements, newspapers and posters bombarded the population with patriotic slogans such as 'twenty-five million Argentines will play in the World Cup'. The opening ceremony, on Sunday 1 June, went without a hitch – without the traditional difficulties of a football Sunday – in front of a President Videla dressed in his civilian suit.[27] *El Gráfico* summed up the excitement and satisfaction that not only the organizers felt:

> For those on the outside, for all the journalists, the insidious and badly intentioned journalists who for months have been organizing a campaign of lies about Argentina this tournament is showing the world the reality of our country and its capacity to do things with responsibility and to do important things well.
>
> For those inside, for those who do not believe that we have in our own house ... after so many hard experiences ... enormous possibilities and this has nothing to do with the football results. Argentina has already won the World Cup.[28]

Videla called it a 'World Cup of Peace' – he got an ovation for that one – and the goals of improving Argentina's international image and repairing the fractured national consensus appeared to have been achieved.

But the enthusiasm with which Argentina overflowed for the World Cup of 1978 was not simply produced by the promotional activities of the dictatorship. It was, as the title of a feature film by Sergio Renán had it, *La fiesta de todos – Everybody's Feast*.[29] There were echoes of 1930, with firms placing television sets in factories and offices, families fitting their lifestyles around the football schedules, cinemas changing their programmes and newspapers publishing special supplements. Every time Argentina played there were huge celebrations in Buenos Aires and the cities of the interior. When Peru were beaten 6–0 and Argentina's place in the final was assured it was estimated that 60 per cent of the population of Buenos Aires went on to the streets to celebrate. Only the Brazilians and Alemann, the Minister of the Interior who had been critical of the cost, were suspicious. The Brazilians, because FIFA had foolishly allowed their game with Poland to be played before Argentina met Peru, which meant, as Argentina and Brazil would have equal points if both won, that Argentina would know exactly how many goals were required to win their place in the final. Alemann, because a bomb exploded at his home at the precise moment when the all-important fourth goal was scored.

After victory in the final against the slightly unfortunate Dutch, parties went on all through the night of 25 June and the next day the Plaza de Mayo was thronged with schoolchildren who were greeted by President Videla.

All the population without exception offered its happiness, its legitimate fervour, showing itself to be hospitable friends of visitors and these people will be the witnesses of our true reality in their own countries without the defamation of this international campaign of falsehoods. The sport was an opportunity, the way to express, as never before, the feeling of national unity and the common hope of peace, unity and fraternity.[30]

But the people too had been in thrall. While it lasted it was something to share and something to savour. It was a breathing space between a horrific immediate past and an anxiously uncertain future.

On the first anniversary of the victory of Argentina over Holland the newspaper *Clarín* organized a great celebration in the River Plate stadium in the presence of the President. In September of the same year, the occasion of the victory of Argentina in the World Youth Cup held in Japan was used to obstruct the work of a committee from the Organization of American States which was investigating violations of human rights. A well-known radio commentator, José María Muñoz, told his listeners to go to the Plaza de Mayo and show the people of the human rights commission that Argentina had nothing to hide. The Plaza de Mayo was the scene of the silent protest by mothers drawing attention to the fact that sons and daughters had disappeared. This attempt to exploit the enthusiasm of football fans against the mothers appears to have backfired, as both members of the commission and the public had the issue placed powerfully in front of them.

The euphoria produced by the 1978 World Cup was not simply the result of government power and in particular its control of newspapers, radio and television. Neither was the enthusiasm shown in the first days of the Falklands War in 1982. But the connection between football, war and politics was close.[31] The chants of the crowds in the streets were from the stadiums. In the final of 1978 they had chanted 'he who does not jump is a Dutchman'; in 1982 he was an Englishman. 'Ar-gen-ti-na, Ar-gen-ti-na' was used in 1982 to support the armed forces in their big match. Leaflets showing the 1978 World Cup emblem, a very young gaucho dressed in football kit accepting the surrender of a defeated British lion, were widely distributed. Official television coverage of the war was shared with football matches. When Argentina played, the games were clothed in patriotic sentiment. The national anthem, a minute's silence for the Argentine dead, followed by flag waving and chants of 'Ar-gen-ti-na'.

Before the end of that war the military dictatorship decided that Argentina would play in the World Cup in Spain. 'The Army of the

Andes in shorts', as one Peronist intellectual labelled them, lost to Belgium just one day before the military surrender in the Falklands. The second stage of the competition was reached but there followed comprehensive defeats by Italy and Brazil and elimination. In the match against Brazil the new hero of Argentine football, Diego Maradona, was sent off.

It is clear that the military dictatorship of Argentina hoped to use the staging of the World Cup in 1978 to enhance the legitimacy of the regime both at home and abroad. In a country where football was so popular a World Cup, and at home, was bound to test people's hopes and feelings of identity. As some Brazilian intellectuals wanted the defeat of Brazil in the 1970 world championships in order to prevent the exploitation of victory by the military government, similar attitudes surfaced in Buenos Aires. No one should underestimate the difficulty of the choice of those who did not support the regime but wanted Argentina to win. As one of them told an American writer, 'for once, however unreal it may be, we have a team – an entity – that is called Argentina'.[32] Ricardo Halac, the playwright, put it more graphically:

> The military men wanted to use the Mundial but they also wanted us to come out champions. Many Argentines who celebrated did not like the military, but we also wanted to be champions. What could we do? Not dance? Boycott the Mundial? Do dictatorships pass away, do Cups remain? We went, we won and we danced.[33]

Such a response was very different from those who accosted the mothers of the Plaza de Mayo, mourning for their 'disappeared' children, and accused them of damaging their country. If all Argentines supported the 'great party' they did not do so for the same reasons. But in the end all this investment in the World Cup could only purchase a breathing space for the government.[34] Football victories, even in World Cups, do not solve economic, political and social problems.

The national euphoria produced by hosting the World Cup was repeated during the early days of the Malvinas/Falklands war in 1982. But again some of the support had complex roots. As in Britain, where groups who detested the Thatcher Government supported a military response to the occupation because they identified the Argentine military government with fascism, so in Argentina there were those who opposed the military regime but were persuaded that the British were imperialists fighting a colonial war.[35] Defeat in the World Cup would not have been the epilogue for the Argentinian military dictatorship. Defeat in the Malvinas/Falklands was.

Football is a political temptation, especially to Argentine nationalists. A group of Peronist Senators demanded that President Alfonsín order the Argentine team not to play against England in the World Cup quarter final of 1986. Two years later Argentine supporters of Newells Old Boys, in Montevideo for the first leg of the Libertadores Cup Final against Nacional, unfurled Peronista banners but put them away after the second Nacional goal. President Menem even donned the Argentine jersey and played a full ninety minutes with the national team in 1989. He once told a British television crew, 'football is the thing that formed me physically and it has given me a great deal of spirituality' and that as a child he had dreamt of playing for Argentina.[36]

Football as political diversion is an old story in South America and by no means restricted to Argentina and Brazil. In La Paz in 1968, for example, the government attempted to distract the workers summoned to march on May Day to protest against low wages and anti-trade union measures by arranging the visit of a leading Argentine team. Televised football was often used to keep people indoors on that dangerous holiday. This was particularly so during the years of General Onganía's rule in Argentina 1966–70, where up to six live matches a week were being shown and the clubs compensated as attendances slumped.[37] Dictators prevented leading clubs from feeling the full impact of their own mismanagement. General Pinochet rescued Everton of Viña del Mar in 1979 and the Rangers club of Talén in 1982 as well as nominating the President of the country's leading club, Colo Colo of Santiago, in 1981 and 1984. He did not want a collapse of Chile's professional league. Similarly the regime of General Stroessner in Paraguay saved two Asunción clubs, Sol de América and Cerro Porteño, when they got into financial difficulties in 1983 and 1985. The military junta in Uruguay did the same for Peñarol in 1978 and 1981. In both countries state funds were used to support the national team: in Uruguay, by organizing a tournament for World Cup winners at the end of 1980 and in the New Year of 1981; in Paraguay by spending one million US dollars on preparing Paraguay for the 1986 World Cup. There have often been rumours that exceptional players were prevented from going abroad by mysterious deals. Is it true or an urban myth that the President of Santos, Athie Coury, who was also a deputy for the state of São Paulo, was warned in 1960 that if Pelé left the club he need not bother to stand for re-election, indeed should start counting the days of his life? Who was Eduardo António Coelho, alleged to have given Santos an interest-free loan of half a million US dollars to keep Pelé? It does seem clear that after the collapse of military dictatorships in the mid 1980s it has become more difficult for clubs to resist offers from Europe for their best players.[38] It is repression or the fear of it which keeps people politically passive in dictatorships, but football, like the television soap opera, plays a part.

CHAPTER SIX

THE REIGN OF PELÉ

O Futebol

Hitting the net
With a dream of a goal

If only
I were Pelé the King
Striking my songs
Home

A painter measuring exactly
To hang in a gallery, no
Brushstroke's more perfect
Than a goal shot
Crisp
As an arrow or a dry leaf.

Chico Buarque, 1989,
quoted in *Independent on
Sunday*, 15 November
1992

With his short legs, his rounded chest sticking out, his cheeky
Job's mug and his diamonded ear, Diego had become a true
Neapolitan for us all. His love of pretty girls and good food, his
mania for racing cars along with his fervent devotion to church
and family – his whole family lives and thrives in Naples at the
club's expense – his nasty character, his feats, his exuberance, his
lack of discipline, all this made him a true and legitimate son of
the city.
Le Monde, 24 August 1989, quoted by Christian Bromberger,
'Foreign Footballers, Cultural Dreams and Community Identity in some North-Western Mediterranean Cities' in John Bale
and Joseph Maguire, eds, *The Global Sports Arena. Athletic
talent migration in an interdependent world*, 1994, p. 178

Pelé was nearly ten on 16 July 1950. That was the day when Brazil, playing at home in their unfinished but still awesome Maracaná stadium and requiring only a draw to win the fourth World Cup, lost to Uruguay. The disappointment touched the whole nation. Pelé himself recalled much later that the unexpected defeat produced 'a sadness so great, so profound that it seemed like the end of a war, with Brazil the loser and many people dead'.[1] Brazil did not play again until April 1952 and not in the Maracaná until March 1954. And they never played in white shirts again.

Until the seventy-ninth minute of that final match everything had gone smoothly for the hosts. They were easily the better-prepared team, having been together for several months at a special training camp close to Rio. Led by the coach, Flavio Costa, the staff included cooks, doctors and a priest. Players' wives were not allowed. Brazil played all their games in Rio apart from the first, a token visit to São Paulo. The other teams had some travelling to do across Brazil's wide open spaces. It was the Brazilian authorities who had insisted on the format of four groups of four in which each team played the other once, the winners making up a final group with the formula repeated. This replaced the straightforward knock-out system of the past.

Excitement and expectation had built up steadily, especially on the radio and in the newspapers as the other twelve competing teams began to arrive. On Shrove Tuesday of 1950, the World Cup had been the parade theme of the great samba schools in the Rio carnival.[2] The trophy itself was displayed in the window of a shoeshop on the Avenida Rio Branco in Rio and thousands of Brazilians filed past as if it was a religious experience. The Maracaná stadium, built by the local municipality, was also a place of pilgrimage. It was the biggest football stadium in the world. It was not really finished – its approaches were like a building site – but it housed the biggest crowds of the tournament by far. A crowd of 199,854 allegedly saw the final, one record destined never to be broken. The Korean War began on the same day as the tournament, but it was on the back pages of Brazilian newspapers.

In fact Brazil began securely enough, with an easy four-goal victory over Mexico. Four days later in São Paulo came an uneasy 2–2 draw with Switzerland. Six Cariocas and five Paulistas made up the team but manager Costa was severely criticized by the locals for not selecting more Paulista players. After that, with all the other matches in the Maracaná, he chose only Rio-based players apart from Bauer and Jair. Yugoslavia meanwhile beat the Swiss 3–0 and Mexico 4–1. Suddenly there was a chance that Brazil might not reach the final pool. Brazil against Yugoslavia on 1 July was crucial. The weekend of 1/2 July was the weekend that World Cup excitement really took hold of Rio. A total of 160,000 spectators filed into the Maracaná for Brazil and Yugoslavia and another 90,000 the next day for the equally critical game between England and Spain. Although July means winter in Brazil, the weather was hot and Maracaná's sixty refreshment stalls ran out of beer. An epidemic of sunstroke overran the ninety first-aid posts.[3] On Saturday the home crowd was anxious, for Yugoslavia only needed a draw to go through. The game started in the most bizarre fashion. The Yugoslavs began with ten men, as Mitic had cut his head on a girder in the unfinished underground of the Maracaná. By the time he arrived, head bandaged, after five minutes, Ademir had scored for Brazil. Zizinho scored a second after half time and ensured a happy ending for the hosts. They were joined in the final pool by Spain, Sweden and Uruguay.

There was a week off before the matches in the final round began and Brazilian confidence and certainty that victory would be theirs appeared to grow with every day that went by. Firecrackers and loudspeakers punctuated the days and nights. The radio continually played a song with the refrain 'Brazil must win ... next time it will be good'. A municipal election campaign in Rio added to the excitement. Flavio Costa was himself one of the candidates and several of the others tried to associate themselves with the Brazilian footballers by using such phrases as 'homage to the champions of the world' on their election addresses and posters. Certainty reached bursting point when the final matches began on 9 July. Brazil slaughtered Sweden – Olympic champions only two years before – by 7–1 in the Maracaná. Ademir scored four and some critics said that it was dream football, instinctive, supernatural (the French were addicted to the latter notion); and it was very impressive, especially the precision of their ball control, passing and shooting and the ease with which they found space. Five minutes before the end 160,000 Brazilians began waving their handkerchiefs in a countdown of ecstasy. Four days later they and the team provided a repeat performance as Spain were outclassed and beaten 6–1. None for Ademir this time but two each for Jair and Chico. It was the similarity of their football to ballet which now struck the watching football scribes of the world. All agreed, no one could live with such play.

Victory must have seemed even more assured when Brazil's progress was compared with the difficulties which Uruguay had with the same opponents. On the day Brazil beat Sweden Uruguay could only draw 2–2 with Spain in São Paulo. On 13 July Uruguay found Sweden just as much of a handful. Again they were 2–1 down at half time and it was only in the last quarter of an hour that centre-forward Miguez scored the victory goals. What all this meant was that although there was no cup final in this tournament the last match amounted to one. If Brazil beat Uruguay or the match was a draw, Brazil would be champions; if not Uruguay would be. Preparations for the triumph of the hosts went on in an atmosphere of carnival orchestrated by a near hysterical media. 'We'll beat Uruguay,' boasted the *Gazetta Esportiva* on 15 July. The *Diário Carioca* of the same day proclaimed: 'World Football has a New Master. Brazil is the name of the new star.'[4] The team manager, Costa, tried to be sensible. 'The Uruguayan team has always disturbed the slumbers of Brazilian footballers. I am afraid that my players will take the field on Sunday as though they already had the championship shield sewn on their jerseys.' He was right, of course. We have already noted the strength and success of Uruguayan footballers and their national team. Brazil had suffered defeat against them eleven times, the latest in the first of a three-match series for the Rio Branco Cup in May 1950. True, Brazil had won the other two, but only by the odd goal in each case.

Perhaps such confidence was a kind of innocence. There was a mad rush for tickets and the unfinished Maracaná struggled to cope with almost 200,000 people. Some broke in without tickets. Before the game the Mayor of Rio gave an oration, relayed over 254 loudspeakers, which included such hostages to fortune as: 'You Brazilians, whom I consider victors of the tournament ... you players who in less than a few hours will be acclaimed champions by millions of your compatriots ... you who are so superior to every other competitor ... you whom I already salute as conquerors...'

Perhaps such pressure began to have an impact on the Brazilian players. Perhaps God was not Brazilian after all. It was a hard match and though Brazil took the lead after forty-eight minutes the sparkle of those victories over Sweden and Spain was missing. Did the players become too careful? Did their anxieties communicate themselves to the crowd or the crowd's worries infect the team? Some journalists later wrote of an air of panic, a sense of catastrophe, but perhaps all this is but the melodrama of hindsight. What we know for certain is that Schiaffino equalized from a centre by Ghiggia after sixty-five minutes. Eleven minutes from the end Ghiggia's right-wing run was ended by a ground shot which beat the Brazilian goalkeeper Barbosa on the near post. The Uruguayan team were beside themselves at the end, especially their thirty-five-year-old attacking centre-half Varela, one of the tournament's lesser-known heroes.[5]

Jules Rimet, the French President of FIFA, after whom the World Cup trophy was later to be named, was due to present the cup to the winning captain in a grandiose ceremony which included a guard of honour from the dressing room tunnel entrance to the centre of the playing area. A few minutes before the end, Rimet left his seat high up in the grandstand. He was rehearsing the speech he would make at the end of the match. The score was still level, which was all Brazil required to be champions. The stadium, he later recalled, was like a sea in a storm with a loud and tempestuous voice. After about five minutes he arrived at the exit of the tunnel which led out on to the pitch. A deathly silence had replaced the tumult. A crowd which a few minutes ago had been expecting victory was mute as if petrified or dead. When the English referee, George Reader, blew the final whistle the shock was such that there was no guard of honour, no national anthems, no speeches to the multitudes and at first, no presentation of the trophy. 'I find myself alone in the crowd (on the field) jostled by my neighbours, the cup in my arms and not knowing what to do. In the end I saw the Uruguay captain [Varela] and gave him the cup, at the same time discreetly shaking his hand...'[6]

As the great crowd dispersed the Brazilian officials and players congratulated the winners with 'a courtesy which was sad and cordial at the same time'. By the time the new champions did their lap of honour the Maracaná was three-quarters empty. It had been a championship surpassing all expectations. The matches were good, the refereeing flawless, no players were sent off and the Jury of Appeal had nothing to consider. The authority and prestige of FIFA in South America had been noticeably enhanced. Even the receipts were higher than expected. But for Brazil it was a wake. People wept in the stands, in the streets and on the buses back to town. The stuff of carnival which had been in place for several days was not needed. After Jacques de Ryswick had sent his last cable he was able to sleep soundly in the quiet city. The *Estado do São Paulo* of 18 July 1950 pronounced that such a blow would not soon be forgotten. The scars would be permanent.[7] But four hundred miles to the west there was a ten-year-old black boy who, sooner than the pessimists had any right to expect, would heal the wounds.

If the 1950 World Cup was a disappointment for Brazil, it was a triumph for South America over Europe. Four years later Europe was victorious and Brazil once more thwarted. In Switzerland Argentina once again refused to compete. The only American representatives were the holders, Uruguay, and Brazil. The Europeans had a new champion from behind the

Iron Curtain. Hungary had won the Olympic football tournament in 1952, although their players could not be called 'amateurs' in any sensible definition of that term, and were unbeaten for four years. They were heavily favoured to win and it was a major surprise when Germany beat them 3–2 in the final, a victory which did something to boost the morale of the Germans in the still austere post-war period.

On the way to the final Hungary had eliminated both Uruguay and Brazil, the former in one of the classic football matches, the latter in one of the more malignant. The Uruguay–Hungary match was a semi-final, which Hungary led by two goals early in the second half. But Hohberg scored twice in the last fifteen minutes for Uruguay to force extra time. It is said that the congratulations of his team after the second goal were so vigorous that he was knocked unconscious. Perhaps that is why he hit the post early in extra time instead of scoring from Schiaffino's pass. Two headed goals from Kocsis in the second period of extra time saw Hungary through. This was yet another formidable Uruguayan team who had already beaten Scotland 7–0 and England 4–2.[8]

Brazil had met Hungary in the quarter final – slightly strange because both had won their groups, but then World Cup draws have never been models of rationality. Only Bauer remained from the eleven beaten in the Maracana four years before. Flavio Costa had been replaced as coach by Zeze Moreira, which one French critic likened to someone with the allure of an Argentine dancer being replaced by an English clergyman. The aim was to produce a team who would play a better collective game. Some of the individual panache which had characterized earlier Brazilian teams might have to be sacrificed in the pursuit of teamwork. Critics would later suggest that the team was frustrated by internal tensions and the usual Carioca–Paulista rivalries.[9] The game was refereed by an Englishman, Arthur Ellis. He had never sent a player off in an international match before but this time he sent three for an early bath. As two of them were Brazilians and they lost the match, it is not surprising that there was considerable criticism of his handling of it in the Brazilian newspapers. He probably ought to have had an interpreter; he would have needed two, of course. He may have overdone the no-nonsense Yorkshireman. His ghosted autobiography implies a mistrust of foreigners of Little Englander proportions. Nevertheless, as has often been said, referees do not commit fouls or throw punches and neutrals thought he had handled a difficult situation well. The Brazilians later claimed provocation following Hungarian fouls but that was one aspect of the game in which they undoubtedly gave as good as they got.[10] Hungary scored twice in the first eight minutes and it was 2–1 at half time. Early in the second half the Hungarians were awarded a penalty from which they made the score 3–1. But with twenty-four minutes still left Julinho scored a second goal for Brazil. It was after that that tempers were really lost and not found again until some time after the final whistle. Boszik (Hungary) and Nilton Santos (Brazil) were sent off for fighting after the Brazilian player had retaliated following a foul. Djalmar Santos chased Czibor about the field intent on assault and battery but was not close enough to prevent him from scoring the fourth Hungarian goal, after which Tozzi was sent off for jumping at Lorant. Players and officials of both sides fought in the dressing rooms afterwards when it was alleged that the Hungarian captain, Ferenc Puskas, not playing in the match because of injury, struck the Brazilian centre-half Pinheiro in the face with a bottle. A famous photograph was published showing two of the Hungarian officials with plasters on their heads. Nobody was punished for these football crimes. In reply to a question about possible suspensions Boszik, a deputy in the Hungarian Parliament, is alleged to have said, 'We do not suspend deputies.'

In 1958 Argentina appeared in the finals of the World Cup for the first time since 1934. Evidence that their oft-repeated boast that their football was the best in the world might be true had been provided by their spectacular victory in the South American championships in Peru in 1957. Five out of six games had been won, twenty-five goals scored and only six conceded. Brazil had been beaten by three goals and Uruguay by four. The inside-forward trio of Maschio, Angelillo and Sivori, the former scoring five against Colombia and two each against Brazil, Uruguay and Chile, had led the celebrations. Opponents christened them the *trío de la muerte* – the trio of death. But Italian scouts were watching and before the end of 1957 Bologna had signed Maschio, Internazionale of Milan Angelillo and Juventus Sivori.[11] As *oriundi* they would soon be playing for Italy, though not in Sweden because Italy had failed to qualify. But such losses did weaken Argentina and defeats by Germany and then a 6–1 drubbing by Czechoslovakia ensured a rough reception when the team arrived back in Buenos Aires. This Swedish frustration, coupled with a home defeat by Russia in 1961, were important moments in a process of reorientation in Argentinian football. In future the famous technique would be stiffened by the ruthless application of physical strength and defensive strategies.

Brazil, for their part, had not looked particularly impressive in Europe in 1956, losing, for the first time, to England and also to Italy, drawing with

Czechoslovakia and Switzerland and winning narrowly in Austria, Portugal and Turkey. The team was much changed since then and only three members of the 1954 side were present in 1958, Djalmar and Nilton Santos and the inside-forward Didi. Wise men looked at the players and predicted less artistry and more concentration on defence. It was the way of the football world. But less artistry did not mean *no* artistry. Brazil still had wonderfully gifted players. The question was, as it always had been, would they produce their best on the day? The Brazilian team was certainly the best prepared, the management being supplemented by doctors, dentists, masseurs – led by the famous Américo – and even a psychologist. Dr Hilton Gosling, who was in charge of the medical team, spent a month in Sweden in 1957 visiting twenty-five towns to find the best headquarters. The players spent a month in two similar places in the state of Minas Gerais on pre-tournament training. The attention to detail was impressive and would lead to high altitude training before the World Cup in Chile in 1962. Brazil seems to have been more advanced in the fields of sports medicine and sports science than many of the more 'developed' countries. As Gosling told journalists, 'We need to know, through the psychologist, such things as if the player is happy playing football or whether his first interest is the money ...'[12] The importance of a relaxed but disciplined atmosphere was illustrated by the card which Pelé sent home to his mum. He told her he was fine but 'don't write, as we are not allowed to receive letters'.[13] Keeping the players in good mental as well as physical shape seems to have worked. At least there was no repeat of 1954.

Pelé nearly did not get to Sweden. He injured his knee playing for Brazil against Corinthians of São Paulo just before the party left for Europe. It is probable that the not-quite eighteen-year-old was taken on the trip for the experience. It was certainly not clear that he would play, and in the first two games against Austria and England neither he nor Garrincha was selected, the latter because of his reluctance to defend, it was said.[14] On the eve of the important third group match against the Soviet Union, an Italian journalist measured the Brazilians' mood and assessed their chances.

How like us these Brazilians are, notwithstanding their medical specialists and professor of psychology! Sometimes I feel as though I'm in the Italian camp, when in spite of all the planning and special preparation some anxiety or other suddenly surfaces. Under these circumstances I cannot say whether Brazil will win the World Cup, even though all in all it has the best individual players and is capable of turning on the most beautiful and at times the most skilled play ...[15]

A football tournament is like a story and, like a story, it does not have to be equally good in every part. Brazil's early chapters in Sweden did not suggest the elegance and excitement to come. Austria were beaten 3–0, but only England were going to allow them to escape without defeat. A Brazil minus both the young mystery man Pelé and Garrincha then met an England who had not selected their young star Bobby Charlton. Brazil had the better of a drab goalless draw. So Brazil had to beat the Soviet Union to be certain of a quarter-final place. Did the psychologist advise the manager, Feola, not to choose Garrincha because he was too unsophisticated and Pelé because he was too young and unaggressive?[16] It is difficult to get to the bottom of these things. In the event, both played, Garrincha apparently by popular request of the players, and the Russians were outclassed. Vava scored the goals after three and seventy-seven minutes. Pelé hit a post and Garrincha spoiled Kuznetsov's afternoon. Wales gave Brazil a hard game in the quarter final, though they were mainly on the receiving end, missing the injured John Charles. Pelé scored the winning goal after sixty-six minutes. Was it brilliant or lucky? It can be seen on video; it was Pelé's first World Cup goal. He has his back to the Welsh goal about ten yards out. The ball is headed forward to him. He takes it on the chest, turns sharply left and volleys the ball with his right foot. It may have touched the boot of a Welsh defender. It still looks pretty good. It was goal number eighty-seven and he was not eighteen until October.

The semi final against the free-scoring French was probably decided by the injury to their centre-half Jonquet. He was limping and useless for the last fifty-five minutes and there were no substitutes in 1958. It was 1–1 when he was injured but Vava scored for Brazil shortly afterwards and Pelé scored a hat-trick in the second half. The host country, Sweden, had won the other semi final and amid terrific enthusiasm took the lead in the final after four minutes on a damp day and a wet pitch not thought to be to the liking of the Brazilians. But once Vava had equalized, the first of two goals made by darting runs and crosses by Garrincha, it was almost a Brazilian carnival, as all the journalists wrote. Pelé scored two memorable second-half goals, the first with a piece of ball juggling that had Brazil stamped right through it like 'Blackpool' is stamped through rock; his second was a strange but effective header. Amid all these fireworks on attack it should be recalled that the Brazilian defence excelled throughout the tournament, and in the final the two Swedish wingers, dangerous in all their matches up to the big day, were blotted out by Djalmar and Nilton Santos. As *The Times* football correspondent wrote, 'In the first final between the New and Old Worlds it was ... the lordly representatives of the New who brought a lustre ... which dazzled ... Here were dark, expressive sportsmen of a distant continent.'[17]

The final was broadcast live in Brazil by all the national radio networks. Most of the population appeared to be listening, some to loudspeakers located in the main thoroughfares of major cities. Later they would be able to see Osvaldo Sampaio's film *The Price of Victory*. President Kubitschek broadcast a message to the nation to mark the victory. The inauguration of the new Federal capital, Brasilia, took place the next day, which was either shrewd planning or a bit of luck. As for the newspapers, none was without a special edition containing detailed and illustrated accounts of this long-promised triumph. When the team arrived back in Rio there seemed to be millions on the streets shouting, singing, drinking and dancing. The carnival bands played and fireworks exploded. The next day the whole party was repeated in São Paulo. Pelé then went home to Bauru to be greeted by yet another parade and a banner which read: 'Welcome Pelé, Son of Bauru, Champion of the World'.[18] The local dignitaries were determined to present him with a car, an item of consumption possessed by few Brazilians in 1958 and a potent symbol of material success. It turned out to be a three-wheel Romisetta which the driver entered by the front. It was the first and most modest of many cars Pelé would own, as 1958 was the first of his many football triumphs.

Pelé was born Edson Arantes do Nascimento in a small town in Minas Gerais called Três Corações on 23 October 1940. As noted earlier, his father was a semi-professional footballer and the family had moved to Bauru when Pelé was six to enable his father to take up a warehouse job and to sign for a local team, Club e Atlético Bauru. Schooling was not a priority for the poor of Brazil, but Pelé did flit in and out of elementary school for six years and did a variety of odd jobs. He also began playing football, at first in the pick-up games, *peladas*, in the streets, on waste ground and in the fields near his home. He eventually joined a team who played without boots and were known as 7 September. It was at this time that he picked up the name Pelé. Nobody knows what it means and he did not like it.

Pelé was soon snapped up for the junior team of AC Bauru. The coach there was Waldermar de Brito, who had played for Brazil in the World Cup of 1938. He was working in the local council offices and keen to return to the big city of São Paulo. Pelé turned out to be his passport. The youth's talent was such that by the age of fifteen he was playing with the men in Bauru's first team. Such a player was bound to attract the attention of the

Pasión de Pueblo, El Gráfico 1956.

Football ... or War? Estudiantes de la Plato, River Plate 1955. The game was abandoned after crowd protest at a River Plate penalty. Two River players escape from the tear gas to the safety of the tunnel.

River Plate champions 1956.

Crowds in front of the offices of *La Prensa* in the centre of Buenos Aires
during the World Cup Final of 1930.

Bangu *c.* 1911.

Flamengo *c.* 1911.

A moment in the 1914 struggle between Brazil and Exeter City.

The first British referee in Argentina. Ike Caswell 1938–39 with justice clearly on his side.

Pelé and Coutinho making *umbanda* blessing before a big game.

No work today: we are off to see Pelé.
Street poster in Mexico City.

Football in the Favellas, 1960.

Three generations of great Brazilian forwards.
From the left: Leonidas, Ademir, Friedenreich.

Building the Maracaná, 1949.

Vila Belmiro, Santos.

River Plate Stadium, Buenos Aires.

Estadio Centenario, Montevideo.

Even a toilet roll can appear exciting on big game days at the Maracaná. (© *Julio Etchart*)

Maradona, 'a raging one-man cornucopia of menace, anger, suspicion, swagger, callousness and contempt – a creepy blustering gangster'.
(© *Alistair Berg*)

top clubs of Rio and São Paulo and several looked at him. It is not clear why none signed him. Bangu was keen, but Pelé's mother did not want him to go to Rio. In the end he went to Santos, the team of the coffee port for whom de Brito had once played. Santos played in the São Paulo state championship but they had never been particularly successful, winning only once in 1935. This was about to change.

Pelé first played for Santos against Corinthians of Santo André on 7 September 1956. He came on as a substitute and scored a goal in a 7–1 victory. He did not miss many games after that. He played seventy-three times in 1957, including his first international for Brazil against Argentina and, as we saw earlier, was selected for the World Cup in Sweden. He played in the last four matches in that tournament and on sixty-three other occasions in 1958. In 1959 he played over one hundred times, in 1960 eighty-two. This punishing schedule went on for the next fourteen years, reaching 1,254 games before he became Brazil's most famous export to the United States in 1975. *La Gazetta Sportiva* noted some of the qualities of his constitution which made all this possible in 1961. His pace revealed 'an athletic component rarely found in a soccer player ... [he had an] excellent build, sprint speed, resistance to fatigue, and a great capacity to absorb knocks'.[19] Lula, the Santos coach, described him in 1962:

> Pelé can no longer be compared to anyone else, because he possesses all the qualities of the ideal football player. He is fast on the ground and in the air, he has the physique, the kick, the ball control, the ability to dictate play, a feeling for the manoeuvre, he is unselfish, good natured and modest. I think he is the only forward in the world who always aims the ball at a precise point in the opposition's net at the moment of shooting for goal.[20]

This encomium was produced after the second World Club Championship final in Lisbon after Pelé had scored a hat-trick in helping Santos to beat Benfica 5–2. Guattiero Zanetti of *La Gazzetta dello Sport* described the goals which left him, and no doubt many others,

> open-mouthed at the complete athletic prowess of this young man ... for the first goal he converted a cross-kick of Pepe's by throwing himself into a long jump of at least seven metres: for the second goal he twice took possession of the ball after starting from a position behind his opponents, putting on sprints worthy of a professional sprinter, trapping the ball in flight in the penalty area, performing a miraculous leap to a height we would not have believed possible; for the third goal he stood up to two very rough fouls which would have sent any other player crashing to the ground ... instead of which we saw the opposing players who lunged at him bounce back and fall. Other champions or so-called champions would have chosen to risk less by artfully taking the foul to obtain the penalty.

Pelé instead accelerated past four opponents and as he was tackled by two defenders shot hard for the space between the goalkeeper and the post. The goalkeeper made a miraculous save but could not hold the ball, which Pelé met on the volley following up and sent into the net. As another commentator said, 'When you have Pelé in the team you start with a 2–0 advantage. What point is there in talking of tactics when that madman is on the field?' And Pelé always looked as though he was enjoying it. Perhaps he ought to have been, because by 1963 he was probably the world's highest-paid athlete. His 1960 contract was alleged to have involved $27,000 US to sign on, a $10,000 home for his parents, a Volkswagen and $150,000 a year win or lose, playing or not.[21]

Santos not only had to find the money for Pelé but also to pay the other members of what had suddenly become the team to beat in Brazil. This was less easy than perhaps it should have been. The Santos ground, the Vila Belmiro, was small, with a capacity of barely twenty thousand. Matches against the leading clubs of São Paulo were played at the Pacaembu stadium, but when the weaker clubs had to be entertained, with the results a foregone conclusion, Vila Belmiro was big enough. The Santos management later became involved in loss-making property speculation. The club also built an expensive new headquarters at the Parque Balneário, compared by critics to the Grand Hotel in Cannes.

An answer to the club's financial problems was the old South American standby of the foreign tour. Air travel facilitated its further development and the 1958 World Cup victory made Brazil and Brazilians attractive propositions for promoters. Everyone wanted to see the club side which contained Pelé, and so many of the other stars of the Brazilian game from Gilmar in goal, Mauro at centre-half, Zito the crucial midfield link and the new young star centre-forward Coutinho. Santos were in great demand. The management said in the early 1960s that they could have played three matches a day. As it was, the tours became a treadmill made necessary by the financial mismanagement of the club. In 1959 Santos played in Sofia on 23 and 24 May, Liège on 26 May, Brussels 27 May, and Ghent 30 May (they lost there). On 3 June it was Rotterdam, 5 June Milan, where they lost again, 6 June Düsseldorf, 7 June Nuremberg, 9 June Geneva, 11 June Hamburg and 13 June Niedersachsen. On 15 June it was back to Holland again and Enschede, 17 June Madrid where they were defeated by Real 5–3, Lisbon on 19 and 21, Valencia on 24, Milan again on 26 June and Santos still had enough energy and motivation to beat Barcelona 5–1 on 28 June. Pelé scored six goals in those last two games, but it was not over. On 30 June

Santos played in Genoa, 2 July Vienna, 5 July Seville. It was a royal progress, and there would be plenty more with Africa, Australia, Asia and the United States added to Europe and South America as the main venues. Record crowds for football matches were established in Japan and the United States to see Santos and Pelé. In the 1960s Santos were the world's leading football team, taking over from Real Madrid. The São Paulo championship was won eleven times between 1955 and 1969. The World Club Championship was won in 1962 and 1963. Their fame spread inside Brazil, where the President declared a national holiday after the first World Club Championship. Suddenly many Brazilian boys wanted to play for them and the club held trials of under-fifteen-year-olds each January. But the strain of constantly playing and travelling began to tell. The exceptional stars lost their edge or retired, to be replaced by good players but no longer the *wunderkinder* of the past. As long as Pelé remained, however, people would still pay their money. Contracts usually insisted he play for at least sixty-five of the ninety minutes. But by 1971 Santos were attracting criticism as the Harlem Globetrotters of world football. They were accused of being concerned only with the gate receipts and the pageantry and not the true competitive nature of the game. The *Miroir du Football* in 1973 claimed they were no longer interested in winning championships at home, indeed hardly ever played there. They never trained but lived only for their world tours.[22] There were scandals in Australia and England when the Santos management waited until the crowd was in the ground and then refused to play unless they were paid more money than had been agreed.[23] Pelé ensured that this era came to an end when he retired from Santos in 1974.

By that time Pelé had played in four World Cups. That of 1962 had been held in Chile where, it was alleged, the President of the Chilean Football Federation had told FIFA 'we must have the World Cup *because* we have nothing'. A new national stadium was built in Santiago and a smaller one at Viña del Mar. Of the other two venues which were used, one was owned by a copper-producing company at Rancagua and the other was located a thousand miles north at Arica. Both were small and down at heel.[24] Government resources were also put into the preparation of the Chilean team and they surpassed all expectations by reaching the semi-final. Unfortunately Chile then met Brazil, a Brazil with only three changes from the 1958 winners. Mauro of Santos replaced Bellini at centre-half and Zozimo came in for Orlando. Pelé was injured after the first two games and did not play thereafter. But Garrincha and Vava each scored twice and

Chile could only manage two in reply. Critics again said Brazil were more cautious than in 1958. Zagallo on the left tucked into midfield to convert the 4–2–4 formation of Sweden into a more security-conscious 4–3–3. The matches were tighter, notably the group game against Spain when Brazil had to score two in the last twenty minutes to win. But the final was won more easily than it might have been against a useful Czechoslovakia because their goalkeeper, Schroiff, had a *very* bad day at the office.

Seeking a hat-trick of victories in England in 1966, Brazil were eliminated in the first round, following defeats by Hungary and Portugal. The Portuguese offered no brotherly love to Pelé by fouling him seven times, eventually forcing his withdrawal from the fray. Another English referee was heavily criticized for not doing enough to protect him. By 1966 many of the players of '58 and '62 were past their best, with eight of them over thirty. There was no Nilton Santos, Mauro, Zito, Zagallo nor Zozimo. Selection mistakes did not help, and later Pelé would suggest that Rio–São Paulo rivalries were once more at the heart of the problem. In both 1958 and 1962 the São Paulo state group under Dr Paulo Machado de Carvalho had been in charge, but Rio had taken over by 1966.[25] Pelé vowed never to play in another World Cup but in 1970 he was yet again to be the star of the show. But before that he was involved in an extraordinary episode.

It began when João Saldanha was appointed to manage the Brazilian team for the 1970 World Cup in Mexico. He had only played junior football but he had coached, taking Botafogo to the Rio championship in 1957. But he then worked in Brazilian radio and became a popular television commentator. His appointment upset some of the São Paulo football establishment, including Machado de Carvalho. His outspokenness and reputation for political radicalism also did not endear him to the military government. He guided Brazil through the qualifying competition, but early in 1969 he was dismissed. He was then quoted as saying that Pelé was short-sighted in one eye and not fit to play in the World Cup.[26] The CBF were asked by the Brazilian Government to provide a full report on the fitness of the players.

Outside these elites, the enthusiasm for another assault on the World Cup by Brazil seemed undiminished. Thirty thousand people turned up to watch a midweek training game between the potential first team and the reserves. On a Sunday when the squad played a practice game in the provinces it was listened to on the radio as if it had been the real thing. Some critics went further than Saldanha, and said that Pelé was finished. Although he had recently scored his thousandth goal, the 941 matches he had played before the 1970 World Cup had taken their mental and physical toll. Moreover FIFA had sold out to European television which insisted that a kick-off time of 4 p.m., 11 p.m. in Europe, was the latest at which they would transmit the matches live. So the games would not only be played at high altitude – Toluca was over 8,000 feet – but in ninety-degree temperatures. It was particularly hot at Guadalajara and León where the Brazilian group matches were to be staged. There was also anxiety, especially in Europe, that the growing intensity of the competition would produce the kind of foul play and violence which had characterized recent World Club Championship finals. But as it was to turn out, the refereeing was good, no players were sent off, no one was seriously injured and there were no unseemly incidents on the field.

In fact, Brazil played with an attacking virtuosity not many had predicted but everyone enjoyed, except the Italians. Pelé was Pelé still, his skill and athleticism there for the whole world to see on the first World Cup televised in colour. Indeed many people not born in 1970 have since been able to see on video or television his outrageous dummy against Uruguay, his shot from the halfway line against Czechoslovakia, his header which Banks saved so amazingly against England. But as we have remarked several times, football is a team game and this Brazil was a team. Purists criticized the defence, but with Gerson, Rivelino and Clodoaldo in midfield and Tostão, Jairzinho and Pelé in attack they had players of imagination and menace. The confrontation in the final with Italy was particularly fascinating because it brought together the high priests of negativity and the *catanaccio* defence against the boys from Brazil. Almost everyone outside the borders of Italy hoped Brazil would win. The Italians represented the forces of darkness, the Brazilians the forces of the new light, as Brian Glanville so feelingly wrote.[27] It was a terrific performance and it moved the *Jornal do Brasil* to exult: 'Brazil's victory with the ball compares with the conquest of the moon by the Americans.' The military government did their best to exploit the victory, as we have already seen. Only recent Italian immigrants to São Paulo were disappointed. In a survey taken right after the 1970 World Cup victory, 90 per cent of lower-class respondents identified Brazilian football with the Brazilian nation.[28] Well they would, wouldn't they? With the footballing miracle went an economic miracle. Growth rates went up, inflation down and Brazil began exporting manufactured goods. For the first time since 1850, coffee ceased to be the largest single export.[29] But the effects of neither miracle lasted for long. The oil crisis of 1973 destroyed the economic miracle, while Brazil remained a country of many poor and some rich. In football too, an era was ending, with the reign of Pelé drawing to a close.

Pelé played his last game for Brazil, an undistinguished affair against Yugoslavia, in July 1971. It ended in a 2–2 draw with the crowd chanting 'stay, stay'. A big effort was made to persuade him to come back when it was seen that the 1974 World Cup team lacked the special qualities characteristic of more recent squads. The President of the CBD, João Havelange, wrote a letter to 'My dear compatriot Edson Arantes do Nascimento',

> We are at the threshold of a new World Soccer championship; our national team will play it with singular responsibilities, in view of the hegemony it has already conquered. In great part, such a hegemony is due to the contribution of our esteemed compatriot, known to all as a football virtuoso...
>
> Our country's printed media, and our radio and television second the aspirations of our people, and persist in publishing views which aim to encourage you to revise your decision of never again wearing the national team's colours. There is a great deal of hope based on the widespread nature of the appeals ... My hopes grow when remembering your devotion, as a citizen and three times world football champion, to the inner yearnings that beat in the heart of Brazil ...[30]

It was quite a propaganda campaign. Forty million viewers saw a television programme in which Elsa Soares led the singing of 'Come back Pelé'. According to Pelé, President Medici asked him personally but the king of football turned down both Presidents. Pelé was by now employed by Pepsi Cola to teach the skills of the game on their international youth football programme. He was also the possessor of a Diploma de Educação Física and star of the instructional film, *Pelé, the Master and His Method*. He was soon to be paid seven million dollars for signing for the New York Cosmos in the North American Soccer League in 1975, nine months after a tearful farewell to Santos.

Pelé had achieved a Brazilian miracle. He had risen from the terrible poverty of Três Corações and Bauru to be a multi-millionaire. He had married a white woman and his children were officially designated white. In 1962 he had been declared a national treasure by the government, and after his thousandth goal in 1969 – which he dedicated to the children of Brazil – a Brazilian Senator offered a paean of praise on the floor of the house including a poem in his honour. But he was not simply a Brazilian icon; he was a world figure. Pelé was the first black man to appear on the cover of *Life*. He was like royalty, and when he met the Duke of Edinburgh at a match in São Paulo in 1964 there was genuine anxiety about who should go to whom; the Duke went to Pelé. He met the Queen in 1968 during her state visit to Brazil when a special Rio–São Paulo game was arranged to show the visitors one of the jewels of Brazilian culture. Visiting Paris with Santos in 1971, he was met at Orly airport by a government minister and then travelled to the centre of Paris in a motorcade along the route normally reserved for heads of state.[31] In an open car Pelé continually waved and threw kisses to the crowds who had turned out to see him. The city centre almost came to a standstill. A ceasefire was arranged in the Nigerian civil war in order to see him play. In 1977 a reception was given at the United Nations to mark his support of UNICEF. When he finally retired from football in the same year he received a tribute from President Carter of the United States,

for the smiles he put on children's faces, the thrills he gave the fans of this nation and the dimension he added to American sports. Pelé has elevated the game of soccer to heights never before attained in America and only Pelé, with his status, incomparable talent and beloved compassion could have accomplished such a mission . . .[32]

In 1981 *L'Equipe* polled the sports writers of twenty major daily newspapers from around the world in an attempt, so beloved of sports journalists, to discover the sports champion of the century. It was expected that the winner would come from an individual rather than a team sport as an athlete, boxer, golfer or tennis player can clearly be seen to be a champion, whereas in team sports such selections are more subjective. The winner was Pelé; he was the number-one player in the number-one sport.[33]

In 1986 Diego Maradona of Argentina was thought to be 'the most extravagantly gifted footballer the world has ever seen'.[34] How can we compare him with Pelé? There are many similarities between the two. Both epitomize the rags-to-riches possibilities in the modern world. Maradona was born in Lanús, in Buenos Aires, into a poor family of Italian descent. Both were spotted early and there is a film of the boy Maradona, in which he juggles the ball with feet and head on what looks like a rough space near a park and says, 'I have two dreams. To play in the World Cup and to be a champion.' Maradona was snapped up by the local club, Argentinos Juniors, at the age of twelve, and had made his league debut at fifteen and his first international appearance for Argentina as a substitute against Hungary at sixteen. Both he and Pelé had similar physical characteristics, which included strong thighs and exceptional balance enabling them to ride tackles. They could kick well with both feet, though Pelé preferred the right and Maradona the left. They had speed and powerful acceleration. Both could do things on the football field which others could not. Maradona's speciality was the *gambeta*, a slalom-like dribble at speed through opposing defences. At Wembley in 1980 his final shot scraped a post after such a run. At Mexico City in 1986 against England, his *gambeta* culminated in the second Argentinian goal, a goal recently voted the best ever by the viewers of a British television programme. Both were Catholic, gave audiences to the Pope and were the guest of kings, Juan Carlos of Spain in the case of Maradona. Both were ambassadors for UNICEF and their countries.

But there were differences, too. Pelé was a one-club man until his late export to the United States. Maradona went from Argentinos Juniors to Boca, to Barcelona, to Naples, to Seville, to Newells Old Boys ... Whereas Pelé went to the World Cup as a seventeen-year-old and starred in the finals, Maradona was left out in 1978. Temperamentally, they seemed at opposite ends of the spectrum. Pelé was not always a gentleman on the field. He was sent off for the first time during his national service when playing for the Brazilian Army against the Argentine Army in Rio in 1960. In the rumpus which followed a general had to be called to restore order. He once said that the same referee had sent him off five times in Brazil. In January 1965 a referee who sent him off was himself suspended. Pelé's most heinous act on the football field probably took place in the Nations Cup in 1964 when Brazil played Argentina. Argentina used Messiano to mark him tightly and after sixty-five minutes, with the ball, and everyone's attention far away, he head-butted the Argentine player and broke his nose. He was not sent off, but his punishment was to be marked by Rattín for the rest of the game, which Argentina won 3–0.[35] But Pelé played over 1,300 matches, many more than Maradona. He was never sent off overseas and his sportsmanship is legendary.

Maradona was detained by police for 'public aggression' after a match in Buenos Aires in 1980. He was suspended for three months following his part in a brawl in the Spanish Cup Final, was sent off during the World Cup in 1982 and on several other occasions. By 1990 he had a reputation for continually complaining to referees during matches. He was often the victim of foul play, most infamously when his leg was broken by Goicoechea in a match between Barcelona and Bilbao in 1983. He did his reputation outside Argentina no good by the 'hand of God goal' against

England in the 1986 World Cup quarter final, though Argentinians saw it as an example of *viveza* – craftiness, a quality to be admired.

It is in temperament and lifestyle that the differences appear to be most marked. Pelé took a degree and became a successful businessman, coping well with the inevitable decline of his athletic prowess. Maradona played brilliantly in Naples for four years but drifted into the world of the Camorra, a world of drink, women and drugs. He became friendly with one of the 'families' and may yet face charges of trafficking if he ever returns to Italy. But as Bromberger has pointed out, the myth of Maradona in Naples has survived all these scandals and many see his downfall as part of the continuing plots against the city. Maradona seemed particularly at home in Naples, his personal style suiting the collective style of the city, as a brilliant and crafty player, 'a wealthy man with the culture of the pauper he used to be'. The two championships won while he was there provided a 'symbolic revenge' for the contempt heaped on all things Neapolitan by the North.[36] How far Maradona is the victim of a football industry which has lost all sense of proportion and believes that anything and anyone can be bought is not easy to say. Perhaps the appeal of Maradona will never transcend the partisan in quite the way in which Pelé's did; in the end it is that quality to which the poll of *L'Equipe* drew our attention when it voted Pelé the world's premier sportsman.

CHAPTER SEVEN

PASSION OF THE PEOPLE?

*At lunch the Brazilian couscous turns out to be fishcakes. When
I ask to see a soccer game the guests get very excited, and when
I mention that I had a long career as a soccer player, I provoke
a general delirium. Unwittingly, I have stumbled upon their
principal passion.*
Albert Camus, *American Journals*, 1989 edn p. 83

*And now I must confess my guilty secret: apart from all the
times I have watched football on the television, I have only
been to one football match in my life, that is to say in the flesh. I
feel I have no right to call myself a good football supporter or,
for that matter, a good Brazilian.*
Clarice Lispector, *Discovering the World*, 1992 English edn,
p. 120

*At the beginning of the match [the crowd] had whistled and
shouted 'Água . . . Água . . .' because in this scorching end of
summer heat water had been strictly rationed in Rio. But as
soon as the Brazilian team had won its ticket to Switzerland, a
single, formidable cry rang out from the masses, 'Vamos Suíça,
Vamos Suíça!' Thousands of shirts were torn off, set alight and
waved about like triumphal torches. For me, the game here had
always been an accessory to the spectacle. In the same way as
man feels crushed by the scene when, from the height of
Corcovado, he gazes with astonishment at the splendours of the
bay of Rio, so football and its players seemed tiny, snuffed out
on the little rectangle of grass, gripped by the immense,
swarming concrete rotunda of the Maracaná. To match its scale,
this game between Brazil and Paraguay would have to have
been played by twenty eight Goliaths . . . Failing which I had
the impression that it was no more than a pretext, an excuse for
the extraordinary striving of the people: a sort of safety valve*

*invented to allow the superabundant life of the people, their
exuberance and need for celebration, to escape.*[1]

The word passion is never far away from any attempt to get under the skin
of football in South America. Passion means 'any vehement, commanding
or overpowering emotion or feeling'. To be passionate about something is
to be more than enthusiastic: it is to be 'ardently desirous' or 'zealously
devoted'.[2] There is no lack of evidence to suggest a growing passion for
football in South America, most clearly seen in the great cities of Buenos
Aires and Montevideo, Rio de Janeiro and São Paulo. Football established
itself in Argentina, Brazil and Uruguay less as a competition between cities,
more on the basis of club rivalry within cities. The city leagues were
dominated by what the British call 'local derbies' between a relatively small
number of clubs; in Montevideo, Nacional and Peñarol; in São Paulo,
Corinthians, Palestra Italia (Palmeiras), São Paulo, Portuguesa; in Rio,
Flamengo, Fluminense, Botafogo and Vasco da Gama; in Buenos Aires
matches between the big five, Racing, Independiente, San Lorenzo, Boca
and River Plate. No city could boast as many professional football grounds
as Buenos Aires and no team from the provinces was admitted to the top
league there until 1939. Local derbies must have intensified the excitement
if for no other reason than the ease with which teams could be followed to
'away' matches.

The clubs represented particular neighbourhoods and in some cases
represented and dramatized other social differences. Once River Plate had
moved their ground from Boca, for example, then the Boca–River matches
became confrontations between the rich and the poor. Similarly in Rio,
Fluminense was associated with the old, high-status families, Flamengo the
team of the poor and the blacks, Vasco da Gama supported by Portuguese
migrants and their Brazilian-born descendants while Botafogo attracted
the modern middle classes.[3] In São Paulo, where the immigration was
much higher, Palmeiras is still run by Italians and their descendants and São
Paulo and Corinthians are the clubs of the middle and lower class
respectively. Of course these neat and tidy interpretations should not be
taken too far. Football clubs attract supporters for many reasons, both
rational and irrational. Fluminense clearly attracted some workers who
wanted to identify with a powerful club supported by the best families, and
over time success and the spectacle provided by outstanding players also
attracts. Moreover the old reasons for supporting one team rather than
another fade. But loyalties once established have a habit of persisting. A

common saying among the football enthusiasts of Buenos Aires is that you can change your wife but your mother and your football club you cannot change. Early in 1985, a wealthy Carioca entrepreneur left 360 million dollars in his will to the Bangu club from the working-class Zona Norte. He had not shifted his allegiance to match his change of fortune.[4]

What was it like to attend one of the leading matches in Argentina on the eve of professionalism? Outside the ground people, often children, were selling things which a spectator might need: parasols, bricks and boxes for the smaller supporter to stand on, oranges and apples, soft drinks, newspapers, pictures of footballers and sweets. Matches often failed to start on time because the field was occupied by more than just the players and officials. Newspaper and, by the late 1920s, radio reporters were irrepressible in their pursuit of the last-minute but first-hand quote. Hordes of small, and not so small, boys, *pibes* in Spanish, would also invade the field, sometimes knocking the match ball out of the hands of the referee and beginning a kick-about of their own. They were also attracted by the free samples of cigarettes and sweets and the balloons dropped from low-flying aeroplanes advertising local products.[5] Actually going to the match quickly became part of the excitements and irritants of Sunday afternoon in Buenos Aires.

> Trams and buses, all sizes, overflowing with passengers, hanging on the steps, the ledge at the back, in fact anywhere where two feet can be planted, while some of the youngsters climb on the roof of the trams. Coming away from the games – not going – they sometimes disconnect the overhead tram guide wires causing chaos among the traffic, and the cacophony of noise becomes deafening.[6]

Surviving newsreels also show lorry loads of supporters heading for the stadiums like an invading army.

Once the game began, crowds tended to be noisy and enthusiastic when their favourites were attacking, silent and anxious when they were defending. The reception of a goal by the home team astonished visitors such as Motherwell's Bobby Ferrier: 'I shall never forget the sight we saw when the only goal of the match was scored. The 50,000 people present waved their handkerchiefs for a full five minutes. They seemed to go mad.'[7] Goals were often greeted by pitch invasions with the scorer kissed and knocked over in the rush to congratulate him, and this in spite of the fences.

Popular support for the game increased throughout the 1930s, 1940s and into the 1950s, reaching a peak in 1954 when the sale of tickets per match averaged 15,056. This figure does not include the many club members who obtained cheap admission to all home games. River Plate claimed 72,000 *socios* in 1958 and fielded nine teams for different age groups every Saturday and Sunday.[8] For the most important matches grounds would be full many hours before the start. When England visited Buenos Aires in 1953 the River Plate ground opened at 10 a.m. and rapidly filled, even though the kick-off was not until mid afternoon.[9] This was the period when spectators at River chanted, '*La gente ya no come por ver a Walter Gómez*' (People are not eating so that they can see Walter Gómez). Gómez was a Uruguayan forward whose attractions contributed to traditional family meals being delayed so that the men could get to the matches. Dances for the young did not begin until 8 p.m. on Sundays in order not to coincide with football and it was the 1960s before earlier starts were introduced.[10] A recent study of workers in the industrial suburb of Avellaneda, home to Racing and Independiente whose stadiums are on the same street, found that not only did each club have a mass following but that football was the principal activity in the many neighbourhood sports clubs – twenty-one with 48,000 members in 1944. Organized games were played every weekend and boys played it every day on the streets, often to the annoyance of some neighbours who asked the police to repress this 'repulsive expression of lack of culture'. It is doubtful if such pleas were successful. The enthusiasm for football was widespread. When the club Social y Deportivo Argentinos de Avellaneda celebrated its tenth anniversary it did so with a dinner and family dance but also with the traditional football match between married and single men.[11]

Newspaper and radio coverage both reflected and contributed to the idea that in Argentina, football mattered to a lot of people. But excitement was further stimulated by papers such as *Crítica*, which in the early thirties gave a medal of honour to the goalkeeper who could keep his goal intact against the free-scoring Ferreyra, and in 1953 by a local firm which was offering bonuses to goalkeepers who saved penalties. It is a mark of football's pulling power that when Eva Perón organized a four-day rally as part of her attempt to become Vice-President of the Republic in 1951 she had the Sunday football programme postponed.[12]

Many stories have been told to illustrate the passion for football in Brazil. A match was being played in Rio in the national championship. Many of the audience at a local theatre had brought transistors. 'All stirred so audibly when a goal was scored that the male lead in the play stopped, looked out, and asked, "What's the score?" Even if it is a myth, it is full of meaning about the pride many Brazilians still feel for their football, and if it isn't ...'[13] From the 1950s until the later 1970s, attendances at football matches in Brazil were higher than in any other country in the world.[14] Brazilian crowds support their teams with a hysterical pandemonium which Europeans find both captivating and inexplicable. It has often been said that the action in the stands is more exciting than that on the pitch. Flags wave, drums beat, songs are sung, confetti, powder and rice thrown: it seems more like the celebration of a wedding, only on a larger scale and more uninhibited. The fireworks fill the stadiums with very loud explosions and a 'magical cloud-like mist'.[15] When all this is performed in a theatre as historic and dramatic as the Maracaná it is not surprising that the impressions of Jacques de Ryswick (third quote at the opening of this chapter) have been often, if rarely so elegantly, repeated. By the sixties another facet of the Brazilian football crowd was the transistor radio held to the ear to listen to the commentary on the match. Samba bands were also a feature. Bands had first played at Flamengo matches in the 1940s and were soon imitated by other clubs.

The first organized fan club was probably also at Flamengo in 1941. By the end of the 1980s they had thirty in Rio alone. Membership can vary from a few hundred to a few thousand. The clubs are self-generated and not promoted by the football club. All the organization is done by the most active supporters. Corinthians of São Paulo are alleged to have the most famous fans, with over 60 per cent of the population claiming allegiance. By the early 1980s, eleven *torcidas* were devoted to them, including the first all-female one. One of them is called 'Camisa 12', shirt number twelve, which says something of their purpose: to be the team's extra man. The members of these supporters' clubs have a wide range of jobs and social backgrounds. In 1977 five thousand of them travelled fifty-one hours in buses to watch their heroes in a quarter final match of the Brazilian championship. Later, 85,000 went to Rio for the semi-final against Fluminense and stayed there for two days celebrating the victory. In 1979 *World Soccer* quoted a fan of Corinthians: 'We are fanatics, but not like the English. Our fans surpass theirs in every category except one – violence. We are more fanatical, better supporters, louder, everything. Soccer means a lot more to us than to them. Yet they're more vicious.' The word for supporter in Brazil is *torcedor*. The verb *torcer* means to twist, turn, fold or bend. So a *torcedor* describes someone very committed to their club, continually crossing fingers in the hope that it will help the team to victory. Many Brazilian supporters go further by seeking the aid of supernatural powers. On the eve of the game offerings are placed at crossroads to bring good luck to favoured teams and bad luck to the opposition. Many will pray to the saints, an amalgamation of African gods and Christian saints, and both spectators and players will make magical gestures. Players, for example, will pour water on their boots and wash their feet with herbs prescribed by a *Pai de Santo*, a type of priest practising the rites of *umbanda* or *candomblé*. Immediately before the game hands are joined in a chain and everyone prays for victory. These practices originated with poor blacks, but they seem to be a regular part of the subculture of football in Brazil over and above the more widespread adherence to particular superstitious practices common among footballers in most countries.[16]

The response to the death of one of Brazil's most famous players, Garrincha, is a telling example of the importance of football to Brazilians. He died after a drinking bout on 16 January 1983 at the age of forty-nine. The days of his fame as a footballer were long since over, and the last decade of his life had been one of declining personal and material circumstances. The previous five years he had lived in a rented house in Bangu. His body was taken to lie in state at the Maracaná stadium. Managers, former players and the supporters of Rio clubs held a vigil and the public queued up to file past the corpse. Flags of Botafogo and Brazil covered the coffin. The burial took place on 21 January in Pau Grande, the small textile town about thirty-five miles from Rio where Garrincha had been born and lived for the first thirty years of his life. At 8.30 a.m. the body left the Maracaná on a fire engine, a similar vehicle to the one in which the world championship-winning team of 1958 had shown themselves to the people of Rio. Representatives of supporters' organizations from various local clubs accompanied the cortege and in windows along the route Brazilian flags and club banners were displayed as they were on the days of important matches in the national championship or the World Cup.

The funeral provoked enormous public interest. The main road out of Rio, the Avenida Brasil, was crowded with people, many carrying national flags, and traffic was stopped while the procession passed. Thousands more had made their way to Pau Grande itself and many of them had to abandon their cars and continue on foot, transistors to their ears as they listened to descriptions of the event. The crowds were similar to those going to or from a big match. Extra trains had been laid on and on a line which passed close by the cemetery engine drivers sounded their whistles. Fixed to a tree at the entrance to a nearby factory a notice read: 'Garrincha – You made the whole world smile. Today you make it cry.'

The cortege took two hours to travel the thirty-five miles. Crowds both inside and outside the church were so large that the priest decided not to celebrate mass but performed a simple benediction over the body. The coffin was lifted on to the shoulders of Botafogo supporters and the national hymn was sung.

Clearly media coverage had something to do with these popular manifestations because of the 'fierceness with which they seized on Garrincha's death and the emotional charge with which they invested it'.[17] But the scale of the demonstration surprised everyone and itself became an event worth reporting. Garrincha was mourned as a hero of Brazilian football, the tragedy of whose decline made it all the more necessary for the media to speak for this inarticulate man who had expressed himself eloquently only on the field of play. It could also be argued that his death symbolized an era of success for Brazil – both on and off the football field – which had gone.

Footballers in South America could rise to heights which others could rarely match. In Argentina and Uruguay as well as Brazil it did not seem quite so ridiculous to speak of football as art. Here was grace under pressure, with individual ball control of an almost magical kind and passing more like a caress than a kick. But there was another side to the passion for football in South America. If the play was more flamboyant and the crowd more colourful, both could erupt into a violence that seemed particularly out of place in an arena of pleasure.

In 1945, the President of Botafogo, emphasizing that several founders of the club had been British and that his club had always respected British sporting traditions, wrote to the British Ambassador in Rio suggesting a visit from a British team. Rio agreed, suggesting such a tour might be extended to other South American countries and provide a money-spinner for the Red Cross.[18] But it was soon clear that British Embassy representatives elsewhere did not think such a visit a good idea. Santiago thought British professionals would indulge on the voyage, get beaten and end by making unsportsmanlike excuses. Buenos Aires was even more doubtful:

> Local interest in football has to be seen to be believed; games between the leaders in the championship draw crowds of 80,000 ... Under their own rules and on their own grounds the Argentine football players are first class and even the best First Division teams from England would have their work cut out to hold their own. Any football team below tip-top standard would do our football reputation more harm than good.
>
> Even then we should have some hesitation in recommending it. The local rules

differ considerably from the English, particularly in regard to charging; an Argentine goalkeeper is a sort of untouchable; as soon as he gets the ball into his hands he is entitled to a free kick. Argentine players and spectators are very excitable and the sight of a twelve stone Arsenal forward charging an Argentine goalkeeper with the ball into the net might easily start a battle...[19]

The writer thought an Argentine team visiting Britain would be safer. If there were any 'incidents' they would only be read about in newspapers and not 'witnessed by about 100,000 excited Argentines'. It would also be returning the compliment for previous visits of British teams and 'you know how touchy Argentines are on such points of dignity'. Montevideo was doubtful, Bogotá, La Paz and Washington definitely opposed. Rio had second thoughts after consulting the 'staff football expert'. Such a visit could not possibly be a success. 'It appears that football in this country arouses passions that can only be compared to the factions of the Green and the Blue in Byzantium. The recent series of the South American Football Championship was notable for the number of free fights ... and to disagreeable incidents of every kind, all exploited to the full by the Press.' Lima was opposed because 'it has been our experience that "latins are lousy losers"'. The South American Department of the Foreign Office rejected the idea.[20]

The British Foreign Office was, of course, an elite within an elite. Its members thought themselves very superior persons indeed. It did not want its well-laid diplomatic schemes disrupted by a lower-class business like football. Nevertheless, it is clear that there were two sides to the passion of the people in South America and it was the other, darker side which fuelled the anxieties of the British Foreign Office and which poses questions which cannot be ignored, no matter how difficult they may be to answer. Was South American football more violence-prone than its European counterpart, and if so, why? Did football players and spectators find it more difficult to accept defeat, more difficult to accept the decisions of the referee, in Argentina, Brazil and Uruguay? These are complex issues which it is not possible to approach systematically in this work. Access to the records of the governing authorities of football would be essential. But what can be done is to explore some examples of actual behaviour over time and to note what contemporaries thought about it. We should keep in mind the cautionary words of Sam Allen of Swindon Town who, when asked in 1912 what he thought of Argentine crowds, replied, 'Partisanship must be encountered wherever football is really known: it is proof of interest in the game.'[21]

Such good sense did not always appeal to commentators in the early days of football in South America. The crowd at a match in São Paulo between Germania and São Paulo Athletic in 1904 was criticized for behaviour which was soon to be all part of the game. But in 1904 the *Jornal do Comércio* disapproved of 'spectators who several times shouted at the players and at the referee when they did something that did not please them, and what most annoys us to say (Oh! Shame) is that even young men from other clubs, interested only in the victory of one team or another to benefit their own team, also over-reacted in a very rude and undignified way'.[22] But as we have seen, the game in Brazil remained firmly in the hands and at the feet of the elites, most notably in Rio and São Paulo, well into the 1920s. Teams would enter the field and raise their right arms with closed fists shouting hip hip hurrah, three times, doubtless after the fashion of the English Corinthians. It meant, according to Waldemyr Caldas, that the spectators were guaranteed an honest match, a playing to win. In their turn the crowd would reply '*Alegua -gua -gua*'.[23]

In Buenos Aires, elite control had never been quite so complete. As early as 1905 a match between Belgrano and Quilmes was abandoned following a pitch invasion after the home team's third goal. The supporters of Boca Juniors were already gaining some notoriety even before 1914. In June 1910, on the ground of the Western Railway Club at Caballito, the Second Division match was prematurely ended by a crowd invasion. The Western Railway's linesman was assaulted by one of the Boca players and the referee by another. The Boca captain apparently made no effort to intervene. There were no police on duty, which cost the home club a fine. The Boca players were suspended for a year and the game ordered to be replayed on a neutral ground.[24] By 1912 the *Buenos Aires Herald* was complaining about 'chronic rowdyism' on local football grounds and in 1914 a Racing official allegedly threatened the referee with a gun at half time during the match against the visiting Exeter City. Blanks were occasionally fired from revolvers during matches and on at least one occasion firearms were used in a fight between rival supporters. After the end of a match between San Martín and Villa Bargano, two people were killed and an old lady who happened to be passing the ground was injured by a stray bullet.[25]

By the 1920s interest in the game in all three countries had grown considerably, especially, as we have seen, after Uruguay's first Olympic victory in 1924. The first fence around the pitch to keep the spectators from the players went up in Argentina in the same year. Yet crowds continued to be very interventionist and games were often interrupted. The Combined Scottish Eleven who toured in 1923 had an amusing example of this when playing a Provincial selection in Buenos Aires. When a corner kick was erroneously awarded to the Scots by the referee a number of spectators formed a line in front of the ball so that it could not be taken. The Scottish player kicked it out for a goal kick in order that the game could continue. Penalties awarded against the home team regularly provoked opposition. When Plymouth Argyle were awarded a penalty against the Rosario League in 1924, first the opposition attempted to leave the field and then a section of the crowd invaded it. It took policemen twenty minutes to clear the ground and restart play. The enthusiasm of Argentine crowds cannot be denied, but they could be brutal too. When the Argentine Amateur Association were three goals down and dispirited towards the end of their match with Motherwell in 1928, the shrill whistles of disapproval were accompanied by shouts of '*tongo*', which implied they had been bribed to lose.[26]

Roberto Arlt, the distinguished Argentine writer, was not a football enthusiast but he drew attention to another aspect of Buenos Aires football fans which was already an established feature in 1929. Groups of fans, identifying with particular clubs, had formed themselves into *barras* or gangs to defend themselves against the *barras* of other clubs. These *barras de hinchas* – Arlt called them groups of ruffians or columns of *malandrines* – went on punitive expeditions in the stadium, spreading terror with their artillery of bottles and bombs of oranges. These are the gangs, he wrote, who burn the benches in the popular sections and invade the pitch to attack rival fans. In some districts they had become a kind of mafia, a small organized group whose armed sallies and fiery eruptions gave them some notoriety, prestige and honour.[27]

Chelsea saw a good deal of the darker side of South American football during their six-week adventure in 1929, most infamously during their fourth match against a Capital eleven played on the ground of Boca Juniors. They were warned by the local English-language press that it was not going to be easy as:

> they would be pitted against ... men who have played football since they were children [who] have probably better stamina, because they eat better and have lived in cleaner air, and they have therefore become faster. Add to that a sufficiency of pluck and a sound knowledge of the intricacies of a non-intricate game and ... you have the reasons why Chelsea must not hope to win more than the gate receipts ...[28]

Moreover, having finished ninth in a modest Second Division in the 1928–9 English season just ended, they could hardly be labelled one of England's premier teams. Nevertheless, there was great interest in the match against the Capital and all other First Division matches scheduled for that day had been postponed. Chelsea lost the match 3–2, although it ended early in what the *Buenos Aires Herald* called 'disorderly scenes'.

They began with a tackle by Wilson on an Argentine forward. He was injured and an 'unruly element in the crowd' ran on to the pitch. One spectator struck the Chelsea captain in the face. Luis Monti, the Argentine international, then deliberately kicked Rodger, the Chelsea centre-half, in the groin. Rodger was removed in pain and there was some fighting on the field. According to the Chelsea director Charles Crisp, one Argentinian player kicked through the glass panel of the dressing room.[29] It was partly a matter of different interpretation of the rules. Shoulder-charges were considered brutal in Argentina, on a level with deliberate tripping and ankle-tapping, but the *Herald*'s reporter claimed that fouls by Monti were greeted with cries of *'muy bien Monti'* from some spectators. He went on to characterize the Argentine football fan:

> [He] is the most wonderful winner in the world ... When Motherwell was beaten, local writers went into learned analyses of Criollo versus British football and came to the conclusion that the former had nothing to learn. The newspapers waxed hysterical, bands of excited and joyous young men paraded the streets. They would have rung the church bells if the latter had not closed for the night ... When Monti ... kicked Rodgers in the groin a happy shout of acclamation went up. When Rodgers fainted and was carried off the field the public cheered ... [The Argentine footballer] must learn to lose as well as to win. In that lies the essence of what football means ... Any player can win gracefully. But it takes a better man to lose gracefully. Locally, they lose disgracefully.[30]

This was not simply the view of the English-language press. The quality Buenos Aires papers, *La Nación*, *La Época* and *El Diario*, all agreed that the visitors were more sinned against than sinning. It did not stop there either because, after waiting for another ninety minutes in the dressing room at the end of the match before being allowed to leave, the Chelsea party found that the tyres of their charabanc had been slashed. As *La Época* said, there was only one expression for it, *'¡Qué vergüenza!'* (How shameful!)

Better referees might have helped. In fact, standards were poor. It does not appear to have been a position enjoying a very high status in South

America. We have already noticed the Amateur League of São Paulo demanding professional referees in 1926, but little appears to have been done. 'Violence has always been present in Brazilian football,' was the resigned judgement of Caldas.[31] It was 1929 before the South American Confederation organized its first meeting of referees from different countries. Touring teams often brought their own: Nottingham Forest did in 1905 and Plymouth Argyle did in 1924. In Argentina most referees seemed none too competent and easily intimidated by crowds who often treated them as criminals. They tended to favour the home side, did not dare to play the advantage rule and blew their whistles for every petty infringement. Nor were they much good at keeping up with play. Their honesty was often called into question. These problems were exacerbated by the establishment of professional football in the 1930s.

As investment in players and stadiums grew, the need to win, already powerful, became even more contagious among club directors, players, and the football public alike. As we have seen, it was in 1932 that River Plate earned their nickname *los millonarios* for their record spending on new players. In such circumstances the scrutiny of the referees' performances became even more intense. Directors regularly criticized them in public and a section of the press were scornfully scurrilous about their mistakes. In such circumstances it was not surprising that self-preservation made them give decisions in favour of the most powerful and popular teams. Their reluctance to award penalty kicks was often commented on: in the 1934 season only thirty-four penalties were given on thirty-nine playing dates. As a later commentator pointed out, to be a referee in Argentina was taking your life in your hands.[32]

Referees were regularly assaulted even in the First Division. On 12 June 1932, for example, one Señor Bruzzone was beaten up by disgruntled fans of Huracán after Racing had won 1–0. Referee De Angelis was assaulted by fans of Ferrocarril Oeste and at La Plata, outraged supporters of another beaten side, Gimnasia y Esgrima, vented their frustrations on referee Gómez. In such a climate of intolerance and anxiety it is hardly surprising that some referees panicked. Señor De Angelis seems to have done that in La Plata on 14 August 1932 when in charge of Estudiantes and River Plate. River were top of the league and leading at half time. De Angelis then disallowed a 'goal' for the home side, and when the players of Estudiantes surrounded him in protest, rushed for the safety of the dressing rooms. When he returned, fifteen minutes later, he had changed his mind and allowed the goal. Rumours suggested that he had been threatened at gunpoint by the President of Estudiantes. It was *el gol de la casilla*, scored in the dressing room, as some contemporaries named it.

Even if not being assaulted, referees were often at the centre of controversy. Gimnasia y Esgrima were making a real challenge for the championship in 1933 and had two points more than Boca, whom they visited on 10 September. They led 2–1 at half time but the referee then gave Boca what everyone considered a most doubtful penalty. A few minutes later Boca scored a third goal amid strong suspicions of offside. The League suspended the referee and the magazine *La Cancha – The Football Ground* – immortalized the events in verse:

> *Por tocar tan bien el pito*
> *en aquella tarde loca*
> *lo nombraron a Angelito*
> *bombero voluntario de la Boca*

> For blowing his whistle so well
> On that mad evening
> They nominated Little Angel
> As volunteer spy for Boca

San Lorenzo went on to win the title, but not before another referee had done his bit to spoil the chances of the outsiders from La Plata. First, with San Lorenzo leading Gimnasia 2–1 at home, the referee gave the visitors a free kick on the edge of the penalty area when the offence looked to have taken place inside. He compounded this by awarding a goal to San Lorenzo after the Gimnasia goalkeeper had appeared to keep the ball from crossing the line. This was too much for the men from La Plata, who staged a sit-down on the field. With no opposition the referee allowed Boca to score another four goals before abandoning the match. Gimnasia never recovered. It seemed to some critics that this was another example of the influence of the over-mighty subjects, Boca, River, Racing, San Lorenzo and Independiente. Referees needed to be more independent. Greater competence might go some way towards such a goal. The Argentinian FA turned to Britain to recruit an experienced British official who would both set a standard of performance and provide training for local referees.

The man selected was a recently retired Football League referee, Isaac Caswell. He came from Blackburn, where he was a Labour councillor. He arrived in Buenos Aires in October 1937 and stayed for three years.[33] For the first three weeks he watched matches and realized that 'British methods' could not be introduced straight away. The first six months were the worst. He later felt the turning point came in a match between Boca and Racing in 1938. After sending off a famous player for arguing he was stoned at the end of the match. The player was later suspended for one month, but gave a radio interview which emphasized his respect for *el árbitro inglés*. Caswell himself commented: 'My firmness in this match, and the fact that it showed I was out for discipline and was not to be deterred either by the fame of players or by clubs, made an impression and changed the situation.'[34]

The Caswell experiment probably influenced the AFA to recruit eight referees from Britain to take charge of all the First Division matches in 1948. Four did not return in 1949, but the first group were joined by four newcomers. By 1950 there were twelve contracted British referees. Some would stay for nine years. They were well paid at over £100 per month and were often able to obtain other jobs. Several taught physical education in the various British schools in Buenos Aires and a few of the more adventurous set up their own businesses. As most of them did not speak Spanish at first each was allocated an interpreter who accompanied them to every match and helped draft the match reports. Each referee was also given a team of three linesmen who would officiate at the reserve team match which preceded the first team fixture on Sunday afternoon, and then run the line in the main match. The British referees were responsible for instructing their apprentices. By 1954 one First Division match per week was being given to an Argentine. In that season Argentine referees had begun a campaign of non-co-operation with the foreign imports. It is clear that not all Argentine referees were bad, but public trust was difficult to win. British referees were clearly neutral and therefore independent. They were not members of any of the clubs. The Rosario teams were especially appreciative of a British referee when visited by one of the Buenos Aires big five clubs.[35]

But the visitors did not escape the intense scrutiny provided by an insatiable press and radio. One referee heard on the radio the victim of a foul for which the referee had awarded a penalty explain how the tackle had really been made outside the area but he, the player, had cunningly fallen inside. Argentine crowds disliked the award of penalties late in a game. When one of the Englishmen gave one to each side in the last five minutes of a match between Racing and Platense he had to be smuggled out of the ground in a police van after stones had been thrown at him. The local press was critical, lapsing into the English 'Get out Mr Turner and bad lucky' (*sic*). Just as well the match had been drawn. All the newspapers classified the referees' performance from very good through to mediocre and poor. Marks were given out of ten. Club magazines could be particularly vitriolic after a defeat.

During the 1950s British referees were in demand throughout South America and were to be found refereeing league and international matches in Brazil, Chile, Peru and Uruguay as well as Argentina. Several accompanied Brazilian and Argentine club teams on tours to other parts of the South American subcontinent. One of the most famous was Jack Barrick from Northampton. He had retired after the 1948 Cup Final in England. He refereed twelve out of the twenty-nine games played during the South American Championship of 1949. He also refereed six of Arsenal's seven games in Brazil in the same year. In eight and a half months he controlled ninety-one games in all, including the most important ones in the championship of the Rio Grande do Sul in Porto Alegre.

What can be said about this strange episode in the history of football in South America? It cannot have been easy for countries wrestling with their identities in a world still dominated by Europe to accept that their own nationals were not capable of controlling the leading players of the national game. On the other hand it was a clear sign to FIFA that a problem had been recognized and a solution was being sought. The overseas referees were mostly British, although there were also some Swedes and at least one Austrian. Britain retained the imperial prestige of the wartime victor as well as the status of the inventor of modern football. British referees were widely thought to be the best, as evidenced by the fact that they were appointed to ten out of the total of twenty-two matches in the 1950 World Cup.[36] Their presence probably did help to improve local refereeing standards. What it also ensured, and this especially in Argentina, was a breathing space in which the smell of corruption could be blown away. It was essential to remove the once widely held opinion that referees were not just bad but bought by the big clubs. The last word should be left to the press of Argentina and Brazil. When Jack Barrick left Pôrto Alegre in 1950 a local paper sadly wrote: 'Mr Barrick's leaving opens a curtain on a black panorama for our football, which he has nearly retrieved from chaos. We shall be like the man who, delighted in Shakespeare plays for several weeks, has to turn back to clown jesters.'

A Buenos Aires newspaper provided the following encomium after

Bob Turner had refereed the second match in the 1957 South American Championships in Peru between the hosts and Ecuador.

> Turner brought to the task all the phlegm of the islands. To arrive recently in a strange country, a Latin American country, which has a reputation for violence; to begin by actually controlling a game in which the local team takes on a country to which it is traditionally antagonistic – Ecuador – and to disallow, in fifteen minutes, two goals for the local team, is a spectacular case of British phlegm ... Mr Turner, without worrying what they might say, disallowed the goals, not just one but two, one after another and for no reason at all! If it had been in my country, commented a Uruguayan, the smell of fried referee would have been in the air, or if it had been in Buenos Aires, we added. Happily for Mr Turner, we were in Lima and here, up to now, the custom of eating referees has not been developed ... Mr Turner will be able to carry on with his contract, and carry on disallowing goals which is where this super phlegm is shown to best effect – super phlegm, personified in the referee called Turner.[37]

One of the insults offered to referees by the crowd in Argentina was to call them *bombero*, which means spy as well as fireman. It is not clear why this term was considered an especially severe term of opprobrium. But referees in South America often had to quell the fires of passion among the players. It was often an impossible task which no amount of British phlegm could help. Referee John Meade discovered this early in his stay in 1950, when an apparently trivial foul five minutes from the end of a match between Huracán and Vélez Sarsfield led to a fight in which all twenty-two players were soon engaged. Police intervention led to the arrest of the players, who were detained in the city gaol for two days and later received suspensions varying from six to fifteen weeks. A Division Two match between Riestra and Los Andes was abandoned in 1957 after nine home players and seven visitors had been sent off. Racing had already secured the championship in 1961 but seven players were sent off for fouls and fighting in their match with Independiente. Eighty-two players were sent off in First Division matches in Argentina in 1964, Independiente accounting for eight. In the 1977 Campeonato Metropolitano it would reach 186. A British referee in charge of Argentina and Uruguay in 1958 thought it the hardest game he had ever tried to control. He had to send off three Uruguayans and two Argentines. In spite of the extensive policing of grounds, the police armed with tear gas and aided by firemen, the fences – supported by moats in the larger stadiums – a well-ordered battle both on the field and off was a common event. The AFA often found itself ratifying the result of a match ended early by 'incidents'. As for the FAA, the players' union, it often laid emphasis on the fraternity of the players but seemed incapable of taking a stand against the savagery which disfigured so many games. Of course some critics spoke out against the violence, notably the famous football journalist Dante Panzeri, but a general feeling of helplessness appears to have prevailed.[38]

Brazil was better but not much better. We have seen how Jack Barrick had real prestige there as a referee. In twenty-three years in the English league he had sent off just six players. In eight and a half months in Brazil he sent off nineteen, including nine in internationals and four during a match between Brazil and Peru. In the 1964 Rio championships one player was being sent off in every six games.[39] In the second leg of the Brazilian Championship Final between Santos and Vasco da Gama in 1965 Zezinho (V.) hit Lima (S.) who got up and hit him back. Both were sent off and in the uproar which followed two more Vasco players and three Santos ones, including Pelé, were sent off. Spectacular eruptions took place on a scale and frequency unknown in Britain and Europe. The last match of the Rio championship of 1966 was between Bangu, already assured of the title, and Flamengo. Bangu led 3–0 when the Flamengo players began fighting. Nine were sent off, but order could not be restored. There were also scuffles in the crowd and six players were later suspended for up to 160 days.[40] In 1967 América versus Olaria was abandoned after eighty minutes and all twenty-two players sent off for fighting, and a Vasco da Gama–Fluminense match came to a similar end following an assault on one player which provoked a mass brawl with twenty-one eventually sent off.[41]

Violence during international matches was also commonplace. At an international club tournament in Montevideo, a match between the local team Peñarol and Rio's Botafogo was abandoned after a goal by the visitors had led to some of the Peñarol players attacking them. Reserves and the police joined in a free for all. Later on the tournament organizers asked the two teams to play the unfinished twenty minutes of the match but Botafogo refused. Peñarol appeared on the field and were declared the winners by the referee. Meanwhile Brazilians complained that they were not allowed to win in Uruguay.[42]

In the 1957 South American Championships held in Lima the British referee awarded a penalty to Brazil in their match against the hosts. He was immediately physically attacked by the home players. The game was abandoned and the referee smuggled out of the city for the night. The next day he was put on a plane back to Buenos Aires for his own safety. In the same tournament the game between Chile and Uruguay was abandoned.

Ambrois had scored for Uruguay but then made an indecent gesture to the crowd. Some of them invaded the pitch and fought with the Uruguayan players and police.

Two years later when the championships were held in Buenos Aires, Brazil v Uruguay was held up for twenty-three minutes in the first half following a brawl between the players which it took police some time to control. There was more fighting at the end of the game.[43] In 1969 Brazil and Peru were involved in a further fracas in the Maracaná. Peru led 2–0 after only nine minutes but it was 2–1 when Gerson of Brazil kicked La Torre of Peru and caused a mêlée which lasted forty minutes. The police eventually calmed things down but the Peruvians returned to their dressing room and only a personal appeal from the CBD President Havelange got them out of it to finish the match. They lost 3–2. João Saldanha, still in his short reign as manager of Brazil, was quoted as saying that he was pleased to see the Brazilian team contained no women.[44]

The violence to which we have drawn attention was a regular part of the spectacular football subculture of South America. While it remained fixed inside the boundaries of the subcontinent it retained for Europeans an exotic, almost humorous quality. It seemed so wild, explosive, extreme and unpredictable, almost like some of the football itself. It was not yet a strategy, a policy deliberately and systematically employed to intimidate opponents. The message of the World Club Championship Final in 1967 between Racing of Buenos Aires and Celtic of Glasgow was that for some clubs it had become such a strategy.

The World Club Championship pitted the winners of the European Champions Cup against the winners of the South American Club Championship or Copa Libertadores de América. This latter competition began in 1960 in imitation of the European Cup, although it has had a much more chequered history than that event, with many changes of format. It has also been close to abandonment on a number of occasions.[45] In 1967 Racing won the South American Club Championship after playing nineteen games: ten in a six-club mini-league; six more in a four-team semi-final group and three matches in the final against Uruguay's Nacional. The home and away legs were drawn without any goals but Racing won the play-off 2–1 in Santiago. Celtic, meantime, played nine matches and won their final against Inter Milan in Lisbon 2–1.

The final of the World Club Championship was to be played over two legs. The first was played in Glasgow, and resulted in victory for Celtic by a single goal. There was a good deal of rough play and what appeared to be systematic time wasting by the players of Racing. The second match was played two weeks later on the ground of Racing in Avellaneda on 1 November 1967. A crowd of about 80,000 had gathered, a typical big-game crowd in Argentina with their pre-match chants, huge banners, confetti, fire crackers and army of photographers and radio reporters on the pitch. The teams came out, the visitors greeted by shrill whistles, the home team noisily acclaimed. It was the usual prologue to a big match.

Before the game began Simpson, the Celtic goalkeeper, was struck on the head by a stone thrown from the crowd behind his goal. He was sufficiently injured to be withdrawn from the match. The stone was thrown by one man, but neither the spectators close to him nor the police were able to identify him. The Celtic manager agreed to go on with the match using his reserve goalkeeper. Experienced football writers watching, such as Francis Thébaud and Dante Panzeri, thought this was a mistake. Celtic should have walked out there and then.

Celtic actually scored first from a penalty by Gemmell after an obvious foul on Johnstone. It was actually the third penalty that might have been given by a Uruguayan referee who seemed intimidated by the atmosphere. Even though the foul was obvious, the Racing players protested and jostled the referee. Raffo equalized for Racing, though clearly offside, as many Argentinian newspapers pointed out the next day. Half time was lengthened because there was mysteriously no water in the Celtic dressing room. Before the match they had not been given a ball with which to warm up. Three minutes after half time Cárdenas gave Racing the lead. The Argentinians now employed all sorts of tricks and brutality to maintain it. The crowd kept the ball but when it came back football did not reappear. 'To intimidate, to strike the Scots, to prevent them from playing was the sole object of these eleven men transformed into specialists of close combat ... who systematically kicked, hit and insulted them when the ball was far away or spat in their faces.'[46] And the referee saw nothing. By now the crowd was chanting 'Ar-gen-tina, Ar-gen-tina'. General Onganía, the Argentine President who was at the match, told El Mundo, 'it was an extraordinary show and I am happy. It is a triumph for Argentina.' Valentín Suárez, President of the AFA, was quoted by the press as saying that 'Celtic is a team that lasts twenty-five minutes'. Many papers in Buenos Aires reproduced the lines 'it wasn't football, but it was a beautiful victory'.

In the event of one victory each, it had been agreed that a third match should be played in the estadio Centenario in Montevideo. Celtic could, and certainly should, have pulled out. But all Celtic did was request guarantees of safety for their players and a change of referee. Perhaps they might have entertained a stray thought of revenge. About 20,000 Argentines crossed the River Plate for the deciding battle. It might have reminded a few with long memories of the first World Cup. Most of the crowd was Uruguayan, warned by loudspeaker announcements that disturbances would be dealt with severely.

At first the referee – from Paraguay this time – appeared to be an improvement. With the players not even acknowledging the Queensberry Rules he brought the two captains together with an interpreter about halfway through the first half to inform them that his patience was at an end. But he had no effect on the combatants. Celtic were literally fighting back. But in this game they came off worse because their obvious transgressions were punished. The more subtle assaults of the players of Racing often escaped, as the foul count of thirty against Celtic and twenty-one against Racing suggests. The referee would later use these figures to justify his sending off of three Celtic players as against two from Racing. First it was Basile and Lennox who went, although most rational observers thought they were hardly equal in blame. Shortly before this the Racing captain, Martín, trying to intervene in one of the many player–referee altercations, was repulsed by a policeman. He reacted as if poleaxed and some of the Argentine newspapers suggested that he had been felled by a Uruguayan truncheon.

The second half began with the sending off of Johnstone, the most dangerous Celtic forward in each of the three games. This is how Francis Thébaud saw the incident.

> Johnstone, in the middle of the pitch, slid the ball to Wallace and got free to receive the return. Martín, without bothering about the ball, threw himself at Johnstone's waist. Both fell and Johnstone struggled and Martín rolled on the ground as if he had been the victim of a blow. Without hesitating, Pérez [the referee] . . . sent [Johnstone] off. Thus he who had been the constant target of all the aggression since the beginning of the match . . . became the victim of a man whose aim was to protect the footballer against the fakers and the foulers. For my part, I have never seen such a staggering decision.

Racing scored a goal and, as the brutalities continued, played for time. Hughes was the next Celtic man to be dismissed. Ruili was sent off near the end for a harmless foul after much worse earlier had gone unpunished.

The lap of honour by the winners did not please the Uruguayan majority in the crowd and Racing were showered with objects as they left the field. Some returned to the centre of the field and waited for police protection. Outside, many people crowded round the exit to the Argentine dressing room. Several police charges were made before they were dispersed. There were stampedes and clashes in the park after the match. As for the headlines in the next day's papers, *La Razón* (Buenos Aires) thought that 'Racing have recovered the glory days of our football'. *Clarín* called Racing 'A champion who was on every field'. But the Uruguayan headlines seemed closer to reality: *El Día*, 'Racing win the World War' and *La Mañana*, 'This was no football, it was a disgrace... The match was a farce and a fraud.' Later, Celtic fined each of their players £250; Racing, it was alleged, bought each of theirs a new car.

Perhaps it needs to be stressed that this account was based on an eye-witness report by a French journalist not especially well disposed to British football and an admirer of the skilful qualities of South American players in general and Argentinians in particular. It should also be pointed out that violent play characterized the World Club Championships of 1968 and 1969 when Estudiantes de la Plata met first Manchester United and then AC Milan. One of the Estudiantes players, Juan Ramón Verón, later claimed that 'we tried to find out everything possible about our rivals individually, their habits, their characters, their weaknesses and even about their private lives, so that we could goad them on the field, get them to react and risk being sent off'.[47] After assaults by Estudiantes players on two of the Milan team President Onganía personally intervened. Such

> shameful behaviour has compromised and sullied Argentina's international standing and provoked the revulsion of a nation... To represent one's country is a supreme honour which can no longer be enjoyed by those who lack the well-known courtesy of the Argentinian people. I have instructed the AFA to take stern steps to defend the good name of our sport...

Goalkeeper Poletti and defender Aguirre Suárez were sentenced to thirty days in prison, the former suspended from international football for life, the latter excluded for five years.[48] These matches gave the World Club Championship an unsavoury reputation and several European teams refused to take part. It was only saved in 1980 by Toyota sponsorship and is now played as a single match, in Tokyo, every December with a crowd made up largely of the company's Japanese employees. Significantly there has been little trouble and some outstanding South American performances, notably in 1981 when Flamengo beat Liverpool 3–0 and 1993 when

São Paulo beat Milan 3–2. These matches cemented an image of Argentine football in Europe: a bewildering mixture of technical virtuosity and physical brutality, intimidation and simulated injury. It was all there again in the World Cup Final of 1990.

It would be too simplistic to assert that the violence of the players directly reflected the passion of the supporters. But it is no accident that the home crowd was long nicknamed the number-twelve player in Argentina. As we have seen, they would often intervene in matches and not just by noisily supporting their own team and shouting insults at the visitors. In 1947 River Plate had already won the championship when they came to the last match of the season away to Atlanta. Atlanta had to win to avoid relegation. As they had lost 8–0 earlier in the season it seemed a tall order. But rumours spread that River were not going to take the match seriously. In such a context the atmosphere at the start was explosive. Was what happened next serious or a mischievous joke? After thirty minutes some *hinchas* of Atlanta came on to the pitch carrying the pennants of their club and River in a necklace of flowers. The supporters of River saw this as a bribery attempt. The River players refused the gift and a fight started which the police eventually controlled. The *hinchas* of Atlanta then threw stones at the River players whenever they attacked their goal. River scored, but the terrified referee disallowed it. But then Alfredo di Stéfano scored from thirty yards and it could not be disallowed. He was later attacked by an Atlanta fan and the game was eventually abandoned.[49]

As one of the leaders of the Racing *hinchas* told a reporter from *La Nación* in 1982, 'our ambition is to be one more person on the playing field'.[50] Each club had long had a significant minority of *hinchas* who on match days rallied to the great *hinchada* banners and flags, often in excess of fifty feet long, which would dominate one side of the stadium. Their role was to support their team and intimidate the visitors but also to promote enthusiasm among their own side and knock any waverers into line. The more active *barras bravas* aimed to confront their opposite numbers on the other side, partly to steal banners and flags as trophies, partly to fight for the honour of club, gang, neighbourhood and self, although it was far from clear that all the members of the most active club *hinchas* came from the same neighbourhoods. Rhythmic chanting of club slogans and songs was used to stoke up the atmosphere. Up to 1967 or so it was still possible to walk around most grounds from the terraces behind one goal to those behind the other. In Argentina, the *hinchas* would make for the goal their side was defending to protect their own goalkeeper as we noted the *hinchas* of Atlanta did in 1947. In Britain the opposite was true. The supporters who gathered behind the goal moved to be at the end which their side was attacking. We will have to return to the nature of the *hinchadas* in a later chapter.

In the 1960s John Gunther thought 'almost' all South Americans were 'football-mad'.[51] This was a pardonable exaggeration. Most of the women certainly were not. Some did attend matches and in Argentina some grounds provided special sections for them, but in general women were excluded from the football subculture. As Betty Milan remembered from her own adolescence in Brazil, no woman could join the male football discussion group. Their role was to serve the coffee. Some did watch and support a team, but they were not expected to understand the game.[52] Men found it more difficult to turn their backs on what was not only the national sport but almost the only one, but some undoubtedly did so, perhaps taking comfort from the occasional anti-football pronouncements of celebrated writers such as Jorge Luis Borges with his tongue-in-the-cheek dismissal of football as a post-colonial replacement for knife-fighting.[53] Football does seem to mean more to more people in South America than in Europe. The best-selling record in Brazil in 1958 was that featuring the voices of the players and officials of the winning World Cup team. In 1959 when the great Argentinian forward Angel Labruna finally retired at the age of forty-two after over a thousand matches and 450 goals for River Plate, he was sent off for a foul in his last match. The friendly meeting between Argentina and Brazil in 1993 to mark the centenary of the Argentinian Football Association ended with Ruggeri (Argentina) and Valdo (Brazil) sent off for fighting.[54] Such events reflect the fact that more people are football-mad in South America than anywhere else.

CHAPTER EIGHT

MEANINGS AND MODERN TIMES

*The first bug fell in Campinas, miles away; it was a caterpillar.
The second bug fell thereabouts too, it was a woolly bear; the
leather ball fell in a field. It was thus that Mannape introduced
the coffee bug, Jiqué the cotton boll weevil and Macunaima the
football; three of the main pests in the country today.*
Mário de Andrade, *Macunaima*, 1928;
1984 English edn, p. 42

What's the Difference?
*The English player has his legs so well protected that they
resemble blown up tyres; but the Brazilian plays with his
stockings fallen down to his ankles most of the time.*
*The Englishman considers a player that dribbles three times
successively a nuisance; the Brazilian considers him a virtuoso.*
*English football requires that the ball move faster than the
player; Brazilian football requires that the player be faster than
the ball.*
*In English football, discipline comes first and the players last;
in Brazil the players come first and discipline last.*
*When the English player loses his calm he generally uses his
feet and sometimes his body; the Brazilian uses his fist.*
*The Englishman goes on the field disposed either to win or to
lose; the Brazilian either to win . . . or to blame the referee.*
From Tomás Mazzoni, Olympicus, *A Gazetta*, June 1949,
quoted in *World Sports* 16, 1950, p. 8

Carlos Fuentes, the distinguished Mexican writer, once said that the
difference between Mexico and Argentina was that the Mexicans were
descended from the Aztecs while the Argentinians were descended from
boats. We have seen how football was also brought to South America by
men disembarking from ships, Italians, Spanish, Portuguese, French and

Germans, but especially the British. We have also seen how the sport was taken up by young men from the urban elites, often educated in Europe, attracted by its excitement and simplicity no doubt, but also by its modernity and the fact that it came with such good references as part of that physical culture that characterized British imperialism. There was no sense that football would become the major sport of South America, but very rapidly it did so as it was taken up by the less well off already living in Buenos Aires and São Paulo, Rio and Montevideo, Rosario and Belo Horizonte and the successive waves of immigrants which both reflected and produced the rapid urbanization of the early twentieth century. Football became part of a subculture to help recent arrivals from the countryside and Europe, often separated by language and traditions, to find their feet both literally and metaphorically in a new and testing world. Football clubs became important social centres.

The popularity of football eventually developed a momentum of its own, but it did not become part of the popular culture without a struggle, especially in Brazil, where vigorous attempts were made to keep it exclusive and to keep out blacks and workers. International competition was important here, demonstrating in a most spectacular way that Jack was as good as his master. First the Olympics and then the World Cup showed that Uruguayans, Brazilians and Argentinians could not only compete with but defeat the nations of the Old World, a Europe towards which so many South Americans still looked for example and approval. Uruguay claimed the football championship of the world in the 1920s and won the first World Cup in 1930. By the thirties Brazil thought their football was the best and in the forties Argentina were certain that *theirs* was. South American superiority was emphasized by the World Cup of 1950 and the genius for football of Brazil further underlined by the World Cup victories of 1958, 1962 and, even more, 1970.

On the eve of the World Cup Finals of 1970 João Saldanha was asked why he thought Brazilian football was the best. He suggested a combination of four major factors. First was the climate, which meant that football could be played all the year round. Second, he considered the poverty of Brazil to be an important element in the production of football players. Most young males in Brazil were forced into taking on adult responsibilities quite early in their lives. This experience sharpened their competitive attitudes. The third factor to which Saldanha pointed was the varied ethnic composition of the population. In particular he claimed that Brazilian blacks, because of their African heritage of centuries of struggle against nature, had developed 'heightened muscular abilities'.[1] His final point was to emphasize that *futebol* was the object of real popular passion in Brazil, obtaining the attention of the majority of the population and having no serious sporting rival.

So far as the first factor is concerned, a climate that allowed all-the-year-round play would seem to be common to most other parts of South America and certainly to Argentina and Uruguay. It must also be true of other continents, notably Africa – even the USA. Perhaps hard, dry grounds and a lively ball do go some way towards an explanation of South American ball control and technique. But the argument that the beach leagues of Rio and in particular the highly visible games on the six kilometres of Copacabana are an ideal preparation for the world's best footballers seems dubious. Trying to control, pass and shoot on soft, dry sand is difficult. Such conditions were not reproduced on the professional grounds.[2] What can be said is that facilities for playing football in Brazil were generally poor, and for most of the population, even in the 1960s, non-existent. There was no sophisticated system of physical education in the schools.[3] Walter Winterbottom, England team manager between 1947 and 1963, told a British audience in 1960 that the range of competition and match play in schoolboy football in England was the envy of the world. But he also claimed that the 'average boy' in South America practised four times as much as the average English boy.[4] Boys played where they could and the beaches were better than nothing. Most of the better players abandoned them for firmer terrain, such as the area reclaimed from the sea close to Flamengo, if they got the chance. São Paulo was no better, with its rapid urban growth of factories and skyscrapers eating up the space, and putting a premium on the provision of all kinds of recreational areas including football pitches. It would also be true to say that poverty was a condition common to all the South American republics and not only Brazil. In both Uruguay and Argentina, for example, it is clear that most professional football players since the 1930s have been recruited from the poorer parts of those societies. Whether the experience of young, poor Brazilians differed in important respects from the poor young males of other parts of South America, or Europe come to that, and whether such differences sharpened determination to succeed or the will to win is a question easy to raise but difficult to answer.

If we turn to the third of Saldanha's factors, that of varied ethnic composition and in particular the 'heightened muscular ability of the blacks' then this does seem to be a characteristic of Brazil not enjoyed by

Argentina certainly and by Uruguay only to a very limited extent. But again it is difficult to accept the argument that Brazilians were best because they were 'made for it'. It was a commonplace in more popular newspapers in many countries, especially after the World Cup victories of 1958 and 1962, to put it all down to the 'animal suppleness' of the blacks and the 'amazing flexibility of their ankles'. This is the famous Czech coach Karel Kolsky, in an interview in 1961: 'A coloured man generally has far greater natural ball sense than a white man; greater flexibility; more elasticity and needs considerably less training to develop and maintain good physical condition . . .' He went on to say that South American players only needed 60 per cent of the training which Europeans required. South Americans began younger and were completely natural.[5] Suppleness and skill were certainly important weapons in the arsenal of the football player but there is no sense in which Brazilians could claim a monopoly of them. It is clear that other South Americans, Europeans and Africans could and did develop such qualities along with the stamina and strength which were also required to succeed in the professional game. There is, indeed, more than a tinge of racism in the notion that black men have special physical qualities. Yet one of Brazil's most respected scholars, Gilberto Freyre, also thought there was something in the ethnic mix of the Brazilian population which made Brazilian football different. Writing in 1945 he asserted:

> . . . our manner of playing football appears to me to contrast with that of the Europeans through a conjunction of qualities of surprise, guile, astuteness, swiftness, and at the same time the brilliance of individual spontaneity which reveals a mulatto quality which, in the art of policies, Nilo Recanha is the greatest example up to the present time.[6]

As we have seen, the professional footballer in South America was mainly recruited from the poor. In Brazil that meant from poor whites but also mulattos and blacks, many of them inhabitants of the *favelas* or young factory workers in the towns and cities. *Futebol* for all those groups, as we have also noted, presented the prospect of escape into a better world, at least a lift out of the direst poverty. For mulattos and blacks in particular boxing, *futebol* and popular music were by far the main lines of opportunity. Until evidence of a much more persuasive sort comes along, it is social rather than ethnic explanations which remain the most convincing, and Brazil appears not too dissimilar to Argentina, Uruguay and elsewhere in the modern world.

Saldanha's final argument was that football was a passion in Brazil which had no sporting rival. As a writer in the French *Football Magazine* wrote in 1963, the passion for the game in Brazil was extraordinary and behind it was

> an immense hope. There are so many of them who hope that they impose their faith on those who have nothing to hope for, being already well off. An ordinary football match in the Rio championships is ... listened to in the streets, cafés and public squares by hundreds of thousands of people who, if they have the means to buy a transistor on hire purchase, don't have enough to pay for a place in the ground. The principal newspaper column is a football one ... The biggest circulation of all papers in Brazil is a sports daily, the *Gazetta Esportiva de São Paulo*.[7]

Football produced this passion partly because it was 'democratic'. It was not exclusive in a society in which people got on because of their family or because they knew someone with influence or even by Presidential decree. In football, only the performance counted. A man's rise or fall depended on competence alone and not on personal relationships in a country where 'the good ones have it all from birth. The footballer, like the samba dancer, did not get it all at birth and did not do much studying on the way either.'[8] Popular attitudes towards work in Brazil do not appear to have had much in common with the Protestant ethic. Popular composers of the twenties and thirties celebrated the figure of the *malandro*, 'a bohemian rascal of folklore' who, with *savoir faire*, moves between the spheres of 'order' and 'disorder' in Brazilian society, taking advantage of the breaches in both:

> Mummy I don't want
> Mummy I don't want
> to work from sun up to sun down
> I want to be a singer on the radio
> a football player...[9]

It was the style of Brazilian football which also contributed to the passion for it. It is not clear whether, in its elite period, Brazilian football was 'gentlemanly and controlled'. But with its takeover by the lower orders it certainly quickly developed a reputation for 'spontaneity' and 'surrealism', especially compared to the more organized physicality of the Europeans. We have already noted the words of Gilberto Freyre on its qualities of surprise, guile and astuteness based on individual spontaneity. The poet Mário Chamrie was saying something similar forty years later. Football had to be graceful to be good, to develop artistically through passing, feinting, dodging, improvisation and, if possible, goals, but 'even if the goal is the real aim of the game, it means less to us than the show'.[10]

The players who most exemplified such qualities were forwards such as Leonidas in the 1930s, Ademir, Jair and Zizinho in the 1940s and Garrincha, Didi and Pelé in the 1950s and 1960s. Garrincha, known as the 'People's Joy', made the spectators laugh, played for the sake of play, it was alleged, and was the epitome of the unpredictable individual, difficult to accommodate to a team pattern, an 'amateur' style of play. He would dribble past the same defender four times. With his deformed legs – like parallel bananas someone thought – his odd walk reminded watchers of Charlie Chaplin. 'The People's Joy took us where we could only imagine going, he made us daydream, and like a magician, left us open-mouthed without ever knowing how he did it.'[11]

Both Garrincha and Pelé were endlessly inventive. Neither, it was claimed, would ever undertake to win at any price. But even foreign players could become adopted Brazilians if they were good enough, so that in 1986, when Michel Platini equalized for France against Brazil, the Brazilian television commentator exclaimed, 'Gooooal! A goal to *our* Platini.'[12] This is the kind of football that Roberto Da Matta is referring to when he writes that football for Brazilians was not a 'sport' as it was for the Americans and the English, but a game. Brazilians, he claimed, speak of the game of football. A game not only implies luck, but depends less on objectivity, force, speed and stamina, and more on cunning. 'This is because it is born as a plaything, as playing with a ball, and later play is not given up but is associated with dexterity... It is exactly because we live under the imperative of play that carnival and football are national passions.'[13]

Indeed they were. But, as we have seen, it could equally plausibly be argued that football was a national passion in Argentina and Uruguay also, no less than in Brazil. It would be a brave man who would argue the contrary with so much evidence available to support the case. All three countries played in a similar style with an emphasis on skilful control and accurate distribution of the ball and a minimum of bodily contact. Perhaps Brazil mixed up the longer with the shorter pass more than the other two; perhaps Uruguay went in for more tackling. Both Argentina and Uruguay produced an equal number of brilliant players who could rank alongside the very best Brazilians: for Uruguay Andrade, Varela, Schiaffino and Santamaría, for example; for Argentina Moreno, Pedernera, Di Stéfano, Rossi and Labruna. In South America both Argentina and Uruguay were thought of as superior footballing powers. Both had won more South

American Championships than Brazil. Both had produced club sides that had been the football wonders of their times. In both countries football was the number-one sport. When the Arsenal manager Tom Whitaker visited Brazil with his club in 1949 he thought he had never seen a more football-conscious nation. But if he had gone to Argentina and Uruguay he would almost certainly have said the same.[14]

Saldanha's combination of climate, poverty, varied ethnic composition and popular passion is three-quarters shared by the other big two South American footballing nations. But what does seem to set Brazil apart from them in the twenty years or so from 1950 during which three World Cups were won is the sophistication of their preparations. Until 1978 Argentina had never punched its weight in the World Cup and Uruguay has had little to show, apart from the semi final in 1970, since 1954. It is a surprise to find a relatively undeveloped country such as Brazil pioneering the use of coaches, doctors and psychologists, indeed a whole team of technicians to back up the team on the field. Clubs in Brazil seem to have realized early the importance of keeping the players together before matches – partly to prevent them losing their edge to excessive sexual, alcoholic, or other indulgence – and employing trained coaching staff. After 1945 all coaches were graduates of the Upper College of Physical Education. For the physical trainers it was a four-year course and a two-year one for the managers. Qualified doctors could not take up a post with a football club unless they had specialized on a two-year course in sports medicine. This emphasis on education, training and preparation seems to have been far ahead of any of the more developed European nations. Brazil *were* the best in 1958, 1962 and 1970. They had some exceptional players in all three tournaments. But as well as outstanding individuals who played with a spontaneity that commentators now look on with nostalgia, they had an infrastructure designed to deal with every problem and a relatively high level of tactical awareness.[15] Argentina were unable to produce such a support group until the appointment of Menotti and state investment for hosting the World Cup in 1978.

Many Argentinians had thought that their football was the best in the world. Moreover they had an explanation for why it was the best. As in Brazil the unique style had been born as poor youths learned the game on any rough patch of ground available where they played their pick-up games – the *peladas* – in Argentina it was the sons of poor Latin immigrants who played football on the waste ground in the city – the *baldío* – and the as yet undeveloped outskirts – the *arrabal* who were responsible for the distinctive way of playing which had become characterisically Argentine by the 1920s. These small but skilful players exemplified *criollo* virtues of agility, virtuosity, individuality and cunning. They practised the deceptive manoeuvre, the subtle stroke, and they did it in particular via the dribble, especially, as we have already noticed when discussing the virtues of Maradona, the *gambeta*, apparently so called because it was like an ostrich running. The authentic Argentine footballer was *el pibe*, the boy, who never stops being a boy – Maradona again? – whose skill and trickery could undermine the most determined defence.[16]

The 1940s in particular seemed like a golden age for Argentinian football with the triumphs of River Plate at home and spectacular club tours abroad such as that of San Lorenzo to Spain in 1946–7 during which the Spanish national side was defeated by 6–1. The South American Championship had been spectacularly won in 1947 and Argentine players began to rebuild their reputations abroad after the end of the war. Brazil and Uruguay dominated the World Cup in 1950 and Argentina regularly beat them, although they had pulled out of the tournament at the last minute. In fact Argentina did not play against another South American country for five years between 1950 and 1955. As we have seen, these were years of government-prompted isolation probably brought about by the loss of leading players to Colombia after the strike of 1948. In general, with a culture firmly rooted in Europe, Argentinians thought themselves superior to all other South Americans and especially in football. They therefore re-entered the World Cup in 1958 with confidence.

The Argentinian experience of Sweden in 1958 provided them with a footballing shock far more severe than that felt by Brazil in 1950. The team lost to Germany in the first match but then beat the Northern Irish 3–1. A draw against Czechoslovakia, already beaten by the Irish, would have ensured a place in the quarter finals. Argentina suffered their heaviest international defeat, 6–1. The Argentines looked slow, their teamwork was poor, and they lacked stamina. The Irish had been warned about Argentine strength and ruthlessness, but standing next to them in the tunnel before going out on to the field Jimmy McIlroy saw 'a lot of little fat men with stomachs, smiling at us and pointing and waving to the girls in the crowd'.[17] When the players returned home they were met at the airport by angry crowds and a spiteful government ordered customs officers to confiscate gifts that the players had brought from Europe for their families.[18] Some newspapers were outspoken in their criticism. 'You must not cry as women for what you did not defend as men.'[19] The myth of the superiority of

Argentine football, so recently buttressed by Di Stéfano's success with Real Madrid and a convincing victory over Brazil in 1957, was exploded, a home defeat by Russia in 1961 further underlining the point that something must be done.

Argentina had a particular way of playing; they even had a word for it, *la nuestra*, based on the skilled ball control of the individual player, the cult of the dribble and the short pass along the ground. But the game in Europe had speeded up and the Argentinian style which Europeans had once thought fast now appeared slow. Argentine players had also fallen behind in physical fitness, heading, tackling and defensive organization. Several Argentinians playing in Europe diagnosed the fault and thought they had a remedy. One of them was Juan Carlos Lorenzo, a player for Sampdoria, Nancy and Atlético Madrid who had also coached in Italy. He was clear that the traditional technical skills of the Argentine players had to be combined with speed and a disciplined defence. Art could be destroyed by physical power. His philosophy was epitomized in the slogan: 'Before we played football, now we run football.'[20] Lorenzo was appointed manager of the Argentine team for the World Cup of 1962 in Chile. The new style was used ruthlessly to defend a one-goal lead against Bulgaria, but that was followed by a 3–1 defeat by England. Failure to score against Hungary in the last match meant elimination from the competition. Tougher defences also became a feature of the domestic game. José d'Amico at Boca built a fearsome defence which conceded only eighteen goals in twenty-eight matches in 1961. This team won the Argentine championship in three of the next four years. In 1963 they were replaced by Giudice's Independiente, whose opponents scored less than a goal a game and who went forty games without defeat based on a *catenaccio* defence – four players strung across the back with an extra defender sweeping up behind – and swift counter-attacks by three midfield players and two forwards. Their attendances averaged over 47,000 in that season.[21]

This was the modernization of Argentinian football, travelling the same road as Italy, Spain and Eastern Europe. The greater tempo, the increased commitment to physical fitness, the accent on defence meant more tackling, more bodily contact, a greater reliance on the 'they shall not pass' mentality. This was the context which eventually produced the 'battles' for the World Club Championship at the end of the 1960s and, as we have seen, intervention by the President of the Republic. Ironically, the new approach did not bring World Cup success for the national team. We have noted the controversy surrounding the defeat at Wembley in 1966. Argentina did not even qualify for Mexico in 1970 following defeats by Bolivia and Peru, and in 1974 they were outclassed by a Cruyff-inspired Holland 4–0.

The year before that, in 1973, Huracán had won the Argentine championship for the first time playing a more attacking brand of football, which seemed to combine the 'traditional' Argentine skills with fitness, teamwork and a sound defence. The manager was César Luis Menotti. He had been an inside-left with Rosario Central, Racing and Boca in the sixties and had also played briefly in the United States. He then became a journalist before taking on the coaching of Huracán. In 1974 he was given the job to prepare the national team which would try to win the World Cup for the first time, and in their own country, in 1978.

From the first day he emphasized his belief in the superiority of Argentine technique. As Huracán had played in the traditional Argentine way, so would the national team. Obviously physical fitness and organization would not be neglected; as we have already seen, the military government invested large amounts of money in preparation for the championship. No previous Argentine manager had had the resources nor had the players together for as long as Menotti did, but not only did the team win with some style: the next year, 1979, Argentina won the junior World Cup in Tokyo led by the seventeen-year-old Maradona. Menotti claimed to have won both with traditional Argentinian footballing virtues. It was success without tricks, by which he presumably meant dirty tricks. 'Our victory is a tribute to the old and glorious Argentinian football.'[22]

It was a victory which could not be repeated in Spain in 1982. Menotti retired and was replaced by Carlos Bilardo. Bilardo had been a mean and testy wing-half in Zubeldía's Estudiantes team which had disfigured the World Club Championship in 1968 and 1969. Bilardo thought all the talk of style mere rhetoric. Winning was everything and it did not matter how it was achieved. In 1986 Argentina had the world's greatest attacking player, but critics were not impressed by the second World Cup victory. For some, doubtless a minority, Bilardo's team contained one genius, Maradona, two excellent players, Burrachaga and Valdano, and eight disciplined Japanese.[23] The symbol of that victory was not the second of Maradona's two goals in the quarter final against England but the first, the one scored 'with the hand of God and the head of Maradona'. By 1990, the Argentine team were playing street-fighter football, going through to the final only after shabby penalty shoot-out victories against Yugoslavia and Italy. The final itself was a tedious and squalid affair, after which Menotti said he was ashamed to be an Argentinian. It is almost as if football in Argentina is part of a Manichaean struggle between good and evil, style and force, as represented by the philosophy of Menotti on the one hand and Bilardo on the other. In both Brazil and Argentina there is some body of opinion that can still assert that winning is not enough, that it has to be with style and panache in what they think of as the true national traditions of the sport. If national style *is* a myth, it is one to which some at least, tenaciously cling.

How can we look for the meanings and wider interpretation of football in South America and particularly in the countries of Argentina, Brazil and Uruguay? It is tempting to suggest it as an opiate of the people, a phenomenon commanding such intense interest over a long period of time that it deflects large portions of the populations from confronting the endemic economic, social and political problems of the region. Indeed in a famous article Janet Lever suggested just that.[24] It would be tempting to agree, but fundamentally mistaken. The euphoria which accompanies victories in the South American Championship or World Cup clearly recedes before the slings and arrows of outrageous ordinary life. A cartoon in the *Jornal do Brasil* in 1981 makes the point well. A group of hungry football fans are shown sitting around a table expecting food to be served. The cook then appears with a pot but it contains not food but a football which the cook throws out to the bewildered-looking group at the table.[25] Great victories are momentary distractions but the harsh realities of poverty and unemployment, class and race quickly return. Football may aid the rule of the rich but it does not by itself eliminate social conflict, indeed can occasionally be used to dramatize it as in the years 1982–4 when the Corinthians of São Paulo, with one of their most famous players Socrates in the vanguard, became involved in the campaign to restore free elections in Brazil.[26]

Another popular account suggests that football was promoted not just by the dominant classes and the media they usually controlled, but even by many intellectuals as a symbol of national unity. So governments of all persuasions have tried to use football in general and the national side in particular to remind people that they are Uruguayan, Argentinian or Brazilian. In her pioneering book *Soccer Madness* Janet Lever argued that because of its popularity and its remarkable three out of four World Cup victories Brazilian football actually did further national unity in that country.[27] We have already explored the ways in which an undemocratic government tried to exploit the victory of 1970. Some opponents of the regime of President Medici suggested victory in Mexico would only

strengthen the dictatorship and that liberals should support Brazil's rivals.
But:

> critical conscience failed to resist our first successful attack. Each victory for the
> 'Canaries' was a spontaneous carnival in the streets of the big cities and when
> Brazil became three times world champion the entire country took to revelry,
> took over the squares, the streets, the alleys for wild celebrations of the
> championship.[28]

The playwright Nélson Rodrigues declared that there was no longer any
need to be ashamed of being a patriot.

In an earlier chapter we drew attention to the way in which, in Argentina
in 1978, opponents of the military regime could not withdraw their
support for the national football team. A similar process was repeated in
Montevideo when Uruguay won the South American Championships – by
then renamed the Copa América – in 1983 and 1987.

When faced with emotional statements such as that of Betty Milan on
Brazil, that 'Football reflected the nationality, it mirrors the nation.
Without football we Brazilians do not exist – just as one could not conceive
of Spain without the bullfight...' one wants to say surely this is an
exaggeration, mere rhetoric. Such victories may promote temporary
euphoria and football may play a part in the formation of local and regional
loyalties but 'without football we Brazilians do not exist'? But then
Roberto Da Matta suggests that it is a particular kind of football which is
being praised here: the football which won three World Cups and
especially the remarkable football that much of the world saw on colour
television in Mexico in 1970. For Da Matta, in *futebol*:

> there is art, dignity, genius, luck and bad luck, Gods and demons, freedom and
> fate, flags, hymns and tears, and above all, the discovery that although Brazil is
> bad at lots of things, it is good with the ball. It is a football champion, which is
> very important. After all, it is better to be champion in samba, carnival and
> football than in wars and sales of rockets. If the serious commentators say we
> suffer from lack of education, inflation, and unequal distribution of wealth,
> football provides a contrast. It shows we can love Brazil with its hymn and its
> flag, maintaining our lucidity relative to the regime we want to transform.[29]

Da Matta has gone on to argue that the most powerful sources of social
identity are not 'institutions, central to the social order, such as laws, the
constitution ...' but the various manifestations of popular culture such as
carnival, popular religion and football. There remain in Brazil many social

identities, with the popular ones rarely converging with the official.[30] But perhaps they did converge, if only briefly, when the third World Cup victory of 1970 was equated with Neil Armstrong's walk on the moon and the transfer of Pelé to the New York Cosmos in 1975 was celebrated as a cultural export from Brazil to the United States. Indeed the export of Brazilian players to Europe is often talked of as an example of modernity being sold to the Old World.[31]

Not all South American thinkers agree with Da Matta's interpretation of the meaning of football. Mario Vargas Llosa refuses to accept that there are any magical or social strengths in football. For him football's importance has been overestimated. Football is simply an empty pleasure. One of the greatest modern writers of Argentina, Jorge Luis Borges, would agree with Vargas Llosa. In 1978 he told journalists that he was going to leave Buenos Aires until the World Cup had passed over. He claimed to prefer the old-style *barrio* 'sport' of knife-fighting to football. 'I still feel that although killing was involved, there was a certain nobility about it, which I cannot find in men kicking a football.'[32] Da Matta might reply that in Europe football could be an empty pleasure, but in Brazil and the rest of South America football is a 'living register of a society's potential'. Maybe, especially when it is as good as it was in 1970 or even in 1978. Then, Brazilian or Argentinian, when the national team plays 'we can finally see, hear, feel, talk and cheer with Brazil' or Argentina.[33] This is how everyone wants it to be. But when the tournament is over, the victory won, there is still limited equality of opportunity, a weak democratic system and societies bitterly divided against themselves, which at worst, as Nicholas Shumway said of Argentina, produce a 'rivalry, suspicion and hatred of one group for another, each with different notions of history, identity and destiny, that lead to bloodletting and frustrate the achievement of a fair and prosperous society'.[34] In such a context football may indeed be a passion rather than a pleasure and may be better than nothing but it is certainly not enough.

CHAPTER NINE

WORLD CUP USA

*I'm convinced after fourteen years in office and of developing
soccer around the world that the organisation of the World Cup
in the USA will be my highest achievement because soccer will
be recognised in that country, where it hasn't been in the past.*
João Havelange, quoted by Alex Fynn and Lynton Guest, *The
Secret Life of Football*, 1989, p. 275

The United States of America owed its selection as host for the 1994 World
Cup to a Brazilian. The decision was taken in 1988 and it seemed to many
of the world's football commentators an astonishing choice, but it was very
much in line with the way in which Havelange had welcomed business
sponsorship not only to revolutionize the finances of the World Cup but to
make FIFA, with himself as President, one of the most powerful
organizations in the world.

Havelange, though a Brazilian, was not a football player, but he did
represent Brazil as a swimmer in the 1936 Olympic Games. At the age of
forty he was in the water polo team which competed at Helsinki and four
years later in Melbourne he led the Brazilian delegation. By 1963 this rich
businessman was on the International Olympic Committee and had been
President of the CBD – the organization with overall responsibility for
Brazilian sport – since 1958. It was this latter position that brought him
close to football, and he was present during the trinity of World Cup
victories in 1958, 1962 and 1970.

It was following that famous Brazilian win over Italy in Mexico that
Havelange began to consider a challenge to FIFA's old order. The football
prestige of Brazil had never been higher, but that would not have been
sufficient to mount a successful campaign against the sitting tenant, Sir
Stanley Rous. FIFA, however, was changing and some dissatisfaction
began to be manifested among new members over the cosy Euro-centrism

of football's world governing body. FIFA was an old-style voluntary organization overtaken by its own success. Membership rose through the sixties, mainly due to the addition of twenty-five newly independent African, Afro-Caribbean and Asian countries. But the Europeans remained dominant and the President had always been a European. Most of the world's top footballing nations were European and it was Europe that provided two-thirds of FIFA's budget. It was Europe, with the Americas, who competed for most of the places in what had become a sixteen-team World Cup: nine finalists from Europe, four from the Americas, the host, the previous winner plus one from Asia had made up the finalists in 1966. The growth of television had increased the visibility and prestige of the World Cup finals. The new nations, many of their governments seeing football as a vehicle to promote national feeling, wanted a share of the finals. By the late 1960s, Africa held the balance of power in FIFA between Europe and the Americas.

In many respects Rous was a typical English conservative. Although he had encouraged the spread and development of the game in Africa, he was out of sympathy with the idea that South Africa should be expelled because of its political system of apartheid. He also found it difficult to solve the problem posed by the reluctance of China to join an organization which also had Taiwan as a member. These issues were political, and Sir Stanley Rous was uncomfortable with the political side of international sport. His attitude to both questions lost him support. There was also opposition to the expulsion of the Soviet Union for refusing to play their return World Cup qualifying match with Chile in Santiago's national stadium in 1973 on the grounds that it had recently been used to house political prisoners after the military overthrow by General Pinochet of the elected Marxist government of Salvador Allende.

Rous had been unopposed since his own elevation to the Presidency in 1961. Havelange, backed by the other Latin American countries, visited eighty-six FIFA member states between 1970 and 1974 in a political campaign unique to the world of international football. What he promised in return for their electoral support was an expanded World Cup finals with twenty-four teams and more places for Third World countries. He also proposed new world tournaments for the under-twenties and the under-sixteens, tournaments which could be staged by relatively undeveloped countries, and wider participation in the Olympic football tournament. In addition FIFA would do more to raise standards via coaching schemes and football seminars. Havelange won the election, but in order to keep his promises he needed money that could only come from big business. The key contact was Horst Dassler, President of the German sports goods firm Adidas. He used his marketing contacts to construct sponsorship packages with some of the greatest international corporations, in particular Coca-Cola, which sponsored the World Youth Cup from 1977 together with a worldwide football coaching and development scheme. In 1985 the new under-sixteen tournament was underwritten by the Japanese company JVC. When the World Cup itself was expanded to twenty-four teams in 1982 it was the rich combination of commercial sponsorship and television revenues·which paid for it. By Italia 90 ten major sponsors were paying over £40 million for the privilege and FIFA had moved into a new building, expanded its bureaucracy and spent generously on its jet-setting officials and the President's Brazilian office.[1] Havelange had also been powerful enough to deliver some of the votes which ensured that Juan Antonio Samaranch would be elected President of the International Olympic Committee in 1980.

João Havelange has turned the World Cup into a vehicle for making money. As he was alleged to have boasted, football sells products all over the world and it was all due to his work. The United States remained the last frontier. So determined was President Havelange to capture it for football that he even talked of abandoning the traditional two halves of forty-five minutes and replacing them with four twenty-five-minute quarters in order to attract American television advertisers. He also mused about widening the goals to promote more scoring. No one can say that the Brazilian lacks a sense of humour. But it is debatable as to whether he was joking when he recently told a journalist that with the break-up of the Soviet Union the world was left with only three major power blocs: the United States, FIFA and the IOC.[2] No wonder he was keen to remain President of the state of football and just before the World Cup began he was elected unopposed for a sixth term at the age of seventy-eight.

But if the Brazilian had never been more satisfied with his performance on the eve of the World Cup, South American football in general and the Brazilian game in particular had found the last decade a difficult one. For one thing Brazil has never really solved the problem of how to run a national championship in the world's fifth largest country, almost forty times the area of Great Britain and Northern Ireland. A national championship was not introduced until 1971, but it has never been run as a straightforward league system with promotion and relegation, as in Europe. In fact the national championship has had many changes of format

– including in 1972 a change in the middle of the season – and even when streamlined has retained an organizational complexity at odds with such a basically simple game.[3] The national championship was added on to the season, producing a large number of games, many of which were one-sided affairs between the top teams, mainly from four or five states in the south east of the country, and much weaker teams from elsewhere. The state football authorities have refused to support any reforms and since 1980 it is their Presidents who have elected the President of the CBF, the Brazilian Football Federation, responsible for running football in Brazil. Such a structure exhausts both players and spectators: the former do just enough in many matches; the latter stay away, only turning up for the really big games. Average attendances had fallen below those of Albania by 1987, when from the 1950s to the 1970s they had been the highest in the world.

Bad management extends to the directors of individual clubs. In January 1989, for example, many people turned up for the big game between Vasco da Gama and Fluminense only to find the gates locked owing to a dispute over admission charges. The crowd was not allowed in until one hour before the kick-off. People were still trying to obtain entry fifteen minutes into the second half. It is a wonder there was no riot. Meantime in Salvador, 110,000 tickets were sold for the Bahia–Fluminense national championship semi-final in a stadium with a capacity of 82,500.[4] But it is the violence on the field which is the most public indicator of the depths to which top professional football in Brazil has been allowed to sink.

Tele Santana, manager of the national team in the World Cups of 1982 and 1986, currently manager of World Club champions São Paulo, said in 1989, 'In Brazil the way you win does not matter. A very violent form of football is being practised.' Players kick each other, foul play is endemic, time wasting and feigning injury rife. The cheats were allowed to get away with it by a politics-obsessed administration.[5] At the beginning of that year a new broom had been taken to the dirty kitchen of Brazilian football. It came in the shape of Ricardo Teixeira, the new President of the CBF. *Placar*, the leading Brazilian football magazine, claimed the appointment was political and the job obtained by gifts of sports equipment and money to some of the more penurious state football federations. Teixeira had had no previous connection with football, but he did possess one quality unmatched by any rivals: he was the son-in-law of João Havelange.

Teixeira soon claimed to have put an end to the violence in domestic Brazilian football. But it seems to have quickly returned because it was one of the main factors behind the government appointment of Zico, the famous Brazilian forward, as Sports Secretary in March 1990. He drew up a plan for the reform of the Brazilian game with failed to obtain the agreement of the Brazilian Congress, provoking Zico to resign.[6] But the violence on the field continued. The start of the 1993 season was disfigured be sendings off – thirty-five in the first thirty-two games – abuse of referees and the failure to discipline wrongdoers. Eight players were sent off in the South American Super Cup match between Grémio and Peñarol in Porto Alegre which finished with players fighting with police. Grémio players and officials had earlier attacked the referee following the awarding of a penalty against them in their national championship match with Santos. Sentenced to play their home games on another ground for the next six months, they were allowed to move to another stadium nearby.[7] Finally, allegations of bribing of referees and match fixing in Rio brought the year to a controversial end. Botafogo, Flamengo and Fluminense announced their withdrawal from the Rio championship and their intention to form a new league. Tele Santana and others have called for a proper investigation and the more general movement in Congress to root out corruption in Brazilian society may soon turn its attention to football. But it will be a tough task. The President of the Rio football federation, Eduardo Viana, was quoted as saying, 'I detest public opinion. The people could all be shot by machine guns, for all I care. I'm the son of a factory owner, the elite, and I'm a right winger.'[8] When Pelé alleged corruption in the running of the Brazilian Football Federation Havelange used his power to ban the world's most famous player from taking part in the draw for USA '94.

Brazilian football has also been affected by an economy in which inflation has been difficult to control, so much so that it was running at 1,500 per cent per year in early 1994.[9] Players can do better in Europe, and over 200 were playing in Portugal alone by the end of the 1980s. It was not only the money which attracted them, of course. There were fewer games to play in Portugal, a better-organized championship, fewer press conferences and fewer periods of 'concentration', with the players in training camps away from their families.[10] Loss of the best players must also have contributed to fewer spectators in the stadiums. Relatively poor performances in five successive World Cups have been linked not only to the loss of players abroad but with anxieties that the greater urban growth of the last thirty years has deprived the poor of places to play football. There is a suggestion that this has allowed more middle-class players from leading educational institutions and sports clubs to come into the national side. Whether this has inhibited their performance is hard to say, but the appointing of seven team managers since 1986 reflects the team's failure to play up to its reputation. For USA '94 it was back to 1970 basics with Carlos Parreira, physiotherapist, then as manager, and Mario Zagalo, manager in 1970, as co-ordinator.

Football in Argentina has also not been without its difficulties in spite of two successive appearances in the World Cup Final. Many league matches attract sparse crowds and the loss of players abroad remains at astonishing levels, 2,509 according to *El País*, between 1980 and 1993. Of these 90 per cent were attackers or creative midfield players, and included the leading goalscorer in every season.[11] The oldest of these players was Ramón Medina Bello at twenty-seven and he did not go to Europe but to Japan to join Yokohama Marinos in the J League. Seventy-five others went to Asia, 537 to Europe and 1,863 to other countries in Central and South America. In some ways these figures are a source of pride among Argentinian football supporters: what other country could survive such losses?

Domestic football in Argentina has also been plagued by crowd violence in the stadiums. No country is free of it, but the Argentinian variety seems more sinister and deep-rooted. Deaths are not uncommon and woundings and arrests regular occurrences. In 1986, the President of San Lorenzo, Alberto Noguera, speaking to a North American audience, claimed that too many fans were just looking for a fight. More importantly, he alleged that clubs gave away tickets to hooligans in an effort to fill the stadiums. He was also critical of the police who, he claimed, provoked violence rather than restrained it. He compared them to the recent military governments who relied on force to achieve order, and there have been other attempts to link the *barra bravas* with the Green Falcons and the Triple A, right-wing death squads who toured the streets in unmarked Ford Falcons during the rule of the military junta.[12] Some individual *barras* have alleged that club directors have provided the groups with tickets for matches and contributions to bus fares for away games. Financial help was also given to some in order for them to travel to Spain for the World Cup in 1982.[13] One Argentine critic has even claimed that club directors have used hooligan gangs to carry out acts of blackmail and violence, often against players who have incurred their wrath. The gangs do seem to have considerable influence inside some clubs. Journalists complained in 1986 that while they had to wait for some time following the end of an evening South American cup game outside River's dressing room, the *barra bravas* had no trouble gaining access.[14] Not surprisingly in such circumstances, players give money to the gangs who also work for politicians. Leading football clubs in

Argentina have had connections with politics since the 1930s at least, as we have seen. The Presidents of clubs like Boca, River and Racing are powerful people. One recent commentator has suggested that in Argentina football clubs are so important as social institutions that they rival those of the state in power. Are River really planning to set up a university?[15]

In 1993 Argentina won the South American Championships. The team was in the middle of a long unbeaten run which had been achieved largely without the help of Maradona. But then came the World Cup qualifying competition and two comprehensive defeats by Colombia. The first, by 2–0 in Bogotá, was not entirely surprising nor unacceptable. But to lose by a record 5–0 in Buenos Aries was a footballing catastrophe and provoked the kind of ludicrous cultural self-examination that seems to accompany such sporting troughs. *El Gráfico*'s headline, '*¡Vergüenza!*' (Shameful!) was one of the more restrained.[16] Fortunately for Argentina, there was a second chance to qualify for the team finishing second in their group. They met the winner of the elimination match between Oceania and Concacaf over two legs.[17] After a shaky 1–1 draw in Sydney against Australia, Argentina, having recalled Maradona, won narrowly in Buenos Aires by a single goal deflected in by an Australian defender. Many thought that Maradona would revive the spirits and fortunes of the team and that qualification for USA '94 was the first sign. But late in March he only played for the first half of Argentina's first defeat by Brazil since 1989. He looked slow and overweight, moving manager Basile to tell journalists, 'Maradona is totally out of shape and our objective is to prepare him slowly for the World Cup.'[18]

If football in Argentina and Brazil has been far from trouble-free in recent years, football in Colombia has been unable to escape contamination by two of the country's most serious social and political problems: violence and drugs. In October 1983 the country's Justice Minister declared: 'The Mafia has taken over Colombian football.' He was later murdered. In 1984 Hernán Botero Moreno, President of Nacional FC and an ally of Pablo Escobar, was extradited to the United States on charges of laundering money from drug-dealing activities. The Colombian League, the Dimayor, postponed all the games for a week in protest. He was later tried and convicted. One of the leaders of the Medellín drug cartel was also a main shareholder in the famous Millonarios club of Bogotá until he died in 1989. In 1986 eight sports officials, including the coach of the national youth team, were murdered. Towards the end of 1988 a referee was kidnapped for twenty-four hours by a group who had sworn to act against referees who were suspected of corruption. Then in November 1989 Alvaro Ortega, a twenty-seven-year-old referee who had controlled only thirteen First Division matches, was shot dead entering a hotel in Medellín after refereeing the match between the local side Independiente and América from Cali. The championship was suspended and the title withheld. Suspicion pointed to members of the Medellín drug cartel, who were thought to bet heavily on matches. The connection between gambling and football in Colombia was given a further graphic illustration in 1990 when a group apparently called Cleansers of Colombian Football claimed responsibility for six murders in the previous week and threatened to murder club shareholders connected with the narcotics trade.[19] Then in September 1990, the South American Football Confederation banned Colombia from staging international matches for a year after six armed men demanded the referee make sure that the local club, Nacional, beat Vasco da Gama from Rio in a South American Cup game. When the managing editor of *El Tiempo*, the largest-circulation daily newspaper in Bogotá, wrote that football was plagued by drug money he was kidnapped and held for eight months. The most notorious of Colombia's drug gangsters was Pablo Escobar. He was a real football enthusiast who built football pitches for the poor and also provided floodlights and other equipment. It seems certain that he was closely involved with the Nacional club, some of whose players visited him in prison and were on friendly terms, most notably the eccentric goalkeeper Higuita, whose spectacular forays from goal were such a feature of Colombia's game in the 1990 World Cup and which led to an embarrassing defeat against Cameroon in the second round.[20] It seems likely that football clubs were helped out of financial difficulties in the 1970s and 1980s by drug money. These funds made possible the buying of foreign stars. Five professional teams were recently thought to be under investigation on suspicion of laundering drug money.

Yet in these difficult circumstances Colombian football has prospered. Nacional Medellín won the Libertadores Cup in 1989 and only lost 1–0, in the last minute of extra time, to the champions of Europe, AC Milan, in the World Cup Championship. Carlos Valderrama became the first Colombian to be named South American Footballer of the Year in 1987. That was an important year, as the South American Youth Championship was won and Francisco Maturana became manager of the national side. He was a dentist and he and his team quickly made a good impression, qualifying for the World Cup in 1990, the first time they had done so since 1962. He believed that Colombians should play in their own style, essentially a short-passing game based on the individual ball control of the players, but he also insisted on the importance of teamwork, maximizing the regional characteristics of the players. So in midfield the need was for hard workers and well-disciplined players, provided by Alvarez and Gabriel Gómez from the Antioquía region where such qualities are commonplace, while the fantasy was left to Valderrama, Asprilla and Rincón, people from Cali and the coast who were harder to discipline but more creative.

The qualification for USA '94 was spectacular: four matches were won and two drawn with the *pièce de résistance* that 5–0 victory in Buenos Aires, a win which prompted the Colombian President, César García, to award the entire team the Boyacá Cross, the highest medal a civilian can receive.[21] This victory was part of a long sequence of forty-one matches with only one defeat, further stimulating popular interest in football in a country which in 1990 was alleged to broadcast 180 radio hours of football coverage every day.[22] Pelé called Colombia the best team in South America and on the eve of the World Cup tipped them as winners. But in *El Tiempo* an astrologer predicted that Colombia would be the surprise team of the tournament.

Bolivia were the fourth South American qualifiers for the 1994 World Cup. With only fourteen teams in their national championship and just over 600 professional players, this small, mountainous country has only a modest football history. Twice before they had appeared in the World Cup Finals, but failed to score a goal in 1930, when losing 4–0 to both Brazil and Yugoslavia, and in Belo Horizonte in 1950 when in a two-team group Bolivia lost 8–0 to Uruguay. In 1963 though, when the South American Championship was held in La Paz and Cochabamba, Bolivia won it, taking as much advantage of the weakened teams sent by Argentina and Brazil, and of the fact that Uruguay sent no team at all, as of the high altitude.

What Bolivia is famous for is coca, of which it grows more than Colombia. Cocaine is one of fourteen alkaloids found in the coca leaf, although in very small amounts, and Bolivia has produced more than its share of drug barons. But in June 1993 coca and football came together in a most interesting way. Bolivia won five successive World Cup matches, four at home and one in Caracas. As the vanquished included Uruguay by 3–1 and Brazil by 2–0, qualification for the World Cup Finals seemed certain. But after the game against Brazil Miguel Rimba, a Bolivian central defender, failed a routine drug test. His sample showed traces of cocaine and he was banned from future World Cup matches. Rimba admitted drinking coca tea before the game in order to settle his stomach. His defenders claimed the coca leaf was not a drug but a legitimate cultural product embedded in the history of all Andean nations. It has been drunk for centuries as both stimulant and digestive and football fans take bags of coca leaves to chew during matches. The traces of cocaine had therefore come from a tea containing coca leaves. FIFA changed its mind and lifted the suspension on Rimba. Perhaps it was impressed by the list of celebrities, including the Pope and Dan Quayle, who have drunk the tea. During the Bolivia–Uruguay match the electronic scoreboard flashed the message 'Coca is not cocaine', further encouraging those keen to promote alternative coca products.[23] With a Basque manager, the growing reputation of the Tahuichi Football Academy in Santa Cruz, and the knowledge that it was they who ended Colombia's long unbeaten run, Bolivia could travel hopefully to the USA.

Not too many South Americans could afford to go to the World Cup, but the media fully intended to bring it to them. In Brazil Rede Globo, the major television network, intended to send ten camera crews to cover all the World Cup venues. Pelé would provide pre- and after-match comments. In all, over one hundred reporters, producers and engineers would be travelling north. Two other networks in Brazil had also obtained rights to transmit the matches and competition for viewers was tough. Nevertheless the advertising spots during the games had been sold out well in advance. Television manufacturers were hoping 1994 would produce record sales for them as two-thirds of the population anxiously watched the first-round games.

All five major television companies in Argentina also had the rights to World Cup football. Channel 13 expected to send sixty staff and use a thirty-strong production company in the United States. Eight reporters from Channel 13 would follow Argentina and their main rivals and Maradona had been hired to provide summaries when he was not playing.

The dominant medium in sports broadcasting in Colombia remains radio, which has the biggest penetration in the country. A pool of six production companies acquired the rights to broadcast the games on the two state-owned channels. The best-known reporters do the radio and not the television commentaries and it is common in Colombia for over half TV viewers to turn off the sound and listen to the radio. Colombia is the only South American country with two all-sport networks.

Bolivian television was also providing blanket coverage of the national team. A TV sports director told an American journalist: 'People are demanding to know who's hurt, what the players are saying, every detail, every word. And not just Bolivia, they want to know how the other teams are doing ... who's in form and who is not.'[24]

It was sensible for Bolivians to want to know how the other teams were doing because Bolivia would not give much trouble to the scorers. Their best player, Marco Antonio Etcheverry, had not played in 1994 due to injury. He eventually did come on near the end of the opening game against Germany but became an early victim of FIFA's determination to eliminate violent conduct when he was sent off for a foolish but mild act of retaliation. Bolivia lost the game to a Klinsmann goal and then proceeded to draw tediously and goallessly with South Korea. Their neat football was finally rewarded by a World Cup Finals goal against Spain but they conceded three and were on their way back to La Paz. As one local newspaper sadly reported, 'Bolivia played like never before but lost like always.'[25]

We have seen that Colombia were highly regarded by the football cognoscenti and they began like world beaters, at least for the first twenty-five minutes, against Rumania. Crisp, short passing repeatedly cut paths through the Rumanian defence but after fifteen minutes it was Rumania who scored via a classic counter-attack. A brilliant pass from Hagi from his own half sent Raducioiu through to score. Worse was to follow when Hagi's cross-cum-shot found the Colombian goalkeeper Córdoba far from home. All was not lost as Valencia at last converted one of Colombia's chances three minutes before half time. But that turned out to be the best that they could do. Another goal near the end by Raducioiu, again with Córdoba badly positioned, meant a 3–1 defeat. This was a setback to Colombian aspirations but it did not seem to preface early elimination with the United States and Switzerland to come. But the pressure about which international sportsmen often complain began to build on the Colombians in an extraordinary way, again drawing attention to the relationship between drugs, gambling, violence and football in that country.

On the day of the match against the USA, threats were telephoned and faxed to Colombian coach Francisco Maturana, his assistant Hernán Darío Gómez and the latter's brother, the midfield player Gabriel Jaime Gómez, that their Medellín homes would be bombed if Gómez played against the North Americans.[26] In Colombia such threats are taken seriously and Gómez was replaced in the team by Hernán Gaviria. This was hardly the best preparation for a football match; but did it explain the feeble performance which followed? Colombia never dominated as expected, even before conceding a goal after thirty-four minutes. An American attack down their left led to a low cross which central defender Andrés Escobar had to stretch to reach: behind him Stewart was coming in dangerously. Escobar prevented the ball from reaching Stewart but only by diverting past his own goalkeeper. Six minutes after half time Stewart scored a second following the kind of passing movement the Colombians had been expected to produce. Ten minutes from the end Balboa, whose father had been a professional in Argentina, delivered an overhead kick from a corner and almost scored what would have been not just a third goal for the USA but the most spectacular of the tournament. Valencia's last-minute goal for Colombia was no consolation. Maturana had substituted de Avila and the highly rated Asprilla at half time but said after the match that he would have like to have taken off all eleven. It was the way the game had been lost which most disgusted him. Inevitably the question was asked, were the players unsettled by the threats? Had the match been thrown to accommodate Colombian gangsters betting against their own country in a match they were expected to win comfortably? Without more evidence, it is football explanations which seem the most convincing. Colombia had never impressed in a major championship. Colombia produces players with imagination and skill but the promise of their short-passing game was not fulfilled. There was a lack of acceleration and above all no width in their play. Against Rumania and the USA, Colombian attacks battered at reinforced central defences whose flanks were never threatened. Everything flowed through the one-paced Valderrama, who is beginning to appear one of football's great under-achievers. Chances were made but not taken and the final irony was the fallibility of goalkeeper Córdoba. Chosen as a safer alternative to the eccentric and tainted Higuita, he found himself blamed for the second and third Rumanian goals. The disappointment in Colombia can be imagined. *La Prensa* ran the predictable headline 'Humiliated by United States' and a fan in the street allegedly told *El Tiempo*, 'If we aren't capable of beating the gringos we aren't worth anything.'[27] So from being among the fancied Colombia were actually the first to be eliminated. A convincing 2–0 victory over Switzerland in their final match further underlined their frustration. But there was worse to come.

Early on the morning of Saturday, 2 July, Andrés Escobar, unfortunate scorer against his own side, was leaving a restaurant on the outskirts of Medellín when he became involved in an altercation with three men. He was insulted, the own goal mentioned and then Escobar was shot and on arrival at the hospital found to be dead. Several arrests were later made and a man called Humberto Muñoz, a bodyguard/chauffeur for a local rancher, admitted the shooting. His employer was also later arrested. Again there has been much speculation about the motive. We have already noted how football clubs in Colombia were invested in by narcotics interests and suggestions were made that Escobar was the victim of disgruntled cartel members who, far from betting against their own team, had backed Colombia to beat USA. We have also seen that leading footballers have been friendly with the traffickers – Higuita with Pablo Escobar for example – and it does not take much imagination to understand that footballers from the slums did not ask questions about the origins of the tips they received for saving or scoring goals. Andrés Escobar, however, was from a middle-class family, a man who could have gone to university but who chose to follow his enthusiasm for football. He played for Nacional in Medellín and although a versatile player eventually became a leading defender. He was always polite and self-effacing and had no known connections with drug dealers. He wrote a column for *El Tiempo* and appears to have been widely respected both on and off the field.

But if we ask why he was murdered it may be less mysterious than some journalists have suggested. Football is part of society and Colombia is a violent place. Ten per cent of the world's murders are committed there and the murder rate is eight or fifteen times that of the United States, depending on which American newspaper you read.[28] Fewer than three per cent of all reported crimes lead to a conviction and killing appears to have become an acceptable way of achieving justice where the law does not work. Escobar may be the first major sportsman to be assassinated but he joins many journalists, over two hundred judges, a thousand policemen and three out of the six Presidential candidates in 1989, all murdered in recent years. Many thousands turned out for the funeral, including President César Gaviria. *El Tiempo* called the murder 'an own goal against the whole country'. In what proved to be his last article for that paper Andrés Escobar asked his readers not to let 'the defeat affect our respect for the sport and the team. See you later, because life goes on.' But for Andrés Escobar, at twenty-seven, it did not. His first own goal was also his last.

Like Colombia, Argentina were also among the favourites for USA '94, a favouritism enhanced by the return of *el pibe de oro*, the golden boy, Diego Maradona. Maradona was fitter and leaner, having lost twenty-six or thirteen pounds (depending on which newspaper you read) and although he could no longer race thirty metres in 3.8 seconds his passing and prompting was at the heart of the 4–0 victory against Greece. He actually scored the third goal himself, a cracking shot from twenty yards with that ever-ready left foot. His excited run to the nearest TV camera was a clear attempt to frighten his critics. Another player, reappearing after a drugs ban, Caniggia, also played with verve and skill and Batistuta scored three goals. As for the defence, the Greeks rarely tested it. It was expected that Nigeria, champions of Africa, would provide a tougher examination.

Argentina versus Nigeria was altogether more competitive and there were signs that the Argentina of Lorenzo and Bilardo was not far away. Argentinian players surrounded the referee after every decision that went against them and many that did not, and *el pibe* himself seemed to want to compete with Jurgen Klinsmann for the title of supreme diving champion of the tournament. The Nigerians did some diving themselves too, but into tackles, so that by half time a nervous referee, threatened by FIFA with being sent home if he did not carry out their instructions, had given twenty-four free kicks against them; Argentina had conceded only one! In goals, though, Argentina were ahead. Siasia had given Nigeria the lead after eight minutes but Caniggia scored twice between the twenty-first and twenty-eighth minutes, the second following a quickly taken free kick by Maradona prompted by Caniggia's quick-thinking run and shout of 'Diego Diego'. There were no more goals, although there might have been. The Nigerians were persuaded or seduced into playing at a slower pace than was good for them. A similar failing would cost them a quarter-final place. But after having played two and won two, Argentina were on their way. At the end of the match with Nigeria, their famous number ten was randomly chosen as one of the twenty-two squad members, one from those who played, one from among the substitutes, to be tested for drugs. He had no trouble providing the sample and was soon telling thirty Argentine journalists:

> The Nigerians played very rough, but it was not their fault. It was the referee's fault. Yes, I am physically hurting, but I am glad we finished the game alive ... I thank the Lord for the great legs he gave me, because I had to do a lot of running today! I would like to dedicate this victory to the people of Argentina![29]

But as everyone knows, both samples were discovered to contain what was described as a cocktail of five banned substances which could have the effect of curbing appetite and enhancing physical stamina.[30] Maradona was immediately withdrawn from the tournament.[31] Argentinians were stunned, if the media are to be believed. One television newsreader in Buenos Aires called it 'total madness, an absolute disaster'. A poll conducted by *Clarín*, the largest-circulation daily, seemed to show people sad rather than angry. But many were emotional, prepared to shed tears on radio phone-ins or in front of hand-held TV cameras on street corners. Some compared the day to that of Perón's funeral in 1974 or the defeat in the Falklands War. Many wanted to believe him innocent. Carlos Ruckauf, the Interior Minister, was quoted as saying that it was 'highly irresponsible to attack him now, when we all cheered his goals' and the Governor of Buenos Aires, Carlos Duhalde, sent Maradona a telegram expressing 'the support of the majority of Argentines'. Channel 13 played Maradona highlights to the music of rock singer Fito Paez's 'You Bring Happiness to my Heart'. There were other voices. Carlos Varela, a radio broadcaster, said 'Maradona was never an example of anything' and Bernardo Neustadt, another famous Argentine reporter, was moved to reflect: 'Ours is a country in which it's the speculators who win, a country that violated its own constitution every time it felt like it. Yesterday, Argentina paid with Maradona [for] a way of life, of not heeding the law.'[32]

Meanwhile the man himself outraged some American opinion by not going home but talking of conspiracies, signing autographs and collecting a reported $1.3 million for offering his opinions to Argentina's Channel 13. George Vecsey of the *New York Times* could not restrain himself in face of the unfairness of it all and called *el pibe de oro* a 'raging one-man cornucopia of menace, anger, suspicion, swagger, callousness and contempt – a creepy, blustering gangster'.[33]

The Argentinian players made predictable statements about winning the cup for Maradona, but the tough question was whether they could win without him. Against Bulgaria in the last first-round match Rodríguez took his place, wearing the number-twenty shirt. He looked lost and ineffective, giving wits the chance to say he was half the player. Argentina had already qualified, so perhaps the 2–0 defeat which kept Bulgaria in the competition did not matter save that Caniggia was hurt and the complexities of the draw sent the blue and whites to Pasadena and Rumania in round two. As they entered the field they were greeted not only by the traditional welcome of confetti from their supporters but also by a thirty-foot-long Argentine flag behind one of the goals inscribed 'Thank you Mrs Tota' (Maradona's mother) and the chanting of the great man's name. It was a football equivalent of the obituary and the match ended Argentina's interest in the tournament. At least it was one of the better games in USA '94. Argentina had plenty of possession and with Ortega now playing the Maradona role their ball control and short passing created several opportunities and by the end they would have had twenty-two shots to Rumania's thirteen. But the Rumanians were the master of the deadly counter-stroke. Hagi – the Maradona of the Carpathians – was into everything and with the help of Munteanu and Dumitrescu was soon dismantling the Argentinian defence. Dumitrescu scored from a free kick after eleven minutes and although Batistuta equalized from a penalty, Hagi's wonderful pass made a second goal for Dumitrescu in the eighteenth minute. Argentina attacked almost non-stop in the second half and Rumania appeared to be wilting in the heat. But after fifty-eight minutes another classic counter-attack saw a ferocious run by Dumitrescu down the left and a perfectly timed pass to Hagi who had himself run forty yards. He scored with a first-time *right*-foot shot, a goal which had neutrals casting off their inhibitions. After Balbo had made it 3–2 in the seventy-fifth minute it could still have gone either way. Rumania were lucky that defender Belodedeci was not sent off for an edge-of-penalty-area foul, a decision which cost referee Pairetto his place in the tournament. Argentina could have won, but like Colombia they neglected the flanks and concentrated on the centre of the Rumanian defence which was at its strongest there. Afterwards Basile told the press that Argentina had 'responded to adversity with fervour, temperament and football. Unfortunately, it wasn't enough.'[34]

Halfway through the tournament and only Brazil remained to represent South America. Brazil were everyone's second favourites but, as we have seen, Brazilian football is not what it was. The twenty-four years since the famous victory of 1970 had been littered with generally undistinguished World Cup performances. Yet the supporters and the media seemed impatient of anything short of victory.

The Brazilian media were ubiquitous, with four hundred reporters at the second-round match against the USA. Even parts of Brazil's practice sessions were shown live on television in Brazil and radio reporters offered live up-to-the-minute comment on such arcane subjects as which players were playing with whom and what this might mean. Is this passion or nightmare? Brazilian newspapers published complicated diagrams of particular moves, and not just ones which had led to goals. All of this attention, all of this print and talk, was in pursuit not just of victory but stylish victory. If stylish victory seemed unlikely then the criticism sharpened to the edge of panic.

Brazil qualified early for round two with comfortable victories over Russia, 2–0, and Cameroon, 3–0. The 1–1 draw with Sweden in the third match was interpreted widely among Brazilian reporters and supporters as failure. Pelé, producing an article for *USA Today*, demanded three changes as Brazil could hardly play worse. Wide currency was given to the news that both President Itamar Franco and manager Parreira's mother wanted to see the young Cruzeiro forward Renaldo included in the team. When the manager's name was reached in pre-game announcements it was always booed by Brazilian supporters in the stadiums. The main criticism was that he was over-cautious, too defensive. This was not the Brazilian way, and many fans claimed to prefer Santana, the coach of World Club champions São Paulo, who had been national team manager in the World Cups of 1982 and 1986. *O Estado de São Paulo* said the best Latin style of football was coming from Eastern Europe.[35] The second-round match with the USA on American Independence Day was awaited with some trepidation.

Brazil won by a single goal set up by Romário and scored by Bebeto fifteen minutes from the end. Brazil had played with only ten men from the forty-fourth minute following the dismissal of left-back Leonardo for a foolish retaliatory elbow to the head of Ramos. It was a disappointing match, with the North Americans very negative in their approach and Brazil poor in the first half and wasting several good scoring opportunities in the second, the main culprits being Bebeto, Romário and Zizinho. Brazil had a total of sixteen shots and the USA four, although most people could remember the North Americans making only one scoring chance and they did not have one worthwhile shot on goal.

In spite of criticisms of the lack of style, and the narrowness of the victory against one of the less fancied teams, Brazilian cities saw what have become conventional street celebrations after the victory. 'The thuds of powerful bottle rockets exploded from the roofs of upscale high-rise rooftops, modest houses and mountainside shanty towns. Flag-waving adults and children flowed into the previously deserted streets screaming BrrrrAAAZiiiLLLL!'[36] During all of Brazil's games national energy consumption was estimated to have dropped by one-third as schools, factories and shopping centres closed.

Holland provided the opponents in the quarter final and for the fifth match in succession Brazil found themselves up against a team concerned mainly with defence. As we have seen, Brazil were also intent on giving nothing and a first-half stalemate ensued. Finally Brazilian pressure produced two goals, for Romário in the fifty-second minute and Bebeto thirteen minutes later, and for thirty minutes it became a real match. Twice the Dutch scored in the space between twelve second-half minutes, first through Bergkamp and then Winter, and either side could have won but Brazil eventually did. With nine minutes left Branco, in for the suspended Leonardo, scored with a free kick from thirty yards. The North American press talked of the Brazilians in terms of the dance – the *capoeira* – and christened them 'magnificent Mononyms' whatever they are, but this seemed part of Yankee overstatement.

The semi-final brought together Brazil and Sweden for the second time in the tournament. An argument could be made that Sweden had played well in the first match. They had been careful and secure in defence but competitive in midfield and purposely dangerous on the counter-attack. The goal they scored in the first half was a classic of its kind and they might have repeated it. They were less impressive thereafter and perhaps lucky to squeeze into the semi-final after a penalty shoot-out victory against Rumania. In the semi-final they gave Tafferel no trouble, their reluctance to get midfield players forward to support their double-marked attackers provoking the suspicion that they were either very tired or playing for another round of penalties, especially once Thern had been ludicrously sent off. After all the defensive planning and determination they finally conceded a soft header to Romário after seventy-five minutes and it was always going to be enough. The Swedes had just three shots on goal in this match.

Brazil were much the better team in the semi-final but they could not make it count and the fact that this was followed by the first World Cup Final to be decided on penalties must be in part a criticism of both the way they played and the calibre of their players. Once again their opponents, Italy, were ultra-cautious and rarely threatened the Brazilian defence, but neither did Brazil exert much pressure on theirs. The first half was interesting enough for the committed and the aficionado alike: the second half was dire. There was little sign of the *jogo bonito* (the beautiful game) from either side. The anxiety at the core was clearly illustrated when Parreira brought on the Corinthians forward Viola, who had not played in the tournament until then, but waited until the final fifteen minutes of extra time to do it. Brazil's victory was ensured when Roberto Baggio shot the fifth Italian penalty over the crossbar.

But a win is a win. This was the record fourth World Cup victory, the *tetracampeão*, and a matter for celebration in the stadium and on the streets. There was some grumbling that it had not been achieved by brilliant goals in open play and that a penalty shoot-out was an unfair way to settle such a championship, but the Monday after was declared a national holiday in Brazil and the team took the trophy to the people on fire engines as in 1958, 1962 and 1970, first in Recife, then Brasilia and finally Rio de Janeiro (but not in São Paulo).[37]

The fact that on the field the final was not a repeat of 1970 except in the names of the finalists alerts us to the idea that if football had changed so had Brazil. In 1970 the victory produced a surge of support for the dictatorship in the context of a media still heavily censored. With a Presidential election due on 3 October there was speculation that the existing Government might reap the benefit in 1994. But the leftist candidate, Luis Inácio Lula da Silva, told a questioner, 'The people know how to distinguish between football and politics. When the festivities are over, the people know how to separate fantasy from reality.' The President of the Vox Populi polling company agreed: 'I think that it is improbable that on October 3 there will be many voters still wearing yellow and green shirts, and still blowing on plastic horns.'[38]

There is an interesting little coda on how Brazil and football's place in it may have changed since 1970. When the players returned home after their victorious adventure in Mexico they were allowed to bring back gifts bought abroad without having to declare them for customs duty. In 1994, Brazilian customs officers in Rio insisted they should pay duty on the twelve tons of high-tech merchandise in the hold of their aircraft. The row which followed lasted for over five hours but, with the approval of the Finance Minister, the party, with its booty, was then allowed through. However opinion polls showed that 70 per cent of people believed they should have paid the duty like everyone else.[39]

We saw at the start of this chapter that João Havelange considered the organization of the World Cup in America would be his highest achievement. How can that achievement be evaluated? The football verdict must begin by stating unequivocally that USA '94 was a better tournament than Italia '90 but then the football in Italy had been so cynical and shabby that FIFA could not have allowed a repeat performance. Yet the suspicion remains that it was not so much a plan to solve the problems of Italia '90 which produced FIFA's prescription for improvement as an attempt to seduce the North American public. After all, the justification for taking the World Cup to the United States was that it would release the forces necessary for the formation of a native professional league. Of that more in a moment.

FIFA's edict had three main prongs. One was to eliminate foul play and particularly the tackle from behind. In general it worked, but the price was a collection of neurotic referees who frequently cautioned and occasionally dismissed players for the commonplace bumps and collisions which are a natural part of a continuous, physical-contact sport. In other words, FIFA lurched uncertainly from the ignorance and permissiveness of Italia '90 to the insensitive interference of USA '94. The second prong of the FIFA fork was the relaxation of the offside law. Whereas the law clearly states that if the attacking player is level with the last defender at the moment when the ball is played to him he is offside, FIFA decided that he would be *on*side. This is authoritarian tinkering with the laws with a vengeance, and it certainly helped Brazil score one and probably two of their goals against the Dutch. The third prong was three points for a win in the first round, and it is hard to know whether that had much effect. Certainly the introduction of a newly designed ball did nothing to improve the game and probably contributed to the poor finishing with which the tournament was plagued, by its lightness and high bounce. Changes in the interpretation of the laws were needed after Italia '90 but so was good sense in applying them, and this seemed to be at a premium in USA '94.

FIFA itself probably contributed to much of the onfield tedium by its acceptance of the demand from European television that most starting times for matches in America should coincide with peak viewing in Europe. This meant football being played not just in great heat, but during the hottest periods of the day, and as one nineteenth-century American general said after a two-year posting to Texas, 'If I owned Texas and Hell, I'd live in Hell and rent out Texas.'[40] Surely a delay of three or four hours would have been a sensible compromise and not undermined European audience figures very much? The heat, together with the travelling, placed a great physical and mental strain on the players and it was largely the result of the pursuit of profit.

One of the criticisms of a twenty-four-team tournament is that it is too long drawn out. That problem ought to be addressed, along with a related one, which is the ludicrously complex method required to decide who plays whom in the second round. It is also ironic that such a long tournament is unable to find a method for settling a drawn final other than by penalty kicks. It seems clear that penalties encourage caution, because managers and players know that a draw provides a 50–50 chance of victory and the defeat does not feel it is as real as one which takes place in open play.

Of course the best team won the cup. Brazil's strength was their sound defence, with often nine men behind the ball when the opposition had possession. The Brazilian goalkeeper, Tafferel, had only twelve saves to make in the six games preceding the final, and not many in the two hours of that either. Neutrals felt that Brazil did not *need* to keep four or five players marking one opposition attacker. These spare defenders rarely moved forward and the midfield was frankly disappointing with Rai dropped and Mazinho and Zinho 'the kings of non-productivity'. The team controlled every game, save the first half of the first-round match against Sweden, and the period in the second half against Holland when the Dutch pulled back to 2–2 but in general lacked thrust. The Brazilians were most dangerous when able to counter-attack quickly with a long ball from defence to the moving Bebeto or Romário, with only two or three defenders between them and the goal. With Italy's game also based on solid defence, it was always likely that without an early goal cautious stalemate would result.

The tournament had no outstanding match nor any outstanding player. There were good matches: Belgium v Holland (although the poor finishing was frustrating); Rumania v Argentina, Germany v Bulgaria, and a number of exciting second halves like Germany v South Korea, Brazil v Holland, and exciting periods of play such as the Roberto Baggio-inspired twenty minutes of the first half against Bulgaria. It was perhaps a pity that Brazil met Sweden and not Rumania in the semi-final. There were many excellent players and for Brazil it was certainly mission accomplished. But will it be remembered even there like the 1970 victory, the 1970 team and the 1970 players are still remembered?[41]

What of the other Havelange aspirations for the World Cup in the United States? It certainly made money, with an expected profit of $20–25 million. Crowds and match receipts touched record levels. The fifty-two games attracted 3,567,415 spectators at an average of 68,604. A crowd of 94,194 saw the final in the Rose Bowl in Pasadena; these spectators paid $43.5 million with an average ticket price of $460 (about £306). Some companies did particularly well, notably the official carrier, American Airlines, the sports kit producers Nike and WH Smith, the British newsagents' group, which also operates the airport and hotel gift stores in the United States that sold three million dollars' worth of World Cup merchandise. The Spanish-language television network Univision more than doubled its advertising revenues compared with the 1990 World Cup, and brewers – not surprisingly – also did well.[42]

The World Cup Final was seen on television in ten million North American households, a bigger audience than for the first six games of the NBA final.[43] Yet on the day that Brazil met Italy an ABC News poll showed that only 22 per cent of Americans found football exciting. What chance the Havelange dream of implanting the world game in the United

States? Of course it is there already. Sixteen million people play it, but they are largely white middle-class children and college boys, immigrants and women. The number of Afro-Americans either playing or interested in 'soccer' is small. All this suggests that a successful professional league is not only a long way off but may be a chimera. The World Cup was a big show, but it was held in a country with its own well-developed sports in which most of the people do not know or care much about football. With the tournament over Tony Meola, the USA goalkeeper in the World Cup, tried and failed to make the grade as a field goal kicker with the New York Jets of the National Football League. Here was a top soccer player prepared to give it all up for a move to the NFL which shows the power of indigenous American sport. After the USA had beaten England in Belo Horizonte in the 1950 World Cup, the coach of that team, Bill Jeffrey, said, 'This is all that's needed to make the game go in the States.' Well, it was not enough and Pelé and the New York Cosmos were not enough and neither will USA '94 be enough.

Postscript

Football now means the score. I am one of those people that think that spectacular play fills one's heart with joy. Fuck it all. But what delights the fan, what the world wants, and in the end what counts, is the goal ...

As a way of demonstrating these two different attitudes to football I am going to tell you a story. One afternoon, at half time, Seone said to Lalín, why don't you pass the ball to me instead of dribbling on your own? Pass it to me and I'll score. Well in the second half he does cross and Seone does score and he runs across to Lalín arms spread wide shouting, 'What did I tell you, what did I tell you?' Lalín replied, 'Yes, but I didn't get any pleasure out of it,' and in that you have all the problems of criollo football.

Ernesto Sábato, *Sobre Héroes y Tumbas – On Heroes and Tombs*, Buenos Aires, 1972 edn, pp. 94–5

In the English-language edition, published in the United States in 1981, these comments in which an old man is comparing Argentinian football of the fifties with the game in the twenties, to the former's disadvantage, were omitted ...

We will play in the way today's football demands. Magic and dreams are finished in football. We have to combine technique and efficiency.

Carlos Alberto Parreira, quoted by *New York Times*, 1 July 1994

People in Europe have difficulty in understanding South Americans. They are not like us. Even within a single national territory they do not all speak the same language or share the same traditions and identities. Economies are often a bewildering mixture of the very modern and the pre-capitalist and a minority of the rich live at a level of opulence unequalled anywhere but often surrounded by a poverty rarely found elsewhere.

But some cultural forms are shared, and football is one of the most notable. As we have seen, the modern game arrived in South America as the pastime of elites emulating the ideals of the metropolis. The British played an important part in its introduction especially around the River Plate but also in Brazil, Chile and Peru. The names of some clubs still bear witness to the nationality of their founders. There was little resistance to this colonial importation. Football was attractive partly because it was modern and European, but once it became a popular spectacle as opposed to an elite recreation South Americans adapted and refashioned it to their own culture. They developed a style and way of playing that was unmistakably their own, based on their mastery of the bouncing ball, the one-touch short pass where the ball is received and immediately transferred to a better-placed teammate, and above all the dribble, where the ball seemed not so much to be kicked as merely touched, in 'a lighter, softer, more affectionate way than it would seem feet are capable of'.[1]

As international sport expanded after the First World War, first the Olympic football tournament and then the World Cup gave birth to world champions. Football played some small part in the making of nations like Argentina, Brazil and Uruguay, all countries in the throes of an intoxicating but alarming immigration and urban growth. Football in South America began to be followed with a passion and commitment apparently unequalled elsewhere. No English political leader, even John Major, could have said, as President Menem of Argentina did, that not only did football 'form me physically' but it also 'gave me a great deal of spirituality'.

There was a negative side to this, as passion could quickly turn to violence both on and off the field. Not only did this produce conflict between clubs and countries in South America; it also damaged footballing relations with Europe, almost bringing about the collapse of the World Club championship. Different interpretations of the laws reflected different attitudes to football and produced occasional outbursts of ill feeling, as in 1966 when the England manager likened the Argentinian players to animals, and in 1986 when the trickery of Maradona's hand-of-God goal was seen as a sign of colonial deviousness. No one in Europe was surprised when a Uruguayan broke the record for the quickest sending-off in the World Cup finals, also in 1986.

Nevertheless South American football at its best was recognized as the sport's highest achievement. After their World Cup win in 1958 Brazil became everyone's second favourite team. Football was something Brazilians did better than anyone else and they did it, thanks to television, as all the world watched. Brazilian intellectuals were able to add football to carnival and music and form a holy trinity of national success and consolation, especially in times of political dictatorship. Football was seen as the only democracy, governed by clear and simple laws which everyone obeyed – most of the time, anyway. At least those who were guilty of infringements were punished – usually – and on the football field there was neither favouritism nor privilege. Even a poor man could triumph in the football meritocracy. It was not who you were but what you could do that counted. Given this context, and it was common to most South American states at different times, it is not surprising that football roused the passions. Unlike everyday life it was a world not corroded by inequality, injustice and corruption. This was Roberto Da Matta's view of the meaning of football for Brazilians and, by extension, most South Americans. It is an attractive theory but it can be opposed and has been, for example, by Mario Vargas Llosa.

Football offers people of all cultures something they hardly ever have – an opportunity to have fun and enjoy themselves, to get excited and to experience intense emotions not provided by the daily routine. A good game of football is intense and absorbing but, Vargas Llosa suggests, an ephemeral experience, 'one in which the effect disappears at the same time as the cause'. Sport in general, and football in particular, is not like a book or a play; it scarcely leaves a trace in the memory and neither enriches nor impoverishes understanding. It is exciting and empty and can be appreciated by all sorts and conditions of men and women, intelligent and unintelligent, cultivated and uncultivated.[2]

When Da Matta was writing in the later 1970s, it was widely accepted that there were two main styles of football – the South American, and especially the Brazilian built around individual initiative, skill, inspiration, even the mood of the players – and the European, a more collective, active, physical, prepared performance in which individuality was disciplined for the good of the team as a whole.[3]

In 1994 it could be argued that this footballing dichotomy of styles no longer exists. All teams now play in a similar fashion with teamwork and organization paramount and the key, a stern defence which is rarely outnumbered but occasionally outflanked and penetrated by swift counter-attacks in which midfield plotters transfer the ball quickly to sniping forwards or auxiliaries make stealthy runs from deep defence in the hope of catching the opposition unawares. Caution is the watchword; the game is not to lose. Perhaps this is an aspect of that globalization or homogenization of the sporting world about which sociologists excitedly chatter.

South American football retains its own history, myths and traditions and they are inextricably linked with the idea of football as reflecting what Argentinians and Brazilians like to think of as their national character and style: and the story they tell themselves about themselves is that their teams 'move on the field to a rhythm that seems programmed by a score'. South Americans discovered a balance between team and individual which made their play effective and graceful at the same time. Europeans still expect them to play that way and South America will continue to export exceptional players. But if the homogenization theory is true something which made football vital and attractive will have been lost.

FOOTBALL STADIUMS IN BUENOS AIRES C.1990

N

1. Boca Juniors
2. Huracán
3. Deportivo Español
4. San Lorenzo
5. Vélez Sarsfield
6. Ferro Carril Oeste
7. Argentinos Juniors
8. River Plate
9. All Boys
10. Nueva Chicago
11. Atlanta
12. Defensores de Belgrano
13. Excursionistas
14. Barracas Central
15. Comunicaciones
16. Deportivo Riestra
17. Sacachispas
18. Lamadrid
19. Lugano

NOTES

INTRODUCTION

1. Simon Collier *et al.* (eds), *The Cambridge Encyclopedia of Latin America and the Caribbean* (1989 edn); E. Bradford Burns, *A History of Brazil* (1993); Edwin Williamson, *The Penguin History of Latin America* (1992); Rory Miller, *Britain and Latin America in the Nineteenth and Twentieth Centuries* (1993). See also Glen Caudill Dealy, *The Latin Americans. Spirit and Ethos* (1992).

CHAPTER 1

1. *Buenos Aires Herald* (henceforth *BAH*), 5 May 1929.
2. By 1904 Thomas Hogg was sub-manager of the London and River Plate Bank. The clubs were Lomas, Flores, Quilmes Rowers, English High School and Buenos Aires Railway.
3. *BAH*, 18 April 1900.
4. Bedford School sent a team to Argentina in 1898. *La Nación*, 4 January 1970; *BAH*, 21 April 1900.
5. *BAH*, 18 May and 1 June 1905, 28 May 1912.
6. Jorge Iwanczuk, *Historia del fútbol amateur en la Argentina* (Buenos Aires 1993), p. 52. This work provides a comprehensive statistical account of the early history of football in Argentina.
7. See Chapter 2, below.
8. Iwanczuk (1993), p. 55.
9. *BAH*, 28, 29 May 1910.
10. *BAH*, 5 February 1905; Iwanczuk (1993), p. 100.
11. *BAH*, 18 May 1905.
12. *BAH*, 10 June 1906.
13. *BAH*, 31 July 1908.
14. *BAH*, 12 May 1912.
15. *BAH*, 30 June 1912.
16. *BAH*, 16 April and 28 May 1912.
17. *BAH*, 22 June 1904; *Liverpool Football Echo*, 24 July 1909.
18. *BAH*, 29 September 1912.
19. *BAH*, 1 December 1912.
20. *BAH*, 15, 22, 24, 29 December 1912.
21. *Uruguay News*, special supplement, 15 January 1893.
22. Much of what follows is based on Juan A. Capelán Carril, *Nueve décadas de gloria* (UFA

1990); José Luis Buzzetti, 'La nacionalización del fútbol' in *El fútbol Antología* (Montevideo 1969); and Julio Marne Rodríguez, 'Selección de Textos y Documentos Históricos'.

23. *BAH*, 11 June 1912.
24. He may have played in the 1–0 defeat of 1892 too. For Hampshire v Corinthians, *Southern Echo*, 21 April 1892 and 6 April 1893. For the early history of football in Brazil, see Tomás Mazzoni, *História do futebol no Brasil 1894–1950* (Rio 1950).
25. Mazzoni (1950), p. 18.
26. Most of these details come from Mazzoni, who also tells a nice story of how the São Paulo club invited a team from Argentina to play cricket in 1892. But it rained for twelve days and they had to return to Buenos Aires without putting bat to ball. Mazzoni (1950), p. 20.
27. Such as António Carlos. Gilberto Freyre, *Order and Progress. Brazil from Monarchy to Republic* (Rio 1970), pp. 118–19; Mazzoni (1950), p. 33.
28. Mazzoni (1950), p. 23.
29. Mazzoni (1950) has the details, pp. 28–32.
30. Mário Filho Rodrigues, *O negro no futebol Brasileiro* (Rio 1964), p. 10, quoted by Waldemyr Caldas, *O Pontapé Inicial. Memoria do futebol Brasileiro* (Rio 1990), p. 76. On Fluminense's early years see also Paulo Coelho Netto, *O Fluminense na Intimidade* Vol. II (Rio 1969), p. 60.
31. On Bangu see Caldas (1990), Chapter 1.
32. Richard Henshaw, *The Encyclopedia of World Soccer* (Washington 1979), p. 153; Ilan Rachum, 'Futebol. The Growth of a Brazilian National Institution', *New Scholar* 7, 1–2, 1978.
33. Quoted by Mazzoni (1950), p. 69.
34. Anatol Rosenfeld, 'O futebol no Brasil', *Revista Argumento* 4 (1974), p. 67; Rachum (1978), p. 188.
35. *Exeter Express and Echo*, 7 July 1914.

CHAPTER 2

1. *BAH*, 31 March and 12 April 1900.
2. *BAH*, 15 May 1900.
3. *BAH*, 23 March 1905.
4. *BAH*, 11 July 1904.
5. *BAH*, 27 June 1904.
6. *BAH*, 16 July 1904.
7. *BAH*, 10 June 1923.
8. *BAH*, 13, 14 June 1905; *El Día*, 1 June 1960.
9. *BAH*, 17 June 1905.
10. *BAH*, 21 June 1905.
11. *BAH*, 21, 23 June 1905.
12. *BAH*, 25 June 1905.
13. *BAH*, 26, 30 June and 6 July 1905.
14. *BAH*, 23, 26 June 1906.
15. Iwanczuk (1993), p. 378; Mazzoni (1950), pp. 64–5.
16. *BAH*, 8 June 1909; *Liverpool Football Echo*, 24 July 1909.
17. See F.N.S. Creek, *A History of Corinthian Football Club* (1933), pp. 82–4.
18. *The Sportsman*, 18, 24 September 1913. Welfare, originally from Liverpool, played for Fluminense and later Vasco da Gama where he eventually became a life President. He taught in an Anglo-Brazilian school. *Sunday Empire News*, 25 June 1950.
19. *BAH*, 13 October 1912, quoting a *Daily Chronicle* article by Allen.
20. *BAH*, 11 July 1912.

21. Iwanczuk (1993), p. 379; *Devon and Exeter Gazette*, 11 August 1914; *BAH*, 17 July 1914.
22. Mazzoni (1950), pp. 99–100.
23. Creek (1933), p. 42.
24. *Express and Echo*, 23 July 1914.
25. *Swindon Evening Advertiser*, 3 July 1912.
26. *BAH*, 15 May and 21 June 1906; 28 June and 13 October 1912; 17 July 1914.
27. *BAH*, 6 July 1905.
28. *BAH*, 6 September and 13 October 1912.
29. *BAH*, 20 May 1906.
30. *BAH*, 31 May 1910.
31. *BAH*, 22 September 1912; José Luis Buzzetti (1960), pp. 7–9; Mazzoni (1950), p. 67.
32. *BAH*, 23 March 1905.
33. Creek (1933), p. 42; *Liverpool Football Echo*, 24 July 1909. On cultural imperialism see Joseph L. Arbena, 'The Diffusion of Modern European Sport in Latin America: A case study of cultural imperialism?', *South Eastern Latin Americanist* 33 (4), pp. 1–8; Allen Guttmann, 'The Diffusion of Sport and the Problem of Cultural Imperialism', in Eric Dunning *et al.* (eds), *The Sports Process. A Comparative and Developmental Approach* (Champaign, Ill. 1993), pp. 125–38. On language see Américo Barabino, 'English Influence on the Common Speech of the River Plate', *Hispania* 33, May 1950, pp. 163–5.

CHAPTER 3

1. Iwanczuk (1993), p. 386. August 15 was the regular date of Lipton Cup matches between Argentina and Uruguay between 1906 and 1918.
2. *BAH*, 14 April 1905. Many other trophies were played for between the different countries of Latin America. With the growth of international football after 1945 most have disappeared, but occasional revivals take place. The Lipton trophy has been competed for five times since the Second World War.
3. *BAH*, 15, 25, 28 May 1910.
4. *BAH*, 31 May 1910.
5. *BAH*, 7 June 1910.
6. *BAH*, 14 June 1910.
7. *BAH*, 18 August; 7, 10, 14 September 1912; Mazzoni (1950), p. 101.
8. *BAH*, 28 September 1914.
9. *Confederación Sudamericano de Fútbol 1916–1991* (Buenos Aires 1991), pp. 86–8.
10. Juan A. Capelán Carril (1990), p. 26.
11. *The Review of the River Plate*, 21 July 1916; *BAH*, 21 July 1916.
12. March L. Krotee, 'The Rise and Demise of Sport: A reflection of Uruguayan society', in *American Academy of Political and Social Science Annals*, 445 (1979), p. 144.
13. *Le Miroir des Sports*, 5 June 1924.
14. *Le Miroir des Sports*, 12 June 1924.
15. Dionisio A. Vera, *Historia del Club Nacional de Football* (nd), pp. 88–9.
16. Iwanczuk (1993), p. 142.
17. Most of this account is taken from Mazzoni (1950), pp. 181–9.
18. See *BAH*, 23, 30 September 1924.
19. *BAH*, 3 October 1924.
20. *BAH*, 4 October 1924; *La Prensa*, 13 October 1924.
21. *BAH*, 19 October 1924.
22. *Le Miroir des Sports*, 12 June 1928; *BAH*, 31 May and 3 June 1928.
23. *Le Miroir des Sports*, 19 June 1928; *BAH*, 13 June 1928.
24. *BAH*, 14 June 1928.

25. British Olympic Committee, *Official Report on 9th Olympiad* (1929), p. 194; *BAH*, 8 June 1928.
26. *BAH*, 14 June 1928.
27. Krotee (1979), p. 146; *El Día*, 20 July 1975.
28. Public Record Office (henceforth PRO), FO 395/434.
29. *BAH*, 23 July 1930.
30. *BAH*, 27 July 1930.
31. *BAH*, 29 July 1930.
32. *BAH*, 30 July 1930.
33. *BAH*, 31 July 1930.
34. *BAH*, 31 July 1930.
35. Both quotations taken from *BAH*, 1 August 1930.
36. *BAH*, 2 August 1930.
37. Gabriel Hanot, a well-known French football journalist with a dislike of the English, later claimed it had been an English referee who had no sense of humour. But there were no English referees in the 1938 World Cup. See *Miroir du Football* (nd). The best account of the World Cup probably remains Brian Glanville, *The Sunday Times History of the World Cup* (1973).
38. FIFA Correspondence Files, Letter from Secretary of the CBD, 28 April 1943, pointing out that the second match with the Czechs and the twelve-hour journey from Bordeaux to Marseilles had given them little time to rest before the Italian match. There should have been three days' respite between games, according to the Brazilians.

CHAPTER 4

1. *BAH*, 29 April 1906 and 12 May 1912; *La Nación*, 14 March 1913.
2. Ariel Scher and Hector Palomino, *Fútbol: pasión de multitudes y de elites. Un estudio institucional de la Asociación de Fútbol Argentino 1934–1986* (1988), p. 233.
3. For these organizational squabbles see Iwanczuk (1993), pp. 132–43; Pablo A. Ramírez, 'Política y Fútbol', *Todo Es Historia* XXI, 248 (February 1988), p. 35.
4. *El Gráfico*, 26 June 1926.
5. *BAH*, 22 May 1929.
6. Iwanczuk (1993), p. 206; *World Soccer*, May 1961.
7. This account owes much to Iwanczuk (1993), p. 224, Ramírez (1988), p. 35 and Scher and Palomino (1988), pp. 26–7. See also *BAH*, 30 April 1931.
8. Scher and Palomino (1988), p. 215.
9. What follows is largely dependent upon Caldas (1990); Robert M. Levine, 'Sport and Society: The case of Brazilian futebol', *Luso-Brazilian Review* 17, 2 (1980), pp. 233–51; Rachum (1978) and Mazzoni (1950).
10. Quoted by Caldas (1990), p. 62.
11. Quoted by Caldas (1990), p. 74.
12. Quoted by Caldas (1990), p. 121.
13. George Reid Andrews, *Blacks and Whites in São Paulo Brazil 1888–1988* (1991), pp. 214–15.
14. See FBF dossiers to FIFA September 1935, FIFA Archives Correspondence with Brazil.
15. Caldas (1990), p. 88.
16. *Western Evening Herald*, 15 July 1924.
17. The membership figures are taken from FBF to FIFA (1935) and Levine (1980).
18. Caldas (1990), p. 135.
19. Levine (1980), quoting from Marcos de Castro and João Máximo (eds), *Gigantes do futebol Brasileiro* (Rio 1965); Rosenfeld (1974), pp. 75–6, 80; Joel Rufino dos Santos, 'Na CBD Até o Papagaio Bate Continência' (At the CBD even the parrot salutes), *Encontro com a Civilização Brasileira*, 5 (November 1978), pp. 125–6. See also Zelbert Moore,

'Reflections on Blacks in Contemporary Brazilian Popular Culture in the 1980s', *Studies in Latin American Popular Culture*, 7 (1988).
20. Scher and Palomino (1988), p. 59.
21. *Miroir du Football* 16, April 1961, p. 22.
22. Pablo A. Ramírez, 'Gloria y Ocaso de los Idolos del Fútbol', *Todo es Historia*, XVIII (1985), pp. 52–63; *World Sports*, August 1939, pp. 140–2.
23. Franklin Morales, 'Fútbol: Mito y Realidad', *Nuestra Tierra* 22 (Montevideo 1969), p. 54.
24. *Miroir du Football* 17, May 1961, p. 21.
25. Scher and Palomino (1988), pp. 85–7; *World Sports* 15, 9 September 1949, p. 39 and 15, 10, November 1949; *Miroir du Football* 17, May 1961, pp. 21–2.
26. *Miroir du Football* 18, June 1961, p. 24.
27. *World Soccer*, May 1961.

CHAPTER 5

1. Quoted by Duncan Shaw, 'The Political Instrumentalization of Professional Football in Francoist Spain 1939–1975', unpublished PhD, University of London, 1988.
2. Scher and Palomino (1988).
3. Rachum (1978), p. 196.
4. *BAH*, 26 June 1906 and 8 June 1909.
5. Mazzoni (1950), p. 66; *BAH*, 23, 24 March and 21 June 1905.
6. FIFA *Handbook* (1937).
7. Quoted by Caldas (1990), p. 100.
8. Caldas (1990), pp. 92–4, Rachum (1978), p. 197. Both quote Mario Filho Rodrigues (1964), pp. 197–8.
9. Caldas (1990), p. 194.
10. Caldas (1990), p. 220; Janet Lever, *Soccer Madness* (1983), pp. 59–69, Rachum (1978), p. 198.
11. John Humphrey, 'Triumph and Despair: Brazil in the World Cup' in John Sugden and Alan Tomlinson (eds), *Hosts and Champions. Soccer cultures, national identities and the USA World Cup* (1994), pp. 65–75.
12. Quoted by Lever (1983), p. 68.
13. This section owes much to Levine (1980), Lever (1983) and Humphrey (1994).
14. Ramírez (1988), p. 35.
15. Scher and Palomino (1988), especially pp. 215–36.
16. Scher and Palomino (1988), p. 77. This section owes much to this work, especially Chapter 4, to Ramírez (1988) and to Alberto Ciria, 'From Soccer to War in Argentina: Preliminary Notes on Sports-as-Politics under a military regime 1976–1982' in Arch. R. M. Ritter, *Latin America and the Caribbean: Geopolitics, development and culture. Proceedings of the 1983 Conference of the Canadian Association for Latin American and Caribbean Studies* (Ottawa 1984), pp. 80–95.
17. *L'Equipe*, 9 January 1953; Ramírez (1988), p. 37; Scher and Palomino (1988), pp. 79–80. Nicholas Fraser and Marysa Navarro, *Eva Perón* (1980), p. 128.
18. Vélez Sarsfield and Huracán also benefited from government money to build their, not so grand, new grounds, opened in 1947 and 1950 respectively. Scher and Palomino (1988), pp. 80–82.
19. Scher and Palomino (1988), p. 85.
20. *The Times*, 23 April 1951.
21. Charles Buchan, *A Lifetime in Football* (1955), pp. 203–4.
22. Scher and Palomino (1988), pp. 88–92.
23. Hugh McIlvanney (ed.), *World Cup '66* (1966), p. 117.
24. Ciria (1984), p. 84.
25. Quoted by Ramírez (1988), p. 42.

26. The most detailed account of these preparations can be found in Mabel Veneziani, 'El Mundial', *Todo Es Historia* XIX, 229 (May–June 1986), pp. 30–54.
27. Veneziani (1986), p. 45. Coca-Cola spent $8 million on the 1978 World Cup. See Vyv Simson and Andrew Jennings, *The Lords of the Rings. Power, money and drugs in the modern Olympics* (1992), p. 46.
28. *El Gráfico*, 6 June 1978.
29. Ciria (1984), p. 84.
30. Quoted by Veneziani (1986), p. 48.
31. This section owes much to Ciria (1984), pp. 85–6.
32. Alastair Reid, 'The Sporting Scene. Ar-Gen-Tina!', *New Yorker*, 7 August 1978, p. 37.
33. Quoted by Joseph L. Arbena, 'Generals and Goles: Assessing the connection between the military and soccer in Argentina', *The International Journal of the History of Sport*, 7, 1 (May 1990), p. 123. The left-wing opposition to the Argentine military government, the Montoneros, also declared the World Cup a 'people's festival' but their hope that supporters at the matches would chant 'Argentina Champions, Videla to the Wall!' was disappointed. Richard Gillespie, *Soldiers of Perón. Argentina's Montoneros* (1982), pp. 257–8.
34. See *Latin American Political Report* XII, 25, 30 June 1978, pp. 196–7 quoted by Neil Larsen, 'Sport as Civil Society: The Argentinian Junta plays championship soccer', N. Larsen (ed.), *The Discourse of Power Culture, Hegemony and the Authoritarian State in Latin America* (1983), pp. 113–28.
35. Apparently including the manager of the Argentine football team César Luis Menotti. On 4 April 1982 he supported the takeover of the Malvinas in the following words: 'Each man has a part in the struggle. In these moments there is national unity against British colonialism and imperialism. We feel immense pain for the brothers in the battle fleet, but we have been assigned a sports mission and we will try to fulfill it with dignity. We are not going to win or lose sovereignty in a [football] match.' See Ciria (1984), p. 89.
36. *BAH*, 22 June 1986; *World Soccer*, December 1988; *Daily Telegraph*, 5 April 1994; Simon Kuper, *Football Against the Enemy* (1994), p. 185.
37. Shaw (1988), p. 134; *La Nación*, 6 May 1969.
38. Shaw (1988), pp. 130–34; *World Soccer*, August 1968 and April 1986.

CHAPTER 6

1. Quoted by Humphrey (1994), p. 66.
2. Jacques de Ryswick, *100,000 Heures de football* (1962), pp. 183–4; Betty Milan, *Football Country* (1989), p. 15. There should have been sixteen teams. Scotland refused to go even though the top two clubs in the British championship qualified, because they did not finish first. Argentina, Czechoslovakia and Turkey all withdrew. France were asked to replace Turkey but after a couple of bad results and on learning that they would not only be in a group with Uruguay and Bolivia but would have to play one game in Pôrto Alegre and the other two thousand miles to the north in Recife, said they would not come if those arrangements remained unaltered. They were not, so France did not.
3. De Ryswick (1962), pp. 187–8.
4. Milan (1989), p. 17; Glanville (1973), p. 68.
5. De Ryswick (1962), p. 195. Varela later claimed that the sight of so many Brazilians so upset at the defeat convinced him that if he had to play the final again he would score against his own team. See Eduardo Archetti, 'Argentina and the World Cup: in search of national identity' in Sugden and Tomlinson (1994), p. 60.
6. Jules Rimet (1954), p. 159.
7. De Ryswick (1962), p. 195; Milan (1989), p. 18. Ademir later said he drove to a remote island after the game and stayed away from Rio for fifteen days.
8. Glanville (1973), p. 99.

9. *Tuttosport*, 6 June 1958.
10. Arthur E. Ellis, *Refereeing Round the World* (1956), pp. 179–81.
11. *World Soccer*, May 1961, p. 33.
12. Stratton Smith (ed.), *The Brazil Book of Football* (1964 edn), pp. 85–94.
13. *The Pelé Albums 1* (1990), p. 41.
14. Robert L. Fish, *Pelé: My life and the beautiful game* (1977), p. 38.
15. *Tuttosport*, 15 June 1958, quoted in *Pelé Albums 1* (1990), p. 49.
16. Fish (1990), pp. 39–59.
17. *The Times*, 30 June 1958.
18. Fish (1990), pp. 57–9.
19. Quoted in *Pelé Albums 1* (1990), p. 109.
20. *La Gazetta dello Sport*, 13 October 1962, quoted in *Pelé Albums 1* (1990), p. 146.
21. *Ebony*, 19 February 1963.
22. *Miroir du Football*, January 1973.
23. A crowd of 38,000 turned out at Plymouth, a Third Division team, and 21,000 at Fulham, then Second Division, in 1973. It was Pelé's only appearance in London. See *Pelé Albums 2* (1990), pp. 535–6, 565–6.
24. Glanville (1973), p. 142.
25. *Pelé Albums 1* (1990), p. 233.
26. *The Times*, 21 March 1969; *World Soccer*, April 1969; Lever (1983), pp. 67–8.
27. Quoted in *Pelé Albums 2* (1990), pp. 456–7.
28. Marplan Survey 160, quoted by Lever (1983), p. 158.
29. *Cambridge Encyclopaedia of Latin America* (1985), p. 275.
30. Quoted in *Pelé Albums 2* (1990), p. 584.
31. *World Soccer*, May 1971.
32. Quoted in *Pelé Albums 2* (1990), p. 738.
33. *L'Equipe*, 16 May 1981.
34. *Observer*, 29 June 1986.
35. *Daily Herald*, 5 June 1964. See also *Pelé Albums 1* (1990), pp. 214, 249, 274.
36. Bromberger in Bale and Maguire (1994), pp. 177–8.

CHAPTER 7

1. De Ryswick (1962), pp. 244–5.
2. *Shorter Oxford English Dictionary* Vol. II (1978 edn).
3. Lever (1983), p. 86.
4. Lever (1983), pp. 138–9.
5. *Western Evening Herald*, 1 August 1924; *BAH*, 9 June 1928.
6. *FA News* II, 8, March 1953, p. 18.
7. *Motherwell Times*, 15 June 1928.
8. *L'Equipe*, 13 May 1958.
9. *BAH*, 15 May 1953.
10. Julio Mafud, *Sociología del Fútbol* (1967), p. 141.
11. Adriana Beatriz Raga, 'Workers, Neighbours and Citizens: A study of an Argentine industrial town 1930–50', unpublished PhD, University of Ann Arbor (1989), pp. 154, 157.
12. Fleur Cowles, *Bloody Precedent* (1952), p. 217.
13. Terry Caesar, 'Bringing It All Down: The 1986 World Cup in Brazil', *Massachusetts Review* 29, ISS 2, p. 277.
14. *FA News* XVII, 12, July 1968.
15. *World Soccer*, May 1979.
16. Rosenfeld (1974), pp. 82–4; Rachum (1978), p. 190; Milan (1989), pp. 37–8.
17. This section is based on José Sérgio Leite Lopes with Sylvain Maresca, 'La Disparition de

"La Joie du Peuple". Notes sur la mort d'un joueur de football', *Actes de la Recherche en Sciences Sociales* 79 (September 1989), pp. 21–36.
18. PRO, FO 371/45052.
19. These warnings went unheeded. Shortly after the end of the war Southampton (1948), Arsenal (twice, 1949 and 1951) and Portsmouth (also 1951) all went on short tours to Brazil. Arsenal played before large crowds in 1949 and made a profit of £8,000, but in their match with Flamengo the prophecy of the Buenos Aires Embassy was proved remarkably prescient. Bryn Jones challenged the goalkeeper and was immediately surrounded by a group of angry defenders. Some of the crowd invaded the pitch and in the fracas which followed, a policeman hit Jones on the head with his truncheon. The match was held up for twenty minutes. Portsmouth did their bit for the reputation of British sportsmanship when they decided to send home Jimmy Scoular after he had been sent off for knocking out an opponent in one of their games. See *FA News* 1, 1, August 1951, p. 23; *Portsmouth Evening News*, 28 June 1951; *Southampton Echo*, 29 April, 17, 19, 21, 31 May and 3, 7, 8 June 1948; Bernard Joy, *Forward, Arsenal!* (1952), pp. 189–90.
20. This did not preclude the South American Department from putting pressure on the Board of Customs and Excise to release a gift of football equipment sent from Argentine clubs to Britain in December 1944. PRO, FO371/44776.
21. *BAH*, 18 June 1912.
22. Mazzoni (1950), p. 48.
23. Caldas (1990), p. 131.
24. *BAH*, 30 May 1905 and 19 June 1910.
25. *BAH*, 28 May 1912 and 7 May 1929.
26. *BAH*, 3 July 1923; *Western Evening Herald*, 11 August 1924; *BAH*, 3 June 1928.
27. Roberto Arlt, 'Ayer ví ganar los Argentinos', reprinted in J. Cau *et al.* (eds), *El Fútbol* (1967), pp. 29–40.
28. *BAH*, 22 May 1929.
29. *BAH*, 3, 23 June 1929; W. Caple Kirby and Frederick W. Carter, *The Mighty Kick* (1933), p. 163.
30. *BAH*, 4 June 1929.
31. Caldas (1990), p. 134.
32. An interesting account of these years on which I have drawn is found in Pablo A. Ramírez, 'Historia negra del fútbol argentino', *Todo Es Historia* XVIII, 232 (September 1986), pp. 42–51.
33. This section is based on *Blackburn Times*, 20 April and 1 October 1937; *Lancashire Evening Telegraph*, 6 June 1964; and Ivan Sharpe, *Forty Years in Football* (1952), pp. 185–7.
34. Sharpe (1952), p. 186.
35. On British referees in South America see *FA Yearbook* 1949–50, pp. 37–40; *FA News* VI, 2, September 1956, pp. 48–51; *The Football Referee*, August, December 1950, May 1956 and May 1958; and private information given to the author. See also *World Sports* 15, 10 October 1949, 15, 11 November 1949, 17, 3 March 1951, 17, 12 December 1951 and 19, 1 January 1953; *Sunday Empire News*, 8 January 1950.
36. *FA Bulletin*, 26 March 1951.
37. The Barrick quotation comes from a cuttings collection kept in Northampton Library. The Turner article is from a scrapbook loaned by Mr Turner.
38. *The Football Referee*, October 1950, p. 11; *FA News* VI, 7, February 1962, XIV, 4 November 1964. Only 96 players were sent off in the whole of the English football league in 1977.
39. *World Soccer*, December 1964.
40. *Pelé Albums 1* (1990), p. 274. *FA News* XVI, 7, February 1967.
41. *FA News* XVII, 6, January 1968.
42. *World Sports* 19, 4 April 1953, p. 39.
43. Private information; *Tuttosport*, 28 March 1959.
44. *Pelé Albums 1* (1990), p. 380; *World Soccer*, June 1969.
45. For details of all the matches see Ron Hockings, *Hockings' South American Cups* (1991).

46. Much of what follows is taken from two articles by Francis Thébaud, *Le Miroir des Sport*, December 1967.
47. Quoted by Kuper (1994), pp. 181–2.
48. *France Football* (1969).
49. *Miroir du Football* 16, April 1961.
50. *La Nación*, 5 August 1982.
51. John Gunther, *Inside South America* (1966), p. 226.
52. Milan (1989), p. 1.
53. Borges wrote nostalgically about the changes which had occurred in the *barrio* of Palermo in Buenos Aires, the cradle of so many *comparitos* (knife fighters), where gymnastics and visits to football matches had become more interesting than death. *Prosa Complets* 1 (Barcelona 1980), p. 49.
54. *FA News* VIII, 2, September 1958 and IX, 4, November 1959; Kuper (1994), p. 172.

CHAPTER 8

1. Saldanha's ideas were quoted by Rachum (1978), p. 200.
2. *Football Magazine*, April 1963.
3. Levine (1980), p. 250.
4. *FA News*, May–June 1960.
5. *World Soccer*, November 1961, p. 9.
6. Gilberto Freyre, *Sociología* 2 (1945), p. 421.
7. *Football Magazine*, April 1963.
8. Betty Milan (1989), p. 11.
9. Quoted by Matthew G. Shirts, 'Playing Soccer in Brazil. Socrates, Corinthians and democracy', *The Wilson Quarterly* XIII, 2 (1989), p. 120.
10. Quoted by Betty Milan (1989), p. 19.
11. Betty Milan (1989), p. 39. On Garrincha see also Stratton Smith (1964), pp. 30–44 and Leite Lopes and Maresca (1989).
12. Betty Milan (1989), p. 28.
13. Roberto Da Matta, 'Notes sur le futebol brésilian', p. 69.
14. *World Sports* 16, 3 March 1950, p. 8.
15. *Pelé Albums 2* (1990), p. 564. See also Alan Wade, *World Sports*, February 1966. They also had strong defences, conceding only four goals in 1958, five in 1962 and seven in 1970 when they scored nineteen in their six games.
16. Similar ideas circulate in Britain about street football being the school where, before the 1950s at any rate, the great professionals learned their skills, especially the idea of the tanner ball player. I am grateful to Eduardo Archetti for allowing me to read his fascinating discussion of the Argentinian case in his unpublished paper, 'Estilo y virtudes masculinas en *El Gráfico*: la creación del imaginario del fútbol argentino' presented to the 48th World Congress of American Studies, Uppsala, 4–9 July 1994.
17. Glanville (1973), p. 123.
18. Osvaldo Bayer, *Fútbol Argentino. Pasión y gloria de nuestro deporte más popular* (1990), p. 86.
19. Bayer (1990), p. 85.
20. Much of this section is based on two fascinating unpublished papers by Eduardo Archetti: 'In Search of National Identity: Argentinian football and Europe' presented to the conference 'Le Football et L'Europe' organized by the European Culture Research Centre, European University Institute, Florence (1990) and 'The Moralities of Argentinian Football' read at the third conference of the European Association of Social Anthropologists, Oslo (1994).
21. *World Soccer*, December 1984.
22. Bayer (1990), p. 133.

23. Archetti (1990), p. 14.
24. Janet Lever, 'Soccer: Opium of the Brazilian People', *Trans-Action* 7, 2 (1972), pp. 36–43.
25. Quoted by Philip Evanson, 'Understanding the People: Futebol, film, theater and politics in present-day Brazil', *South Atlantic Quarterly* 81, 4 (1982), pp. 399–412.
26. This curious episode is described by Shirts (1989), pp. 119–23.
27. Lever (1983), p. 6. See the reviews of *Soccer Madness* by Alan M. Klein, *Sociology of Sport Journal* 1, 2 (1984), pp. 195–7, and John Humphrey and Alan Tomlinson, 'Reflections on Brazilian Football: a review and critique of Janet Lever's *Soccer Madness*', *Bulletin of Latin American Research* 5, 1 (1986), pp. 101–8.
28. Betty Milan (1989), p. 12.
29. Roberto Da Matta, *Explorações: Ensaios de Sociologia Interpretativa* (1986), quoted by Caldas (1990), p. 132.
30. Quoted by Shirts (1989), p. 122. See also William Rowe and Vivian Schelling, *Memory and Modernity: Popular culture in Latin America* (1991), especially pp. 138–40.
31. *Pelé Albums 2* (1990), pp. 455, 607. Between 1980 and 1988 Caldas calculated that the CBD had recognized the transfer of 987 players to Europe: Caldas (1990), pp. 202–3.
32. Reid (1978), p. 46. See also João Máximo, quoted in the *Observer Colour Supplement*, 17 May 1970: '[Football] is a limited instrument of expression. A people cannot fulfil itself through a game. In the end, by distracting from more fundamental issues, football can be said to do considerable harm!'
33. Roberto Da Matta, *Carnivals, Rogues and Heroes. An interpretation of the Brazilian dilemma* (1991 edn) p. 15.
34. Nicholas Shumway, *The Invention of Argentina* (1991), p. 299.

CHAPTER 9

1. Details can be found in Alex Fynn and Lynton Guest, *The Secret Life of Football* (1989), pp. 266–80 and Simson and Jennings (1992), pp. 37–47.
2. *Washington Post*, 12 April 1994.
3. *Pelé Albums 2* (1990), p. 516; *World Soccer*, September 1988. The complexity means that the best team often does not win. Socrates called it a stupid system in 1992 when the best team in Brazil was São Paulo, the best in the national championship Vasco but the champions were Flamengo. *World Soccer*, September 1992.
4. *World Soccer*, May 1989.
5. *International Herald Tribune*, 14 June 1989.
6. *World Soccer*, February, June 1991.
7. *World Soccer*, March, December 1993.
8. *Independent*, 6 January 1994; *Guardian*, 6 January 1994.
9. *Financial Times*, 12 March 1994.
10. *World Soccer*, November 1989. When São Paulo met Milan in the World Club Championship at the end of 1993 it was their ninety-fifth competitive game of the year. *Guardian*, 11 December 1993.
11. *El País*, 14 March 1994. *La Hora* claimed 1,332 footballers were exported from Uruguay between 1957 and 1984. *World Soccer*, May 1988.
12. See *Journal of Sports History* 13, 2, Summer 1986, p. 157, and Amilcar Romero, 'Muerte en la Cancha' (Death in the Stadium), *Todo Es Historia* XVII, 209, September 1984, pp. 8–44. For further explorations of violence in Argentinian football see Eduardo P. Archetti, 'Argentinian Football: A ritual of violence?', *The International Journal of the History of Sport* 9, 2, August 1992, pp. 209–35.
13. *La Nación*, 4, 5, 6 August 1982.
14. Kuper (1994), pp. 191–2; *BAH*, 31 October 1986. Two of the journalists claimed that they were robbed at the dressing-room door.
15. A claim made by Kuper (1994), p. 193.

16. *El Gráfico*, 7 September 1993.
17. Oceania comprised Australia, Solomon Islands, Western Samoa, New Zealand, Fiji, Tahiti and Vanuatu. Concacaf involved twenty-three countries in Central and North America and the Caribbean. The USA qualified as hosts, Mexico won the group and the runners-up played off against the winners of Oceania.
18. *Washington Post*, 27 March 1994.
19. *World Soccer*, January 1989 and January, April 1990.
20. *Sports Illustrated*, 23 May 1994. Higuita served a prison sentence in 1993, apparently for withholding information from the courts.
21. *Washington Post*, 4 March 1994.
22. *World Soccer*, November 1990.
23. *Guardian*, 21 May 1994; *The Economist*, 14 August 1993.
24. *Washington Post*, 29 May 1994; *Financial Times*, 7 April 1994.
25. *Time*, 18 July 1994.
26. Much of what follows is based on *Guardian*, 24 June 1994; *New York Times*, 24 June 1994 and the *Washington Post*, 24 June 1994.
27. *Guardian*, 28 June 1994; *New York Post*, 22 June 1994; *Washington Post*, 24 June 1994.
28. For this section see *New York Post*, 5, 6 July 1994; *Guardian*, 5 July 1994; *Washington Post*, 4 July 1994 and *Sports Illustrated*, 8 July 1994.
29. *Village Voice*, 12 July 1994.
30. *New York Times*, 1 July 1994; *Independent on Sunday*, 3 July 1994.
31. João Havelange was quoted as saying: 'I, as President of FIFA, will do everything possible to avoid a situation that will be the end of Maradona's career.' *Washington Post*, 3 July 1994, quoting the *Dallas Morning News*. Perhaps he did. FIFA's verdict was announced on 24 August: a fifteen-month suspension and a small fine of about £10,000.
32. *Guardian*, 2 July 1994; *Washington Post*, 1 July 1994.
33. *New York Times*, 1 July 1994.
34. *Washington Post*, 4 July 1994.
35. *Time*, 18 July 1994.
36. *Washington Post*, 5 July 1994.
37. *New York Post*, 18 July 1994; *New York Times*, 18 July 1994.
38. *New York Times*, 18 July 1994.
39. *Guardian*, 30 July 1994.
40. I owe this reference to David Ward.
41. This was based on watching a lot of football matches on television and also on *Financial Times*, 16/17 July 1994; *Guardian*, 16 July 1994; *Independent on Sunday*, 24 July 1994; *New York Post*, 22 June 1994; *Washington Post*, 17 July 1994; *Weekend Australian*, 23/24 July 1994.
42. *New York Times*, 19 July 1994; *Financial Times*, 15 August 1994.
43. *New Yorker*, 1 August 1994.

POSTSCRIPT

1. Mario Vargas Llosa, *La Vanguardia*, 3 July 1982.
2. Mario Vargas Llosa, one of the world's most interesting contemporary novelists, wrote a regular column in *La Vanguardia* during the 1982 World Cup. He did accept that certain sporting moments lived 'like an old love in the memory of the aficionado'. *La Vanguardia*, 13 June and 3 July 1982.
3. Although, as we have seen in the post-war World Cups, it was Brazil who led the way in sophisticated preparations and Europe who largely followed their example.

INDEX

BOOKS FROM THE LATIN AMERICA BUREAU

¡SALSA!
Havana Heat, Bronx Beat
Hernando Calvo Ospina
Translated by Nick Caistor

'A marvellous book. I am deeply grateful to Hernando Calvo for helping our audiences understand the roots of our rhythms.'   *Celia Cruz, the 'Rumba Queen'*

'Calvo shows a real affinity and respect for our music.'   *Willie Colón, top salsa musician*

Hot, like a chilli sauce, but with a smooth blend of Latin sounds. This is what Latin record companies tried to convey when they gave 'salsa' its name.

Though it was coined as a musical term in the 1970s, the rhythms of this vibrant music are much older, beating like a pulse through the last 500 years of Caribbean history.

Salsa! takes the reader on a fascinating journey through the development of Latin America's most popular music. A journey which begins on a slave ship and ends amidst the cut-throat, commercial music business of the 1990s. En route, the author explores the extraordinary cultural melting pots of Cuba and New York which hold the key to salsa's creation.

Evocative use of song lyrics bring colour and passion to a book which is equally accessible to the salsa enthusiast and novice alike.

Hernando Calvo Ospina is a Colombian journalist, writer, and avid salsa dancer. He is author of books on Peru, and Pablo Escobar.

April 1995   160pp   photos   ISBN 0 906156 98 X   £9.99

Distributed in North America by Monthly Review Press, 122 West 27th Street, New York, NY 10001

REBEL RADIO
The story of El Salvador's Radio Venceremos
José Ignacio López Vigil

'Engrossing, self-effacing and hilarious'   *New York Times*

El Salvador. The civil war. The guerrillas need a radio station to win hearts and minds. Radio Venceremos. An underground station that keeps broadcasting whatever the cost - under helicopter attack, against high-tech jamming, on the run from endless army offensives.

Fast-moving, in turn funny and tragic, **Rebel Radio** is about history in the making as the men and women of Radio Venceremos relive their war.

José Ignacio López Vigil is a broadcaster, writer of radio soap operas and author of books on radical radio in Bolivia and Nicaragua. Based in Lima, Peru, he is the Latin American representative of the World Association of Community Radio Broadcasters.

April 1995   256 pp   photos   ISBN 0 906156 88 2 (pbk)   £8.99

Published in North America by Curbstone Press 321 Jackson Street, Willimantic CT 06226

LAB books are available by post (plus 10% UK postage, 20% overseas) from Latin America Bureau, Dept V, 1 Amwell Street, London EC1R 1UL. Write for a free catalogue.

The Latin America Bureau is an independent research and publishing organisation. It works to broaden public understanding of human rights and social and economic justice in Latin America and the Caribbean.